Organizing for Cyber Power

Organizing for Cyber Power examines how states organise to develop and employ offensive cyberspace operations (OCO) as an instrument of national security under conditions of time compression, partial intelligence, attribution friction, and technical volatility. Its central claim is conditional: offensive capability contributes to strategic value when it is integrated across strategic authority, operational planning, and tactical execution, and embedded in institutional arrangements that sustain legal compliance, political oversight, intelligence-driven targeting, and risk governance.

The book introduces the Multi-Level, Multi-Dimensional (MLMD) Framework as a structured map linking strategic, operational, and tactical decision-making with cross-cutting political, ethical, and technological dimensions. MLMD is used to trace dependencies that shape whether policy intent can be translated into authorised, feasible action without losing control over effects that may propagate across interconnected systems.

Across three parts, the analysis develops conceptual foundations for cyber power and deterrence, then applies the framework to governance and institutional design, including Sweden's cyber deterrence posture, vulnerability exploitation and its ethical implications, and whole-of-society partnership configurations. A policy-to-payload workflow and deconfliction model clarifies where authorisation, intelligence, engineering, and defensive activity collide and where escalation exposure concentrates.

The final part connects theory to practice through cases and prospective analysis, including WannaCry and an exercise-based cyber range scenario, before deriving institutional implications and future policy directions. The book is written for policy-makers, practitioners, students, and scholars who require a coherent way to analyse how cyber power is organised and governed as lawful statecraft in a contested domain.

Organizing for Cyber Power
Offensive Cyberspace Operations and National Security

Dr Gazmend Huskaj, CISM

CRC Press
Taylor & Francis Group
Boca Raton London New York

CRC Press is an imprint of the
Taylor & Francis Group, an **informa** business

Designed cover image: Shutterstock ID: 2497488765

First edition published 2027
by CRC Press
2385 NW Executive Center Drive, Suite 320, Boca Raton FL 33431

and by CRC Press
4 Park Square, Milton Park, Abingdon, Oxon, OX14 4RN

CRC Press is an imprint of Taylor & Francis Group, LLC

ISBN: 978-1-041-10465-0 (hbk)
ISBN: 978-1-041-10466-7 (pbk)
ISBN: 978-1-003-65518-3 (ebk)

DOI: 10.1201/9781003655183

Typeset in Latin Modern font
by KnowledgeWorks Global Ltd.

Publisher's note: This book has been prepared from camera-ready copy provided by the author.

To those closest to me:
For patience during long seasons of work.

To the practitioners who carry decision burden under uncertainty:
For the discipline of restraint.

To those who build, govern, and oversee cyber power:
In service of lawful statecraft.

"I believe it is possible for actions in cyberspace
to have a deterrent effect and contribute
to the Nation's overall deterrence posture."

— Gen. Paul Nakasone

Contents

List of Figures and Tables

Preface

This book examines how states organise to develop and employ offensive cyberspace operations (OCO) as an instrument of national security. Its central claim is conditional: offensive capability contributes to strategic value only when it is integrated across strategic authority, operational planning, and tactical execution, and when it is embedded in institutional arrangements that sustain legal compliance, political oversight, intelligence-driven targeting, and risk governance under time compression.

The audience is global. The book is written for policy-makers and officials who shape mandates, authorities, and oversight; for practitioners who design and coordinate programmes across defence, intelligence, and cybersecurity; and for students who require a structured entry point into the relationship between deterrence, intelligence, and the operational character of cyberspace. The analysis is grounded in doctrine, policy documents, and scholarship. It does not provide operational guidance, targeting methods, tradecraft, exploit techniques, or capability inventories. Where open evidence is incomplete, the argument remains bounded by what can be substantiated.

The instrument is the Multi-Level, Multi-Dimensional (MLMD) Framework. MLMD maps strategic, operational, and tactical levels alongside cross-cutting political, ethical, and technological dimensions. The framework is used to trace how deterrence purpose, intelligence requirements, and OCO means interact across levels of decision-making. The intent is to make dependencies visible: strategic intent can be undermined by operational coordination latency; operational plans can fail if intelligence and authorisation timelines are misaligned; tactical success can generate strategic risk when effects propagate beyond intended boundaries.

The book is structured in three parts. Part I establishes the conceptual foundations for analysing OCO as politically directed and legally bounded activity under technical volatility. It introduces MLMD and specifies why integration across levels is a recurring condition for political usability. Part II applies the framework to institutional design and governance. It examines how authorities, oversight, intelligence integration, and vulnerability policy shape the feasibility of maintaining usable options under constraint. Part III turns to practice through cases and prospective analysis. It examines how time compression, partial visibility, and interaction effects shape outcomes, and it develops implications for policy design and capability development.

Readers may approach the book in two ways. A sequential reading develops the full causal argument from theory to implications. A modular reading is also supported. Policy-makers may begin with the framework chapter and the governance chapters to identify design choices and oversight trade-offs. Practitioners may focus on the integration chapters that address authorisation pathways, intelligence dependencies, and risk governance. Students may use the framework chapter as a conceptual map and then read the cases as applications that demonstrate how the same constraints recur across contexts.

The purpose of this book is to clarify conditions under which offensive cyber capability can be developed and employed under political control and legal constraint, and to specify institutional arrangements implied by this requirement. It aims to support analysis, policy design, and informed discussion of cyber power in national security policy practice.

Use of Generative AI Tools

The author discloses the use of Generative AI tools during the preparation of this manuscript, in accordance with Taylor & Francis guidance. OpenAI ChatGPT (model label shown in the interface: "GPT-5.2," including "Thinking," accessed in 2025) and Google Gemini (model label shown in the interface: "Gemini Pro," accessed in 2025) were used in a limited supporting capacity for idea exploration, drafting support, and language editing, including improving clarity, readability, and internal consistency across chapters.

OpenAI Codex (accessed in 2025) was used as software-engineering support to diagnose LaTeX compilation and layout issues and to suggest corrections to author-written LaTeX source files. The author implemented and verified any changes.

AI tools were also used to support the drafting and refinement of decision exercises by assisting with phrasing variants and presentation. The author designed the exercises and validated the final versions.

All AI-assisted outputs were reviewed, verified, edited, and approved by the author. The author remains solely responsible for the originality, validity, and integrity of the manuscript, including all arguments, interpretations, and conclusions.

Acknowledgements

The author thanks Dr Paul de Souza (Cyber Security Forum Initiative), Dr Josef Schroefl, Col (Austrian Ministry of Defence; European Centre of Excellence for Countering Hybrid Threats), and Dr Robert Black (University of Manchester) for their proposal reviews and for recommending that the project be pursued. Responsibility for all remaining arguments and interpretations rests with the author.

Author

Dr Gazmend Huskaj heads the Global Cyber and Security Policy Programme at the Geneva Centre for Security Policy (GCSP), which supports international cooperation through executive education, diplomatic dialogue, and policy research. Over the past two decades, he has held roles spanning early deployments in multinational peace support and humanitarian operations, served as Head of the Security Information Coordination Cell within the United Nations, and served as Director of Intelligence for cyber-related issues within the Swedish Armed Forces.

A military veteran, he has served more than five years in conflict and post-conflict regions. In 2014, he was recognised by the European External Action Service (EEAS) for a contribution to the "EU as a Global Security Provider" forum at a global policy event that connected over 2,000 experts from 114 countries. In 2023, he received Best Virtual Poster for "Offensive Cyberspace Operations for Cyber Security."

Dr Huskaj holds Master of Science degrees in Security and Risk Management (University of Leicester) and Information Security (Stockholm University). He is a Certified Information Security Manager (CISM) and an alumnus of executive programmes at Harvard Kennedy School and the Geneva Centre for Security Policy's European Training Course in Security Policy. He has also completed advanced studies at Cranfield University, the University of St Andrews, and KTH Royal Institute of Technology. His doctoral research examined offensive cyberspace operations and analysed their implications for national security policy, organisational design, and governance.

Part I

Cyber Power and Offensive Operations

1

Offensive Cyberspace Operations

This chapter examines why many cyberliterate states treat defence as insufficient for securing national security interests in cyberspace. Adversaries can exploit globally connected information systems at relatively low marginal cost and at high operational tempo. Because cyberspace compresses decision windows and enables repeated intrusion attempts even when baseline hygiene improves, defensive measures can raise the cost of individual attacks yet leave adversary decision-making largely unchanged when the adversary's strategy depends on sustained activity rather than isolated events.

A further pressure towards active contestation follows from attribution frictions. Attribution can be established in some cases, yet it often arrives under time pressure, evidentiary ambiguity, and political contestation. Because these conditions complicate a timely and publicly defensible response, adversaries can treat the expected costs of continued probing as negotiable. States that seek to influence adversary behaviour may therefore integrate offensive cyberspace operations (OCO) as one instrument within deterrence and defence postures, subject to legal authority, political control, and oversight.

The scope and stance of this chapter are conceptual and explanatory. It analyses how doctrine and scholarship account for why OCOs are integrated into national security practice under specified conditions. The chapter does not provide operational guidance and does not propose target sets, operational methods, or national implementation choices. Where the chapter refers to claims of "necessity" in doctrine or scholarship, it treats them as conditional arguments to be assessed against legal constraints, ethical limits, and escalation dynamics.

The chapter specifies how access dependencies, intelligence requirements, and technical volatility propagate constraints across strategic, operational, and tactical levels. It then defines OCO as a purposeful sequence of planned actions and outlines mechanisms through which OCO are theorised to impose costs and signal resolve under uncertainty, preparing the analytical basis for the multi-level, multi-dimensional (MLMD) framework developed in Chapters 2 and 3.

The central argument of this book is the following conditional claim: offensive capability generates strategic value only when it is integrated across strategic, operational, and tactical decision-making and embedded in institutional, legal, and societal arrangements that enable coherent authorisation, planning, and execution. Within this book, these institutional, legal, and societal arrangements are analysed through political authority, ethical constraint, organisational design, and technical feasibility.

1.1 Cyberspace as a Domain of Strategic Competition

Cyberspace constitutes a domain of strategic competition because national security and economic activity depend on internetworked information systems whose disruption, manipulation, or compromise can generate political consequences. This dependence creates

DOI: 10.1201/9781003655183-1

incentives for adversaries to conduct cyberspace operations for cyber attack or cyber exploitation in pursuit of their security interests. Because the technical and organisational properties of the domain reduce the constraining role of geography that characterises land, air, sea, and space, an actor can deny, manipulate, or extract information without physical proximity to the target (Joint Chiefs of Staff, 2018). Consequently, states face a persistent requirement to protect systems and data while also influencing adversary decision-making under uncertainty.

The literature associates this problem with deterrence concepts that emphasise altering an adversary's risk calculus, including through cost imposition and signalling, as discussed by Snyder (Snyder, 1961). Because cyberspace enables repeated interaction at high tempo, a state may seek instruments that go beyond passive defence and episodic response. Therefore, doctrine and scholarship discuss the integration of OCO as one component within deterrence and defence postures when the intent is to contest adversary activity and impose costs aligned with political objectives (Huskaj and Axelsson, 2023; Huskaj, Blix, and Axelsson, 2024).

Cyberspace also creates incentives for capability development because defensive measures alone may not secure national security interests against adversaries that exploit global interconnectivity and the practical difficulties of timely, publicly credible attribution. Attribution can be established in some cases, yet uncertainty and time pressure can complicate response decisions and enable continued probing behaviour. Because adversaries often rely on continuous activity rather than isolated events, scholarship argues that states may adopt a posture of continuous engagement in which security is pursued by contesting adversary operations that seek to establish or maintain persistent access within internetworked information systems (Fischerkeller and Harknett, 2017).

Managing the requirement to contest adversaries while maintaining strategic stability creates an alignment problem across levels of decision-making. Tactical technical actions can generate political consequences, and political objectives can constrain operational feasibility; therefore, analysis benefits from a framework that links strategic intent to operational design and to tactical execution. The MLMD framework is introduced for this purpose because it specifies how legal authority, organisational arrangements, intelligence requirements, and technical feasibility interact across strategic, operational, and tactical levels when states integrate OCO into deterrence and defence postures.

Cyberspace as Statecraft

At the strategic level, cyberspace can function as an instrument of statecraft because states pursue political objectives through internetworked information systems that shape governance, economic activity, and military operations. When states integrate OCO into national security strategy, the stated intent in doctrine and scholarship is often to impose costs, collect intelligence, and signal intent in order to influence an adversary's expectations and behaviour. Because influence depends on how an adversary anticipates consequences, the ability to generate denial or manipulation effects is frequently presented as a mechanism for altering the adversary's risk decision-making (Huskaj, 2017).

Cyberspace also reshapes power relationships because the resources required to generate certain offensive capabilities differ from those associated with conventional military force. This condition widens the set of actors able to conduct consequential operations and contributes to a higher tempo of interaction, which increases the number of decision points that states must address (Valeriano, Jensen, and Maness, 2018). Because capability diffusion interacts with continuous exposure and attribution frictions, uncertainty can increase regarding who can act, when action occurs, and how intent is interpreted under evidentiary ambiguity. As discussed in intelligence theory, this uncertainty can reduce the predictive value of assessments that rely primarily on aggregate measures of military strength (Warner, 2014; Johnson, 2003). Consequently, states may invest in intelligence capabilities and integrate OCO as part of a broader posture intended to improve detection, enable timely disruption, and reduce the operational space available to adversaries.

Attribution constraints can weaken deterrence by punishment because adversaries may attempt to obscure identity through technical routing, deceptive indicators, or the use of intermediaries (Rid and Buchanan, 2015). Because reduced confidence in responsibility complicates timely and proportionate cost imposition, decision-makers may face delays in generating domestically and internationally defensible responses. Consequently, states can become more reliant on intelligence assessments that reconstruct behaviour over time, which can increase opportunities for continued intrusion. This dynamic explains why scholarship often treats OCO as relevant to deterrence and defence under conditions where defensive measures alone do not change an adversary's expectation of anonymity or plausible deniability.

The Operational Level: Intelligence and Access

At the operational level, cyberspace operations depend on organisational arrangements that generate, sustain, and employ capabilities under legal authority and oversight. Because access to adversary systems is contingent on technical conditions that change over time, doctrine and scholarship treat continuous intelligence support as a recurring prerequisite for offensive action. This logic follows because intelligence assessments shape what can plausibly be reached, what can be influenced, and when operational opportunities exist (US Joint Chiefs of Staff, 2013). Consequently, operational feasibility is often framed as a function of intelligence quality and timeliness rather than of force concentration in physical space.

Cyberspace challenges inherited security assumptions because critical systems can be affected without geographic proximity or territorial penetration in the conventional sense. As long as connectivity exists, operations can be conducted remotely, which reduces the protective value of distance that traditionally constrains many forms of coercion and interference (Lynn, 2010). Because this condition expands exposure across governmental, military, and economic systems, states face repeated interactions with adversaries who attempt to obtain and maintain access. Doctrine has conceptualised this interaction as an ongoing contest over presence and initiative, including through the concept of "persistent engagement" (Nakasone, 2019; U.S. Cyber Command Public Affairs Office, 2022). Consequently, the operational problem becomes one of sustaining monitoring, collection, and readiness under uncertainty while remaining aligned with political intent and legal constraint.

Cyberspace also alters decision-making because hostile activity frequently occurs below thresholds associated with armed conflict while still producing cumulative effects that can degrade national security interests over time (Huskaj, 2023*a*). Because adversaries can combine espionage, disruption, and influence activities in ways that remain difficult to classify in real time, policy-makers may face fewer unambiguous moments for authorisation and public justification of response (Schmitt, 2017). This ambiguity complicates escalation assessment because it can be unclear when activity shifts from intelligence collection to preparation for disruption or degradation. Consequently, doctrine and scholarship often treat operational design as tightly coupled to intelligence support, since intelligence conditions the timing, scope, and feasibility of offensive action without implying a stable boundary between competition and conflict.

The Tactical Level: Vulnerability and Exploit

At the tactical level, cyberspace operations depend on technical interactions with specific software and hardware components, where access and effects are mediated by vulnerabilities and their exploitation. Tactical activity conditions feasibility because operational possibilities are bounded by what can be reached, what can be influenced, and what remains stable long enough to support a planned sequence of action. Consequently, tactical outcomes often constrain higher-level decision-making because they determine whether a given political intent can be translated into an operational design without assuming controllability or permanence.

A recurrent claim in the security literature is that offence and defence are structurally asymmetric because an attacker may require a single workable access path, whereas defenders confront a broader set of potential access vectors across complex systems (Saltzer and Schroeder, 1975). This asymmetry matters at the level of analysis because it helps explain why exposure persists even when defensive practices improve. Consequently, states and other actors face incentives to treat access as a scarce and time-bound condition, which links tactical volatility to strategic uncertainty about what can be achieved and with what risk.

Tactical constraints are also organisational because critical digital infrastructure is frequently owned and operated by private entities rather than by the state. This ownership structure creates dependency because governmental and military functions rely on services maintained by commercial actors whose incentives, governance structures, and operational priorities differ from those of public authorities. Consequently, coordination across government, industry, and, where relevant, academia becomes a recurring condition for managing security and resilience at scale, including for intelligence integration and incident response (Huskaj and Axelsson, 2023; Mandsager, Cole, Drew, and McLaughlin, 2022). This book treats such coordination as an analytical problem of institutional alignment rather than as a prescription for national implementation choices.

The Strategic Necessity of Offence

Cyberspace constitutes a domain of strategic competition because it enables actors to generate political, economic, and military effects through actions taken within networked systems that support societal functions. This condition follows because global interconnectivity, reliance on privately operated infrastructure, and the diffusion of technical capability compress decision windows and increase uncertainty about intent, attribution, and feasible response. Consequently, tactical interactions with specific systems can scale into strategic consequences without providing the signalling clarity associated with many conventional forms of coercion.

These characteristics incentivise states to treat hostile cyber activity as a persistent feature of competition rather than as an episodic crisis. Because cumulative activity can degrade security interests over time, doctrine and scholarship often frame state responses as a portfolio of measures that combine defence, intelligence, and, in some cases, offensive action under legal authority and oversight. Consequently, the analytical problem becomes one of explaining when and how OCO are integrated into deterrence and defence postures, and how alignment is maintained across strategic intent, operational design, and tactical feasibility. This purpose motivates the MLMD framework developed in the subsequent chapters.

1.2 Defining Offensive Cyberspace Operations

OCO are purposeful actions undertaken to advance national security objectives by altering the confidentiality, integrity, or availability of adversary digital systems. Scholarly research describes these operations as sequences of planned activities executed by organised groups that seek to influence how information is processed, stored, or transmitted within target environments (Huskaj and Wilson, 2020*a*). The offensive character derives from the intent to generate effects that shape adversary decision-making or impose costs that support strategic aims. This focus on purpose distinguishes OCO from routine network interaction because the operation's organisational design, technical preparation, and decision authority are aligned towards producing effects that alter an adversary's operational conditions. OCO therefore project power in and through foreign cyberspace by combining access, exploitable vulnerabilities, and payloads to conduct a cyberspace attack (CA) or cyberspace exploitation (CE) under policy direction to advance national security objectives (Huskaj et al., 2024).

Doctrinal and Theoretical Foundations

U.S. doctrine reinforces this understanding by situating OCO within the military effects framework. Joint Publication 3-12 defines OCO as operations intended "to project power by the application of force in or through cyberspace" (Joint Chiefs of Staff, 2018). This definition positions OCO within a broader family of cyberspace activities that includes defensive operations and Department of Defense Information Network (DODIN) functions (USAF LeMay Center, 2023). However, a theoretical analysis reveals that OCO relies on a specific triad of components: access, vulnerabilities, and payloads. Access provides the pathway to the target; vulnerabilities constitute the flaws in hardware, software, or human configurations that enable entry; and payloads are the mechanisms that execute the desired effect (Huskaj et al., 2024). Thus, OCO are complex technical chains where success depends on the synchronisation of these three elements, enabling force projection through various effects.

Doctrinal frameworks distinguish between two primary categories of offensive effects: deny and manipulate. These categories provide a structured means of linking technical actions to intended outcomes, enabling planners to select effects that correspond to strategic requirements, escalation thresholds, and the reversibility of consequences.

Deny actions reduce an adversary's ability to use targeted systems by degrading, disrupting, or destroying their functionality. Degrade effects reduce system capacity and impose friction that alters adversary timelines or burdens decision processes. Disrupt effects interrupt operations for bounded periods, often creating opportunities for coordinated actions in other domains. Destroy effects eliminate system functionality entirely and thus carry implications for escalation, restoration timelines, and the resilience of the affected infrastructure (Joint Chiefs of Staff, 2018).

Manipulate actions serve different purposes by altering sensor readings, data integrity, or system behaviour to influence adversary perception or operational choices. This modifies data or system logic to influence adversary behaviour without necessarily producing visible damage, often supporting deception or exploitation objectives (USAF LeMay Center, 2023).

Doctrine enables decision-makers to map intended outcomes to offensive actions, ensuring coherence between strategic purpose and technical execution (Huskaj, 2024*c*). This clarity is central because OCO needs to be integrated with other instruments of state power to achieve meaningful political effects.

The Intelligence-Operations Nexus

Intelligence preparation is foundational to OCO because operational feasibility depends on understanding how target systems function and how their vulnerabilities can be leveraged. Intelligence collection identifies system architecture, defensive behaviours, access pathways, and potential cascading effects (US Joint Chiefs of Staff, 2013). These insights determine which offensive actions are possible, which are proportionate, and which align with strategic objectives. Access generated through intelligence collection often becomes the basis for offensive options because it reveals the internal logic of targeted systems and the conditions under which effects might be realised. The relationship is therefore structural: without detailed intelligence, OCO cannot be calibrated to the operational environment, and its strategic utility diminishes. Intelligence preparation thus functions as the interpretive layer that links political aims to operational design.

This interdependence produces the intelligence gain–loss (IGL) dilemma. Executing an offensive effect may expose the access pathway or vulnerability that enabled intelligence collection, prompting adversaries to modify their systems and thereby eliminating future insight (Huskaj and Iftimie, 2020). Decision-makers therefore face the question of whether the immediate benefits of imposing costs outweigh the strategic value of continued visibility into adversary behaviour (Axelrod and Iliev, 2014). High-tempo operational environments compress this decision cycle because opportunities for imposing costs may be brief, creating situations where assessments may be made under uncertainty. Research by Maschmeyer indicates that such conditions can constrain deliberation and force states to prioritise either near-term disruption or sustained awareness, depending on strategic priorities and operational timelines (Maschmeyer, 2021). This dilemma is inherent to the offensive domain and may be managed through institutional frameworks that govern targeting decisions.

Institutional Oversight and Strategic Alignment

States develop formal processes to evaluate these trade-offs because offensive actions carry risks related to attribution, escalation, and the loss of intelligence advantage. Legal and policy frameworks require that decisions regarding access, vulnerability use, and payload selection be reviewed to ensure alignment with national strategy and to limit unintended effects (Bronk, 2016; Valeriano et al., 2018). While intelligence collection aims to remain persistent and minimally observable, offensive action may reveal presence or intent, increasing the likelihood of detection and retaliation (Gartzke and Lindsay, 2017; Moore, 2022). These considerations necessitate institutional integration across intelligence, legal, operational, and political authorities to ensure that OCO remains aligned with national interests. The feasibility of offensive action is therefore shaped not only by technical capability but by the organisational processes that govern decision-making under uncertainty (Mandsager et al., 2022).

Taken together, these elements demonstrate that OCO function as instruments of statecraft when they integrate strategic purpose, doctrinal guidance, intelligence dependence, and institutional oversight. OCO requires organisational coherence because effects generated within digital systems can propagate across political, military, and societal domains. Their value arises from the ability to impose costs, shape adversary behaviour, and influence operational conditions in ways that defensive measures alone cannot achieve. Understanding OCO therefore requires attention to strategic intent, the doctrinal tools available to decision-makers, and the intelligence structures that condition operational feasibility. These foundations establish the conceptual basis for analysing offensive operations within the broader competitive environment developed throughout this chapter.

1.3 From Defence to Offence: Historical Evolution

This historical account draws disproportionately on United States doctrinal and policy sources because the United States has published the most extensive open-source material on the organisation, legal framing, and doctrinal codification of cyberspace operations. This visibility creates an empirical asymmetry: U.S. documents provide unusually granular reference points for tracing how OCO were conceptualised, authorised, and integrated into broader security postures, whereas comparable material from many other cyberliterate countries remains less accessible or is articulated through different institutional genres. Consequently, U.S. doctrine is used here as a transparent baseline for tracking conceptual and organisational development in open sources, rather than as a claim that other states follow the same trajectory or adopt identical thresholds, authorities, or practices.

The strategic conception of cyberspace has evolved from a technical focus on information security to the integration of offensive capabilities into national power. During the 1970s and 1980s, early networks such as ARPANET were restricted to government and academic use, leading policy-makers to view security primarily as a matter of data protection. Willis H. Ware's influential 1967 analysis identified system vulnerabilities, but the prevailing objective was to secure information residence within closed systems rather than to project power through them (Ware, 1967). This defensive orientation persisted until the integration of digital systems into military command-and-control architectures created new dependencies. The recognition that these dependencies could be targeted transformed the domain from a protected space into an operational environment. This transformation occurred because military planners realised that if their own reliance on digital systems created vulnerabilities, the same condition applied to potential adversaries. Consequently, the assumption that networks could be secured solely through perimeter defence began to erode as the strategic value of exploiting adversary dependence became apparent.

Early Information Warfare and Doctrinal Consolidation (1991–2000)

The 1991 Gulf War marked the transition towards "information warfare." U.S. planners considered using cyber techniques to disable Iraqi infrastructure, including telecommunications and electrical generation. Although kinetic strikes were ultimately preferred due to legal uncertainties regarding collateral damage to civilian facilities such as hospitals, the debate established a precedent: digital systems were valid military targets (Kaplan, 2016). This period demonstrated that the technical capability to disrupt adversary systems existed, even if policy frameworks were not yet mature enough to authorise its use. The reluctance to employ these tools stemmed from the difficulty of predicting cascading effects within dual-use infrastructure, where military and civilian networks often converged. The result was a doctrinal shift where military organisations began to view information not just as a resource to be protected, but as a weapon system to be employed, contingent upon the development of precise targeting protocols (Dahm, 2021).

Following the Gulf War, doctrinal development moved away from the broad umbrella of information warfare—which included psychological operations and electronic warfare—towards precise definitions of Computer Network Attack (CNA). By 1998, Joint Publication 3-13 defined CNA as operations to "disrupt, deny, degrade, or destroy" information systems, formalising the distinction between technical intrusion and operational effect. This codification was required because the expanding connectivity of military networks demanded specific authorities and rules of engagement (ROE) different from those governing traditional electronic warfare (Denning, 1999). Electronic warfare typically targeted the physical layer of the electromagnetic spectrum, whereas CNA targeted the logical layer of data and protocols. The establishment of these definitions provided the institutional legitimacy required for states to begin investing in dedicated offensive capabilities, moving the discipline from theoretical experimentation to operational readiness. This bureaucratic formalisation allowed states to segregate intelligence collection (Computer Network Exploitation) from destructive action (CNA), creating distinct legal and operational lanes for each activity.

Catalytic Incidents and the Failure of Static Defence (2000–2010)

By the mid-2000s, the strategic balance shifted as policy-makers recognised that passive defence was insufficient to counter determined adversaries. The 2010 observation by U.S. Deputy Secretary of Defence William Lynn that cyberspace had become "a race between offense and defense in which offense has the upper hand" reflected a growing consensus that static defences could not guarantee security against sophisticated threats (Lynn, 2010). This assessment was driven by a series of catalytic events that demonstrated the utility of offensive operations for political and military coercion. The 2007 attacks on Estonia illustrated how distributed denial-of-service (DDoS) campaigns could disrupt national governance without kinetic violence. By overwhelming banking and government servers, the attackers imposed significant political costs while maintaining plausible deniability. The 2008 Russo-Georgian War advanced this logic by synchronising cyber attacks with conventional military manoeuvres, establishing that cyberspace operations could function as a force multiplier in armed conflict. These incidents proved that cyber power could be used to shape political outcomes and operational environments, validating the requirement for offensive options that could respond to or preempt such coercion (EBSCO Knowledge Advantage, 2021; White, 2018).

The operational scope of OCO expanded significantly with the discovery of Stuxnet in 2010. By physically destroying centrifuges at Iran's Natanz facility, this operation demonstrated that code could generate kinetic equivalence, crossing the threshold from digital disruption to physical destruction (Huskaj and Wilson, 2021). This capability implied that cyberspace operations could achieve strategic disarmament objectives previously reserved for aerial bombardment or special forces. Stuxnet also revealed the importance of supply chain vulnerabilities and the necessity of intelligence preparation, as the operation required detailed knowledge of specific industrial control systems (ICS). The implication was that air-gapped networks were no longer invulnerable, forcing states to reconsider the survivability of their own critical infrastructure. The success of Stuxnet incentivised other actors to develop similar capabilities, initiating a proliferation cycle where the ability to target industrial processes became a standard component of advanced cyber arsenals.

Targeting the Private Sector and Critical Infrastructure (2012–2016)

The subsequent proliferation of destructive tools reinforced this offensive imperative. The 2012 Shamoon attack on Saudi Aramco and the 2014 attack on Sony Pictures Entertainment proved that state actors would target private sector entities to impose economic and political costs (Javers, 2016; Frizell, 2015). These incidents expanded the target set beyond military networks to include critical infrastructure and commercial assets, creating a security environment in which civilian entities became primary belligerents. The Shamoon attack, which wiped data from over 30,000 workstations, demonstrated that adversaries could inflict massive recovery costs to signal displeasure with national policies. The Sony attack illustrated how offensive cyber capabilities could be used for coercion against corporate entities to suppress free speech or shape cultural output. The implication was that the distinction between military and civilian targets had eroded, requiring national security strategies to account for the defence of the private sector through active means (Huskaj and Axelsson, 2023).

This trajectory towards kinetic and coercive effects continued with the attacks on Ukraine's power grid in 2015 and 2016. Unlike Stuxnet, which was covert and sabotaged, these operations were overt and disruptive, cutting power to hundreds of thousands of civilians during winter. These incidents demonstrated that adversaries could leverage access to Operational Technology (OT) to hold civilian populations hostage, thereby exerting psychological and political pressure on the government. The Ukraine cases highlighted the integration of cyber attacks into hybrid warfare doctrines, where digital disruption is used to degrade societal resilience and amplify political instability. This development forced Western planners to acknowledge that critical infrastructure protection required more than compliance standards; it required the capacity to detect and disrupt adversaries who had already pre-positioned themselves within critical networks (North Atlantic Treaty Organization, 2025*b*; Leidos, 2025).

The Strategic Pivot: Defend Forward, Persistent Engagement (2016–Present)

The limitations of defensive postures became acute with the rise of Advanced Persistent Threats (APTs) engaged in industrial-scale espionage. Campaigns such as those attributed to PLA Unit 61398 (APT1) and the 2014 breach of the U.S. Office of Personnel Management (OPM) revealed that adversaries could maintain long-term presence within secured networks to extract strategic intelligence (Mandiant, 2013; Wikipedia contributors, 2015). These intrusions demonstrated that perimeter defence could not prevent determined state actors from gaining access. The OPM breach, involving the exfiltration of sensitive clearance data on millions of government employees, represented a counter-intelligence catastrophe that fundamentally altered the U.S. assessment of Chinese cyber strategy. The strategic implication was that security required the ability to contest the adversary's freedom of action outside one's own networks. This requirement necessitated a shift from reactive investigation to proactive operation, where defenders actively hunt threats within their networks and, eventually, in external networks (Park and Kim, 2025).

In response to these structural conditions, national strategies underwent a fundamental revision in the late 2010s. The 2018 U.S. Department of Defence Cyber Strategy formalised the doctrine of "Defend Forward," which posits that security is achieved by disrupting malicious activity at its source before it reaches national networks (Joint Chiefs of Staff, 2018). This doctrine relies on the concept of "Persistent Engagement," which argues that because adversaries are continuously active below the threshold of armed conflict, stability is maintained only through constant interaction and the imposition of friction (Fischerkeller and Harknett, 2017; Healey, 2019). This strategic pivot validated the integration of OCO into the national security toolkit. It rejected the premise that cyber deterrence functions like nuclear deterrence—through the threat of catastrophic punishment—and instead posited that deterrence is cumulative, achieved by denying adversaries the benefits of their campaigns through continuous operational contestation (Montgomery and Borghard, 2021; U.S. Cyber Command Public Affairs Office, 2022).

Operation Glowing Symphony (2016), which dismantled ISIS propaganda infrastructure, provided the operational proof of concept for this proactive approach (Rhysider, 2019). By authorising U.S. Cyber Command to degrade server infrastructure and disrupt communications globally, the operation demonstrated that OCO could successfully reduce the capability of a non-state actor to inspire and direct violence. This marked a definitive step away from treating cyber threats solely as law enforcement or intelligence problems. The success of such operations solidified the view that offensive capabilities are essential for degrading adversary capacity in real-time.

Thus, the historical evolution from the passive security models of the 1970s to the persistent engagement of the modern era illustrates a clear causal trajectory. The increasing dependence on digital infrastructure created vulnerabilities that defensive measures alone could not mitigate. Adversaries exploited these vulnerabilities to project power, disrupt governance, and destroy physical assets. Consequently, states were compelled to adopt offensive capabilities to restore deterrence and manage escalation. This shift was not merely technical but conceptual, redefining cyberspace as a domain of constant contact where security depends on the ability to seize the initiative. This historical context provides the necessary foundation for understanding the specific adversary behaviours—from Russian hybrid warfare to Chinese industrial espionage—that define the contemporary offensive imperative described in the following section.

1.4 Why Offence Has Been Framed as Strategically Necessary

The transition from a defensive paradigm to one that embraces OCO was not a matter of choice, but a response to structural necessity. This necessity arises from the empirical reality that defensive postures, no matter how mature, have failed to constrain adversary behaviour or alter the strategic calculus of hostile actors. The operational environment is defined by continuous campaigns that operate below the threshold of armed attack, creating conditions where passive resilience alone cannot prevent the erosion of national security interests. To understand this shift, one has to analyse the structural asymmetries of the domain, the logic of cost imposition, and the requirement to integrate effects across the strategic, operational, and tactical levels of war.

The Structural Asymmetry of Defence

The primary driver of the offensive imperative is the inherent structural asymmetry of the cyber domain, where the initiative rests almost exclusively with the attacker. Defensive measures are structurally reactive; they depend on the identification of vulnerabilities, the application of patches, and the monitoring of networks for known signatures. This dependency creates temporal and informational constraints because defenders are required to react to adversary behaviour that may already have progressed through several stages of the kill chain. Research demonstrates that defenders rarely possess complete visibility of their own systems, a condition exacerbated by the reliance on complex global supply chains and commercial-off-the-shelf technologies (Bronk, 2016).

This lack of visibility enables adversaries to conduct reconnaissance, escalate privileges, and establish persistence well before defensive mechanisms are triggered. The time gap between an adversary's initial access and their detection—often measured in months—provides a window of opportunity for data exfiltration or the pre-positioning of disruptive payloads. Because adversaries can exploit zero-day vulnerabilities or leverage legitimate credentials to disguise their activity, defence-only postures cannot reliably prevent adversaries from gaining footholds in critical systems, nor can they guarantee expulsion once access is established (Huskaj and Wilson, 2021).

Furthermore, the interconnected nature of digital infrastructure means that vulnerabilities in peripheral systems can cascade into critical assets. States depend on technologies produced by diverse suppliers, creating uncertainty regarding hidden vulnerabilities or unanticipated interactions between components. Adversaries exploit these systemic characteristics by targeting widely deployed software or hardware, enabling them to affect multiple targets simultaneously through supply chain intrusions. The implication is that defence alone cannot eliminate risk because the structure of the digital ecosystem creates opportunities for adversary action that cannot be fully mitigated through passive hardening (Anderson, Ablon, Kuehn and Libicki, 2017). Consequently, states require the capacity to look and act beyond the perimeter of their own networks to identify threats and degrade adversary capabilities before they are deployed.

The Rationale of Cost Imposition and Pre-emption

The second dimension of this necessity is the requirement to impose costs in a domain defined by persistent competition. For decades, Western cyber strategy relied on the assumption that resilience would deter aggression—that if defences were strong enough, the cost of entry would dissuade adversaries. Empirical evidence has invalidated this assumption. Adversaries such as Russia, China, and Iran interpreted the absence of offensive responses as a signal that hostile campaigns could be conducted with impunity (Huskaj and Axelsson, 2023). By operating continuously below the threshold of armed conflict, these actors generated cumulative strategic effects—intellectual property theft, democratic interference, and critical infrastructure mapping—without triggering the consequences associated with kinetic warfare.

OCO became necessary to correct this strategic imbalance. Offensive actions provide the means to intervene in adversary campaigns, disrupting their reconnaissance, degrading their attack infrastructure, or manipulating their systems to reduce operational freedom. These actions serve a dual function: they impose friction that makes adversary operations more costly and less effective, and they signal resolve by demonstrating that intrusive behaviour will be contested (Fischerkeller and Harknett, 2017). The condition of continuous competition requires states to act "left of boom," intervening at the early stages of adversary preparation. Pre-emption is central to this logic because adversaries often act with speed and ambiguity. Waiting for an attack to manifest on friendly networks cedes the initiative and accepts the risk of irreversible damage. Research indicates that pre-emptive action, when grounded in solid intelligence, can reduce escalation risks by disrupting operations that would otherwise produce strategic harm (Maschmeyer, 2021).

The strategic logic of shaping adversary behaviour is therefore grounded in the recognition that passive defence is static, whereas the threat is dynamic. Adversaries constantly adapt their tactics, techniques, and procedures (TTPs) to bypass security controls. To maintain stability, states face incentives to adopt active measures that alter the adversary's decision-making calculus. By targeting the resources adversaries value—their tools, their infrastructure, and their anonymity—offensive operations create a deterrent effect that denial mechanisms alone cannot achieve (Valeriano et al., 2018).

Integrating the MLMD Framework

The strategic argument for integrating OCO is clarified when analysed through the MLMD framework. Defensive postures tend to be organised around technical controls and incident response, whereas many cyber campaigns generate effects through interacting dependencies across political intent, organisational design, intelligence support, and technical execution. Consequently, a defence-only posture can fail even when local technical measures improve, because misalignment across levels creates gaps that adversaries exploit.

At the tactical level, operational feasibility is conditioned by the properties of software and hardware systems, including vulnerability discovery, patch latency, and the diffusion of malicious tooling. These properties create recurrent opportunities for intrusion and persistence, which means that tactical defence can reduce exposure but rarely eliminates it. Consequently, the analytical issue is that tactical actions constrain what is possible at higher levels, because political objectives and operational plans depend on whether access can be created, maintained, and controlled under changing technical conditions.

At the operational level, cyberspace operations depend on intelligence support, organisational integration, and decision processes that translate political intent into authorised activity. Adversaries can use distributed infrastructure and intermediaries to stage activity across jurisdictions and sectors, which complicates monitoring, attribution, and response. Consequently, the operational problem concerns how states manage campaigns as continuing interaction rather than isolated incidents, including how intelligence, legal review, and command arrangements shape what options remain available under time pressure (Joint Chiefs of Staff, 2018).

At the strategic level, the cumulative effects of persistent campaigns can impose political and economic costs, degrade trust, and constrain freedom of action without producing a single decisive incident. Defensive measures can reduce specific harms, but they do not by themselves generate the coercive and signalling options that states may require when adversaries treat cyberspace as a domain of continuous competition. Consequently, offensive capability is analysed here as a policy instrument whose strategic value depends on whether it can be authorised, governed, and aligned with political objectives under conditions of uncertainty (Huskaj et al., 2024).

The MLMD framework is therefore used as an explanatory model of alignment. The framework links strategic purpose, operational governance, and tactical feasibility to show why technical action can diverge from political intent when intelligence is incomplete, time is compressed, and effects propagate across interconnected systems. This framing prepares the subsequent chapters by specifying the analytical dependencies that shape whether OCO can contribute to deterrence and defence without implying operational guidance.

Connecting Necessity to the Adversary Threat

The claim that the offence is framed as strategically necessary follows from how the domain operates under persistent competition. Structural exposure, recurrent vulnerability discovery, and the tempo of activity create incentives for adversaries to sustain campaigns that generate cumulative effects while remaining below traditional thresholds for armed conflict. Consequently, the analytical question is not whether defence has value, but under which conditions defence alone is unlikely to alter adversary behaviour, and why some states therefore integrate offensive capability as part of a broader posture.

This necessity is driven by observable patterns in adversary practice, including the use of long-term access, staged infrastructure, and iterative campaign design across espionage, disruption, and influence. The following section therefore examines how major state threat actors have operationalised these patterns in open sources, and how variation in their objectives and constraints shapes the requirements placed on deterrence and defence.

1.5 Adversaries and the Offensive Imperative

The strategic rationale for OCO arises directly from the behaviour of adversaries whose campaigns exploit the structural characteristics of digital systems. These campaigns are persistent, multi-vector, and deliberately positioned below the threshold of armed attack.

Their cumulative effect is to impose continuous operational strain on defenders while reshaping political and military decision environments. Because these behaviours exploit ambiguity, jurisdictional gaps, and the asymmetries of initiative inherent in cyberspace, defensive measures alone cannot meaningfully constrain adversary action. The offensive imperative therefore emerges as a structural condition of the threat environment: states require the ability to intervene inside adversary campaigns, disrupt preparation activities, and impose costs that alter adversary calculations. Without this capability, states remain confined to reactive postures that permit hostile actors to accumulate strategic advantage over time.

Russia: Hybrid Warfare and Norm Contestation

Russia exemplifies how cyberspace operations are integrated into a broader hybrid warfare strategy designed to influence, coerce, and destabilise without triggering overt escalation. Russian operators maintain persistent access within foreign networks to facilitate intelligence collection, reconnaissance, and the placement of tools that can be activated during crises. This persistent access is central to Russia's approach because it expands the set of options available at politically advantageous moments, allowing the Kremlin to shape decision-making indirectly. The 2015–2016 intrusions into Ukraine's power grid illustrate this logic: the disruption of electricity during a period of heightened conflict signalled Russian operational reach and magnified psychological pressure on the population (Huskaj and Axelsson, 2023). Defensive measures could not prevent such positioning because Russian access preparation occurred months in advance, demonstrating why states require offensive tools capable of degrading Russian infrastructure and interrupting its preparation cycles.

Russian campaigns also illustrate how adversaries exploit ambiguity to sustain operational tempo while avoiding decisive retaliation. By conducting intrusions that fall short of physical destruction or obvious kinetic correlation, Russia creates uncertainty about attribution, intent, and proportionality. This ambiguity impedes timely response and allows Russian operators to continue probing defences, manipulating political narratives, and eroding public trust. Russian interference in democratic processes, such as the 2016 U.S. election, demonstrates how cyber intrusions and information operations function jointly to weaken institutional legitimacy (Huskaj and Axelsson, 2023). Because defensive mechanisms cannot constrain the ambiguity Russia weaponises, states face a structural disadvantage unless they can impose costs on Russian operators. OCO therefore serve as a means to reduce Russia's freedom of manoeuvre, degrading its command-and-control assets and signalling that persistent hostility will incur operational and reputational consequences.

A further dimension of Russian activity involves norm contestation. Research demonstrates that Russia uses cyber operations to challenge Western interpretations of sovereignty, non-intervention, and responsible state behaviour (Huskaj, Sallinen and Nicander, 2021). By conducting disruptive actions below the armed-attack threshold, the Kremlin signals that these norms are negotiable and that cybersecurity is a domain where persistence yields strategic gain. This behaviour encourages other states to emulate ambiguity and probes the limits of tolerance within liberal democracies. The implication is that defensive measures, which rely on stabilised norms and predictable behaviour, are inadequate in a competitive environment where adversaries actively reject such norms. Offensive capabilities thus become necessary to defend not only national systems but also the normative foundations of the international order by demonstrating that norm violations carry operational consequences.

China: Civil-Military Fusion and Latent Access

China presents a different but equally consequential challenge rooted in systematic intelligence extraction, industrial policy, and long-term strategic positioning. Chinese cyber campaigns target research institutions, defence contractors, government agencies, and private firms to acquire intellectual property, technological insights, and sensitive data that can accelerate domestic development (Bengtsson and Huskaj, 2021). The 2014 breach of the U.S. Office of Personnel Management (OPM), in which millions of personnel records were exfiltrated, demonstrated the scale and strategic value of long-term data acquisition (Mandiant, 2013). Chinese operators sustain such campaigns because they assess that information superiority contributes directly to national rejuvenation and military modernisation. Defensive measures cannot constrain this behaviour because opportunities for access proliferate across sectors and jurisdictions. The implication is that states require OCO that can disrupt Chinese operational infrastructure and impede the processes enabling persistent intelligence extraction.

China's strategy also involves developing latent disruption capabilities designed for activation in crisis scenarios. This requires maintaining covert footholds in operational technology networks—such as energy, water, and transport infrastructure—without triggering detection. Such latent access can be used to impose societal disruption, delay mobilisation, or influence crisis decision-making. Because latent disruption relies on long-term persistence, defensive mechanisms alone cannot reliably eliminate it. OCO become necessary to hunt, identify, and degrade these covert access points and the supporting infrastructure that enables them. Persistent engagement, as articulated in U.S. doctrine, emerged partly as a response to such systematic preparation, recognising that preventing adversaries from shaping the battlespace requires continuous action "left of boom" (Nakasone, 2019). The logic is clear: only by contesting adversary presence proactively can states reduce the strategic value of latent disruption.

In addition to operational considerations, China engages in normative contestation by advancing the principle of "cyber sovereignty," advocating for state control over domestic information spaces and challenging the liberal vision of an open, global internet (Huskaj et al., 2021). This normative challenge supports Chinese strategic aims by legitimising information control and creating international acceptance for domestic restrictions that also shield offensive preparations. Defensive measures cannot address this dimension because it originates in diplomatic and ideological arenas. Offensive capability therefore becomes part of a broader strategic posture that signals resilience, imposes costs for coercive cyber activities, and reassures allies facing similar campaigns. The requirement is not to impose norms unilaterally but to ensure that hostile norms do not translate into unchallenged operational advantage.

Iran: Asymmetric Retaliation and Proxy Networks

Iran illustrates a third category of adversary that uses cyberspace as an asymmetric tool to compensate for limited conventional military capability. Iranian campaigns often combine disruptive attacks with espionage and retaliatory actions. The 2012 Shamoon attack on Saudi Aramco, which wiped data from tens of thousands of computers, exemplifies Iran's willingness to impose high-impact disruption in response to geopolitical tensions (Huskaj and Wilson, 2020*a*). Such operations rely on identifying vulnerabilities within civilian infrastructure and exploiting them through wiper malware capable of producing rapid and irrecoverable damage. Defensive mechanisms cannot eliminate these risks because Iran employs adaptable proxy networks and distributes operational tasks across loosely affiliated groups. OCO are therefore required to degrade

Iranian access, disrupt operational readiness, and reduce the feasibility of high-impact retaliation.

Iran's extensive use of proxies complicates attribution and slows diplomatic responses. Proxy groups receive support in the form of tools, training, and infrastructure, enabling them to conduct intrusions, data theft, and disruptive attacks across multiple sectors. This distributed structure creates a buffering layer that shields Iranian decision-makers from immediate consequences while permitting sustained low-intensity hostility. Defensive measures are ill-suited to counter this arrangement because they do not address the infrastructure and enabling relationships that empower proxies. OCO are necessary to target these enabling structures—such as shared servers, communication channels, or tool repositories—thereby reducing Iran's operational reach and raising the costs of attributional ambiguity. By limiting Iran's proxy-enabled manoeuvre space, offensive operations help restore strategic balance.

Iranian campaigns also function as signalling mechanisms designed to convey resolve and retaliatory capability. Cyber operations allow Iran to impose costs on adversaries while avoiding the political risk of kinetic escalation. For example, after the downing of a U.S. surveillance drone in 2019, the United States reportedly conducted a cyberspace operation disabling Iranian missile-related systems in lieu of kinetic strikes (Huskaj and Wilson, 2020*a*). This episode illustrates how cyber operations become tools within broader deterrence dynamics, enabling controlled responses that shape adversary expectations. Because Iran monitors geopolitical developments for opportunities to impose cyber costs, defensive mechanisms alone cannot prevent opportunistic retaliation. Offensive capabilities are required to reduce Iran's operational readiness by degrading its ability to execute rapid retaliatory actions.

North Korea: Regime Survival and Disruptive Revenue

North Korea represents a distinct threat actor whose cyber operations focus on revenue generation, disruption, and political signalling as means of regime survival. Cyber operations compensate for economic isolation and sanctions by enabling theft from financial institutions, cryptocurrency exchanges, and commercial entities. The 2016 Bangladesh Bank heist and subsequent campaigns demonstrate that North Korean operators use credential theft, phishing, and lateral movement across financial networks to acquire substantial funds for state objectives (Huskaj and Wilson, 2020*a*). Defensive measures cannot eliminate the incentives underlying these operations because the regime depends on cyber-enabled revenue streams to support its strategic programmes. OCO are therefore necessary to degrade North Korean infrastructure, disrupt laundering mechanisms, and impose costs that reduce the profitability of cybercrime.

North Korea also employs disruptive operations, including ransomware and destructive malware, to signal capability and raise the cost of international opposition. The 2017 WannaCry campaign, attributed to North Korean operators using repurposed exploits, demonstrated how indiscriminate propagation can generate global systemic risk (Huskaj and Wilson, 2021). Because these tools can be rapidly adapted and deployed with minimal warning, purely defensive measures cannot reliably pre-empt disruptive action. OCO that target North Korea's command-and-control structures, malware repositories, and operational infrastructure reduce the regime's readiness and complicate efforts to conduct rapid disruption. By degrading external access points in third-party jurisdictions, offensive operations also limit North Korea's ability to exploit global connectivity.

The Necessity of Intervention

Across all four adversaries, a common pattern emerges: hostile campaigns exploit persistence, ambiguity, and asymmetric incentives to achieve strategic effects without escalating to armed conflict. Defensive postures alone cannot disrupt adversaries' operational preparation, reduce their freedom of manoeuvre, or prevent cumulative advantage. The offensive imperative therefore reflects a structural reality: to restore strategic equilibrium, states need to possess capabilities that allow them to act within adversary campaigns, impose costs, and reduce the expected utility of hostile action. This is not a normative endorsement of aggression but an analytical recognition that the absence of offensive capability cedes initiative to adversaries whose operations are already persistent, adaptive, and strategically motivated.

The offensive imperative also arises from the need to protect allies and maintain credibility within collective defence frameworks. Persistent adversary campaigns often target multiple states simultaneously, exploiting differences in national regulation, capability, and attribution processes. Without offensive options, states cannot credibly contribute to collective defence, leaving gaps that adversaries can use to undermine alliance cohesion. NATO's designation of cyberspace as an operational domain reflects recognition that deterrence and defence require proactive measures that integrate offensive capabilities where legally authorised. The experience of hunt-forward operations conducted by partners illustrates how targeted, proactive actions can remove adversary footholds and enhance shared resilience.

These dynamics indicate why many states treat OCO as central instruments of contemporary statecraft. Adversary campaigns create structural conditions that defence alone cannot mitigate; states are required to disrupt preparation, remove access, and impose costs to influence adversary behaviour. Russia's hybrid integration of cyber and information operations, China's industrial-scale intelligence extraction and latent disruption, Iran's asymmetric retaliation and proxy networks, and North Korea's revenue-driven campaigns collectively illustrate a threat environment defined by persistence and adaptability. Offensive capability provides the means to counter these behaviours by intervening early, shaping adversary expectations, and restoring strategic balance. As subsequent chapters demonstrate, the challenge for democratic states is not whether to develop offensive capabilities, but how to integrate them within legitimate governance structures while maintaining strategic, ethical, and operational coherence.

1.6 OCO as Instruments of Statecraft

Having established why many states integrate OCO under conditions of persistent adversary activity, this section treats OCO as instruments of statecraft alongside the organisational and technical activities that enable their use. The core claim is that offensive capability generates strategic value only when it is embedded in a wider portfolio of diplomatic, informational, economic, military, and intelligence measures and governed through legal authority and political oversight. Because cyberspace operations occur under attribution frictions and compressed decision windows, the statecraft problem concerns alignment between intent, escalation management, institutional control, and technical feasibility. The section introduces cyber statecraft as the organising concept for analysing how OCO can be selected, sequenced, and constrained to support national objectives without implying operational methods or target choices.

Defining Cyber Statecraft

Cyber statecraft refers to the art and practice of employing cyber capabilities to advance national objectives through the integration of diplomatic, informational, military, and intelligence instruments of power. It represents the extension of traditional statecraft into the digital domain, characterised by non-territorial terrain, private-sector dominance, and accelerated decision cycles (Chas and Barrinha, 2024).

Recent policy-oriented studies by the University of Bath, King's College London, and RUSI arrive at a convergent understanding, conceptualising cyber statecraft as a "whole-of-society" endeavour that mobilises state, private, and civil actors to uphold responsible, democratic cyber power (Chas and Barrinha, 2024). Within this framework, intelligence provides the epistemic foundation for state behaviour in cyberspace: it reduces uncertainty, supports targeting, guides deterrence, and ensures that cyber operations remain aligned with ethical and legal norms.

Having established how adversary behaviour generates an offensive imperative, we now examine how OCO function not solely as technical countermeasures, but as integrated instruments of statecraft. In a domain characterised by continuous contact and ambiguity, states require structured means to influence adversary behaviour, protect national security interests, and manage escalation. OCO provides these means by enabling governments to project power and impose costs in ways that passive defence cannot. Joint doctrine captures this role by defining OCO as activities "intended to project power by the application of force in or through cyberspace" (Joint Chiefs of Staff, 2018). This definition situates OCO alongside other military capabilities, indicating that cyber tools are employed to achieve political and military objectives rather than to conduct isolated technical activities. The implication is that OCO may be needed to be integrated into broader strategic planning and governed through institutional arrangements that align technical capacity with national objectives.

Deterrence, Cost Imposition, and Signalling

OCO contribute to deterrence when they support both denial and punishment strategies under conditions of ambiguity and speed. Denial occurs when states use OCO to degrade or disrupt adversary attack infrastructure—such as botnets or command-and-control servers—thereby lowering the expected payoff of future campaigns and increasing operational friction for attackers (Van de Velde, 2023). By reducing the adversary's confidence in their own tools, denial strategies alter the cost-benefit calculus of aggression. Punishment strategies, conversely, rely on the credible threat of imposing costs on adversaries that cross defined thresholds, including destructive attacks on critical systems or persistent espionage against sensitive targets (Huskaj and Moradian, 2018). Because cyberspace is characterised by frequent, low-intensity operations below the threshold of armed attack, states employ sustained campaigning rather than episodic retaliation to shape adversary calculations (Van de Velde, 2023). The result is that OCO becomes central to deterrence strategies that seek to alter adversary decision-making by making hostile campaigns more costly and less predictable in outcome.

Beyond formal deterrence, OCO provides calibrated tools for disruption and shaping that operate below the threshold of war. States use targeted actions to deny (degrade, disrupt, destroy) or manipulate (alter data, spoof) adversary systems to interfere with specific operational chains (Huskaj and Wilson, 2020*a*). Manipulation actions are particularly potent instruments of statecraft because they can misdirect adversary assessments or decision-making without immediate detection, creating a "fog of war" effect within the digital domain (Huskaj, 2024*c*). These actions are selected because they generate specific political or military effects, such as delaying an attack, constraining coordination, or undermining confidence in internal reporting. The strategic value lies in expanding the policymaker's toolkit beyond the binary choice of inaction or kinetic force, enabling responses that can alter adversary behaviour while managing escalation risks.

Operational Design and Capability Governance

To fulfil these functions, OCO depends on integration with national strategy, doctrine, and institutional design. Technical capabilities do not generate strategic value unless they can be authorised and employed within decision-making timeframes that match the operational tempo of the adversary (USAF LeMay Center, 2023). Governments may therefore have to define clear authorities, command relationships, and approval processes that specify who can initiate planning and who can authorise execution. These arrangements determine whether offensive options are available when needed and whether they can be coordinated with other instruments of state power, such as sanctions or diplomacy. The implication is that organisational design is a determinant of deterrence credibility; poorly structured authorities can paralyse the state even when it possesses superior technical capability (Huskaj and Moradian, 2018).

Governance of offensive capabilities may also be required to address the full lifecycle of the triad of access, vulnerabilities, and payloads, as each element carries distinct risks and opportunities. Decision-makers face the Vulnerabilities Equities Process (VEP) dilemma: determining which discovered vulnerabilities to retain for potential offensive use and which to disclose to vendors for patching (Huskaj and Wilson, 2020*a*). This choice directly influences both national security (by enabling OCO) and broader cyber hygiene (by securing domestic systems). Furthermore, states may control how tools are developed, tested, and stored to avoid theft, reuse by adversaries, or unintended proliferation—risks highlighted by the leakage of tools like EternalBlue (Huskaj and Wilson, 2021). Access to foreign networks can be governed through compartmentalisation and audit mechanisms to prevent unauthorised use and to ensure that offensive actions do not conflict with ongoing intelligence requirements (Bronk, 2016; Valeriano et al., 2018). The implication is that capability governance is a core component of strategic management, ensuring that the pursuit of offensive capacity does not generate unacceptable systemic risk.

Legal and Ethical Constraints

Legal and ethical frameworks shape the legitimacy and feasibility of OCO as instruments of statecraft. In the absence of a comprehensive global cyber treaty, states apply existing principles of international law—sovereignty, non-intervention, and the prohibition of the use of force—to the digital domain (Mandsager et al., 2022). Guidance such as the Tallinn Manual 2.0 and the Newport Rules of Engagement Handbook clarify when a cyberspace operation may amount to a use of force or an armed attack and outline requirements for necessity, distinction, and proportionality (Schmitt, 2017; Mandsager et al., 2022). OCO depends on planning and execution through rigorous processes that incorporate legal review, assessment of potential cascading effects, and evaluation of escalation risks. The implication is that state practice is bounded by these norms; operations that ignore them risk undermining the very international order the state seeks to defend (Huskaj and Wilson, 2020*a*).

Ethical considerations, particularly regarding anticipatory ethics, further constrain planning. Decision-makers may weigh the potential for collateral damage—such as the disruption of civilian services—against military necessity. The risk of unintended cascading effects in interconnected systems means that even targeted operations can have broad consequences. Ethical governance requires that these risks be anticipated and mitigated during the design phase of an operation, ensuring that the means employed are proportionate to the ends sought (Huskaj and Wilson, 2020*a*).

The Intelligence-Offence Nexus

Intelligence requirements play a central role in determining the feasibility and risk profile of OCO. Offensive actions depend on precise, timely knowledge of target networks, their dependencies, and their defensive postures—knowledge that can only be generated through sustained Cyber Intelligence, Surveillance, and Reconnaissance (Cyber ISR) activities (Huskaj, 2024*c*). This dependency creates a structural convergence between intelligence collection and offensive action: the same accesses and vulnerabilities that enable espionage often enable attack (Huskaj and Wilson, 2020*a*).

This convergence produces the IGL dilemma. Using an access for a destructive attack typically reveals the method to the adversary, who will then patch the vulnerability or reconfigure the network, thereby closing a valuable intelligence window (Axelrod and Iliev, 2014). Decision-makers may constantly weigh the immediate tactical benefit of an offensive action against the long-term strategic value of continued intelligence collection. This calculation requires close coordination between intelligence agencies and military commanders to ensure that short-term operational gains do not compromise long-term situational awareness (Maschmeyer, 2021). The implication is that OCO cannot be planned in isolation; intelligence integration is a structural requirement for its effective design and employment.

Synthesis: Multi-Level Integration

These considerations specify how OCO function as intelligence-dependent instruments of statecraft whose feasibility and consequences are produced through interacting constraints at the strategic, operational, and tactical levels of the MLMD framework:

- At the strategic level, OCO supports national objectives by providing options for deterrence, signalling, and cost imposition. They allow the state to alter adversary expectations and manage escalation without resorting to kinetic war (Huskaj and Moradian, 2018).
- At the operational level, OCO depend on robust institutional designs—clear authorities, legal oversight, and intelligence integration—to ensure that campaigns are feasible, legitimate, and aligned with broader government actions (Huskaj and Wilson, 2020*a*).
- At the tactical level, OCO relies on the specific technical triad of accesses, vulnerabilities, and payloads. These assets can be discovered, validated, and maintained through sustained Cyber ISR activities, governed by strict lifecycle management to mitigate risk (Huskaj, 2024*c*).

The implication is that OCO design and use are conditioned by institutional arrangements that determine what can be authorised, sustained, and controlled under operational tempo. Strategic purpose shapes the types of effects that can be justified and signalled; operational governance and intelligence integration shape whether options can be generated and sequenced in time; tactical volatility shapes whether planned effects remain feasible once execution begins. The credibility of OCO as statecraft therefore depends on maintaining alignment across these constraints, because misalignment allows technical action to diverge from political intent or to exceed what oversight and escalation management can support.

1.7 Central Argument of the Book

This book advances a central claim: defence alone cannot secure national security interests in cyberspace under conditions of continuous adversary activity. OCO are required because adversaries conduct campaigns that exploit networks. A posture focused exclusively on defence places policy-makers, responding only after adversaries have achieved access, identified targets, and prepared payloads. The result is that states absorb harm to confidentiality, integrity, and availability while lacking instruments to alter adversary decision-making or impose costs (Huskaj, 2023*b*; Joint Chiefs of Staff, 2018). Offensive capability generates strategic value only when it is integrated across strategic, operational, and tactical decision-making and embedded in institutional, legal, and societal arrangements that enable coherent authorisation, planning, and execution.

A strong objection holds that even when states organise offensive capability, OCO may generate limited strategic value. The mechanism is that secrecy constrains signalling, attribution uncertainty delays or narrows response options, and technical volatility reduces control over how effects unfold. Under these conditions, vulnerability retention can leave widely used systems unpatched, and tool leakage can increase exposure for the initiating state and its partners. Misinterpretation under compressed decision windows can further increase escalation risk. The argument of this book addresses the objection by specifying that strategic value is conditional: offensive capability contributes to national security when it is integrated across strategic, operational, and tactical levels and embedded in institutional arrangements that support timely authorisation, intelligence-informed targeting, traceable risk governance, and legally bound selection of effects (Rid and Buchanan, 2015; Huskaj and Wilson, 2021; Maschmeyer, 2021).

Defence is insufficient because the technical and organisational properties of cyberspace favour persistent intrusion. Attackers need to identify one exploitable weakness in a system or operational process, while defenders may need to maintain the integrity of interconnected systems over time and across multiple domains. Legal constraints and attribution challenges further restrict the range and timing of defensive responses, particularly when hostile activity remains below the threshold of armed conflict. These conditions create an environment in which breach and compromise are recurrent outcomes, even for states that allocate resources to defensive capabilities. The implication is that a defence-only posture accepts an asymmetric baseline that leaves the strategic initiative with adversaries (Huskaj and Wilson, 2021; Bronk, 2016).

These structural conditions also create the IGL dilemma because using access for disruption can reveal methods and collapse collection windows. The implication is that shaping adversary behaviour requires integration between intelligence objectives and offensive options, since poorly sequenced action can reduce situational awareness and narrow future response space.

OCO are required for credible deterrence and strategic stability because they provide states with the capacity to shape the adversary's calculus under these structural conditions. Here, strategic stability denotes the capacity to manage escalation exposure and preserve political control while contesting persistent campaigns below the armed-conflict threshold. The ability to conduct tailored deny and manipulate actions against adversary systems demonstrates that a state can impose costs, degrade hostile infrastructure, and disrupt campaigns before they generate unacceptable harm (Van de Velde, 2023; Huskaj and Moradian, 2018). This capacity strengthens deterrence by signalling that hostile operations will trigger responses calibrated to political objectives and legal constraints. At the same time, integrating OCO with legal oversight and intelligence integration allows decision-makers to manage escalation risks by selecting operations that are proportionate, discriminating, and responsive to updated situational awareness (Fischerkeller and Harknett, 2017).

OCO contribute to national security only when they are embedded within institutional arrangements that integrate strategic, operational, and tactical levels. At the strategic level, political leaders may define objectives, thresholds, alliance commitments, and legal parameters that guide offensive planning. At the operational level, intelligence organisations, cyber units, and civilian agencies may coordinate to generate access, select targets, and align campaigns with national security interests and international obligations. At the tactical level, technical operators can implement the actions that produce denial or manipulation effects under constraints derived from law, policy, and ROE (Huskaj, 2024*c*; USAF LeMay Center, 2023). Offensive capability generates value when these levels are aligned because institutional coherence permits timely authorisation, coordinated intelligence integration, and controlled execution. When they are fragmented, offensive capability produces uncertainty, operational friction, and potential instability.

This argument structures the rest of the book. Theoretical chapters explain how deterrence, intelligence, and offensive action interact in cyberspace and why integration across these domains is required for statecraft. The MLMD framework then provides an analytical tool for tracing how decisions at the strategic, operational, and tactical levels propagate across political, ethical, organisational, and technical dimensions. Subsequent chapters examine a dedicated national case study in Chapter 4, analyse vulnerability governance and anticipatory ethics, and assess organisational arrangements for a whole-of-society approach to OCO. The concluding synthesis returns to the central claim advanced here and evaluates how the findings clarify the conditions under which OCO can strengthen national security while preserving strategic stability.

1.8 Roadmap of the Book

The structure of the book is designed to operationalise the central argument that OCO can be integrated across strategic, operational, and tactical levels and embedded within institutional, legal, and societal arrangements. The chapters follow a sequence from theoretical foundations through framework development to empirical application and synthesis. This progression is required because the conditions under which OCO contribute to national security cannot be assessed without a clear conceptual vocabulary, a structured analytical model, and a detailed examination of state practice. The result is a coherent path that links abstract reasoning to practical implications for national security interests.

Chapter 2 develops the theoretical foundations for the book by integrating deterrence theory, intelligence theory, and OCO theory into a single conceptual architecture. The chapter is organised by the levels of analysis used in the MLMD framework: deterrence theory specifies strategic purpose and credibility conditions for denial and punishment; intelligence theory explains how collection and assessment reduce uncertainty, enable lawful targeting, and compress decision cycles under operational tempo; and OCO theory specifies the tactical means through which access, vulnerabilities, and payloads are combined to generate authorised effects. Across these levels, the chapter treats legality, proportionality, vulnerability governance, and oversight as constraints that condition credibility because they shape what can be executed, what can be signalled, and what can be controlled. The synthesis prepares Chapter 3 by showing how ends, ways, and means remain aligned only when deterrent intent, intelligence integration, and technical feasibility are coordinated under defined authority (Snyder, 1961; Schelling, 1966).

Chapter 3 introduces the MLMD framework as the core analytical instrument of the book. It formalises how strategic, operational, and tactical levels interact in the design, authorisation, and execution of OCO while treating political authority, ethical constraint, and technological feasibility as cross-cutting conditions. The framework clarifies how strategic intent and legal mandate delimit operational options, how intelligence integration and campaign design shape what can be executed and when, and how tactical choices about access, vulnerabilities, and payloads can generate second- and third-order political and ethical consequences. The purpose is analytical rather than procedural: MLMD supports systematic tracing of dependencies, frictions, and trade-offs across levels and dimensions, and it provides a structured basis for applying the same lens across empirical cases (Huskaj et al., 2024).

Chapters 4 to 6 apply the MLMD framework to empirical and organisational material. Chapter 4 presents a focused national case study that uses publicly available sources to examine how a cyberliterate state articulates objectives, allocates responsibilities, and manages exposure to persistent adversary activity under legal and political constraint (Huskaj and Axelsson, 2023). Chapter 5 examines vulnerability exploitation as an IGL and anticipatory ethics problem by analysing how decisions to discover, retain, and disclose zero-day vulnerabilities trade operational leverage against systemic risk, legal constraint, and normative consequences, drawing on cases such as Stuxnet, Heartbleed, and WannaCry and on institutional mechanisms such as the United States Vulnerabilities Equities Process (Huskaj and Wilson, 2021; Huskaj and Wilson, 2020*b*). Chapter 6 analyses capability generation as an institutional alignment problem by examining how government, industry, and academia contribute inputs that condition offensive capability development and readiness, and how oversight and coordination shape the boundary conditions for employment (Huskaj and Axelsson, 2023). Together, these chapters demonstrate how the MLMD framework supports analysis of institutional arrangements without implying operational guidance.

Chapters 7 to 9 synthesise and extend the analysis. Chapter 7 uses a paired design—WannaCry as an uncontrolled real-world incident and a cyber range scenario as exercise-based material—to show how OCO unfold under time compression, partial intelligence, and technical volatility and what these constraints imply for maintaining alignment across the strategic, operational, and tactical layers specified in MLMD (Huskaj and Iftimie, 2020; Huskaj and Blix, 2022; Huskaj, 2024*c*). Chapter 8 extends MLMD into a prospective analysis by examining how technological acceleration—particularly AI-enabled tooling and quantum risk—interacts with legal authority, ethical constraint, alliance practice, and evolving normative interpretation to shape what can be authorised and controlled under narrowed decision windows (Huskaj, 2026). Chapter 9 synthesises the book's conceptual and empirical findings to restate and evaluate the central causal claim—strategic value depends on integration across levels and embedding in legal, institutional, and societal arrangements—and to specify where additional governance safeguards, institutional reform, or conceptual refinement are required (Huskaj, 2024*c*).

Decision Exercise: Authorising Persistent Engagement Under Ambiguity

Scenario. A partner government requests a time-limited hunt-forward deployment after credible reporting indicates persistent access in its energy-sector networks. The same actor is assessed to be running influence activity against the partner's election administration. Public attribution remains contested, and the partner seeks visible reassurance. Technical reporting suggests the access path may close if exposed, and the operational window is assessed as short.

Analytical question 1—Strategic purpose and success condition. State the strategic purpose of approving the deployment (denial, signalling, reassurance, intelligence, or a bounded combination) and specify one observable outcome that would indicate that the purpose has been met. Explain why that outcome is a credible indicator under attribution frictions and time compression.

Analytical question 2—IGL and sequencing. Identify the principal IGL trade-off created by acting now. Specify what information should be preserved, what can be risked, and how this assessment should shape sequencing and limits on action.

Analytical question 3—Authority, oversight, and escalation exposure. Specify the minimum authorisation and oversight conditions required to proceed (legal basis, political approval threshold, inter-agency coordination, and partner constraints). Explain how these conditions reduce escalation exposure while preserving timely decisions.

Short task—MLMD mapping (one page). Create a 3-row mapping (Strategic / Operational / Tactical) listing: (i) the decision at each level, (ii) the key dependency at that level (authority, intelligence, feasibility), and (iii) one failure mode where misalignment would cause technical action to diverge from political intent.

2

Towards a Theory of Cyber Power

This chapter provides the theoretical foundations needed to analyse offensive cyberspace operations (OCO) as instruments of statecraft. It integrates deterrence theory, intelligence theory, and OCO theory into a single conceptual account of how states project power through cyberspace under conditions of time compression, partial intelligence, and technical volatility. This integration is required because each theory, treated in isolation, explains only part of the causal chain. Deterrence theory specifies strategic purpose and credibility conditions, but it does not explain how intelligence and technical feasibility constrain what can credibly be threatened or executed. Intelligence theory explains how uncertainty is reduced, but it does not by itself account for how collected access and knowledge are converted into authorised effects. OCO theory specifies the technical means of action, but it does not explain how those means remain aligned with political intent, legal authority, and escalation management. The synthesis in this chapter therefore specifies the analytical requirements that the Multi-Level, Multi-Dimensional (MLMD) framework formalises in Chapter 3 (Huskaj et al., 2024).

The scope and limits of this chapter are conceptual and explanatory. It synthesises open-source scholarship and doctrine to explain how deterrence theory, intelligence theory, and OCO theory function as analytical constructs and how they relate. It does not provide operational instruction, target-selection guidance, technical procedures, or tradecraft. Technical terms (for example, "access," "vulnerability," and "payload") are used only to describe dependencies that shape feasibility, credibility, and governance. Any illustrative cases are used to clarify causal linkages, not to describe methods for conducting operations.

The structure of the chapter follows the levels of analysis central to MLMD. At the strategic level, deterrence theory explains how states seek to impose costs or deny benefits in order to alter an adversary's decision-making under uncertainty (Snyder, 1961). At the operational level, intelligence theory explains how direction, collection, analysis, and dissemination reduce uncertainty, support lawful targeting, and compress decision cycles under operational tempo (Omand, 2021). At the tactical level, OCO theory specifies how access, vulnerabilities, and payloads are combined to generate authorised effects within and through cyberspace (Joint Chiefs of Staff, 2018). By mapping these theories across political, ethical, and technical dimensions, the chapter shows why cyber power depends on alignment between intent, intelligence support, and technical feasibility. The conclusion synthesises these components and prepares Chapter 3, where MLMD is formalised as a framework for structured analysis of planning, authorisation, and assessment.

2.1 The Need for an Integrated Theory of Cyber Power

Cyberspace operations present a unique strategic domain where states can project influence, collect intelligence, and deliver effects faster than in other domains (Huskaj, 2024*c*).

DOI: 10.1201/9781003655183-2

However, understanding this domain through only one theoretical lens is insufficient; it leads to partial comprehension of cyber capabilities and their uses. A fragmented view risks misaligning strategy with means and tactics. For example, deterrence without integration and intelligence collection lacks credibility; intelligence collection without offensive capabilities provides insights but not the capacity to act when needed; and OCO without a clear policy or deterrence risk uncontrolled escalation (Huskaj and Axelsson, 2023).

The purpose of this section is to motivate an integrated approach, which explains three foundational theories: deterrence theory, intelligence theory, and offensive cyber operations theory. This section demonstrates how each operates across different levels and dimensions, including the strategic, operational, and tactical levels as well as political, ethical, and technical dimensions (Huskaj et al., 2024). An integrated approach is necessary for policy design, governance, and force development in an environment characterised by uncertainty and operational tempo. The necessity of integration lies not only in generating a comprehensive understanding of cyberspace operations but also in sustaining coherent decision-making under conditions of high operational tempo and uncertainty.

Deterrence Theory: The Strategic Purpose

Deterrence theory provides a rationale and tools for how states can influence an adversary's choices before the adversary can cause harm (Huskaj and Moradian, 2018). In the cyber domain, this deterrence approach is strained because of inherent secrecy surrounding offensive tools, the ephemeral nature of vulnerabilities, and difficulties in demonstrating credible offensive power without revealing technical details that could compromise their utility.

Strategic practice has evolved from episodic crisis management into steady-state competition where routine operations shape adversary behaviour without necessarily triggering overt conflict. The doctrine of Defend Forward exemplifies this shift towards proactive cyber operations; the purpose is to disrupt and deter adversaries "left of boom," meaning to disrupt a threat early enough to prevent the "boom": the moment an attacker successfully executes malware, encrypts data (ransomware), or steals sensitive files. In other words, before they can act against national interests.

Defend Forward blurs the distinction between defence and offence by emphasising anticipatory action. Persistent Engagement serves as the operational construct that underpins Defend Forward, involving constant interaction with adversary capabilities, contending activities, learning from each encounter, and shaping the digital environment to maintain initiative. The logic mirrors other deterrence postures: just as navies patrol to preserve freedom of navigation, cyber forces patrol the networked domain to deny adversaries operational freedom. This is a shift away from an absolute prevention of hostile acts towards continuous management within tolerable bounds of competition, as argued by Fischerkeller and Harknett (Fischerkeller and Harknett, 2017).

Four-star general Paul Nakasone, former head of the National Security Agency and USCYBERCOM, operationalises this with persistent engagement: directing forces to act persistently in order to contest adversary behaviour below the threshold of armed conflict (Nakasone, 2019). Deterrence is sustained through continuous action supported by timely intelligence on adversary intent, capability, and opportunity for attack. In other words, deterrence in cyberspace is not about preventing hostile acts absolutely; rather, it involves managing these activities within tolerable bounds of competition.

Intelligence Theory: The Operational Understanding

Intelligence theory provides a conceptual framework for understanding how information is directed, collected, processed, analysed, and disseminated in order to reduce uncertainty about adversarial intentions and capabilities, and to support decision-making in the development of policy, strategy, and operational plans for cyber operations (Huskaj, 2024*c*). The intelligence cycle—direction, collection, processing, analysis, and dissemination—organises this effort and links information requirements to operational outcomes, while, in practice, functioning as an iterative and interactive process rather than a strictly linear sequence. In the context of OCO, elements of the cycle may overlap and compress in time, because intelligence collection and CE can continue alongside active operational engagement. Multiple intelligence disciplines contribute to this environment.

The purpose of intelligence is to provide decision-makers with information collected, processed and exploited from numerous sources. This can be information about the threat actor's capabilities, intent and opportunity, but also about one's own information systems that are critical for supporting the mission. In other words, intelligence in cyberspace operations consists of two types: intelligence for supporting cyberspace operations and intelligence for cyberspace operations to support other domains (Joint Chiefs of Staff, 2018). Therefore, as in the other domains, the first step is to generate an understanding of the operational environment, which in this case is cyberspace. It consists of three layers: the physical network layer, the logical network layer and the cyber-persona layer (Joint Chiefs of Staff, 2018).

Signals intelligence (SIGINT) supports the identification of command-and-control systems; open-source intelligence (OSINT) contributes to the identification of operators, tools, and organisational structures; and human intelligence (HUMINT) can enable close or privileged access to targets. Other intelligence disciplines, such as imagery and measurement techniques, may support targeting and assessment where relevant. These activities represent an extension of traditional intelligence, surveillance, and reconnaissance (ISR) functions into cyberspace. Cyber ISR focuses on mapping digital terrain, identifying exploitable dependencies, and providing situational awareness in cyberspace to support military planning and operations (Huskaj and Iftimie, 2020; Joint Chiefs of Staff, 2018). Intelligence theory also engages with the ethical and legal dimensions of cyber operations by informing assessments of proportionality, necessity, accountability, and escalation risk. At the operational level, intelligence connects strategic intent to tactical execution by translating policy objectives into feasible plans for action while managing uncertainty across an operation's lifecycle. Where such integration is absent, tactical success may fail to produce intended strategic effects (Huskaj, 2024*c*).

OCO Theory: The Tactical Means

OCO theory explains how states can project power through digital means, in a manner consistent with doctrine such as Joint Publication 3-12 (Joint Chiefs of Staff, 2018). Offensive activity within OCO encompasses both cyberspace exploitation (CE) and cyberspace attack (CA), and may shift between these modes as access is gained, maintained, and, when authorised, converted into operational effects. At the tactical level, offensive operations rely on a technical triad of access, vulnerability, and payload, coordinated through TTPs that typically progress from reconnaissance to action on objectives, often with an emphasis on limiting detection. In this sense, OCO theory defines the what: the executable means through which deterrence can be rendered credible and intelligence preparation can be translated into operational action (Huskaj, 2024*c*; Joint Chiefs of Staff, 2018).

Synthesis: The MLMD Framework

The structure of this book follows the MLMD framework. It is grounded in the triad of deterrence theory, intelligence theory, and OCO theory. Here, theory denotes a systematic means of ordering relationships among observed elements to explain how the world works and to improve informed action (Dubin, 1978; Lynham, 2002). By contrast, doctrine denotes an established corpus of guidance within a profession such as the military (Harper, 2024).

MLMD arranges these theories into a coherent analytical structure. Deterrence specifies the strategic purpose by shaping expected costs and benefits. Intelligence reduces uncertainty by directing collection and producing decision-relevant assessments. OCO supplies the authorised means for generating effects at the tactical level in support of political intent.

These theories are mutually reinforcing: deterrence provides the strategic purpose; intelligence provides understanding of the operational environment, including adversary targets; and OCO delivers action against those targets. Together, the three theories form the conceptual foundation of the MLMD framework, describing how ends, ways, and means align in OCO (Huskaj, 2024*c*).

Purpose and Approach

The analytical aim of this chapter is to synthesise deterrence theory, intelligence theory, and OCO theory into a coherent conceptual framework that explains how strategic intent, operational preparation, and tactical execution interact across political, ethical, and technical dimensions. The purpose is to specify how this interaction conditions the organisation, governance, and employment of OCO for policy design and capability development. This enquiry addresses two practical challenges: first, the fragmentation of theory and doctrine that separates strategic intent, intelligence preparation, and operational capability; and second, the requirement to align ethical–legal governance with technical feasibility and decision tempo. These challenges motivate an integrated framework in which intelligence is treated as an operational precondition for authorised action and OCOs are analysed as politically directed and ethically bounded practices as well as technical activities (Huskaj and Wilson, 2021; Joint Chiefs of Staff, 2018).

The chapter develops this synthesis through conceptual and doctrinal analysis supported by illustrative cases. The analysis draws on strategic reasoning about deterrence and state behaviour, on scholarship that conceptualises intelligence as a decision-support process, and on military cyber doctrine to specify categories, authorities, and practice. Short comparative vignettes—Estonia 2007, Stuxnet 2010, and APT10 2013–2017—are used to demonstrate how deterrence, intelligence, and OCO interact across strategic, operational, and tactical levels and within political, ethical, and technical dimensions. The cases are used to clarify causal linkages between intent, preparation, and execution rather than to provide historical reconstruction (Joint Chiefs of Staff, 2018; Huskaj, 2024*c*).

Three implications follow from this integrated stance. First, deterrence in cyberspace remains viable when it is anchored in demonstrable capability and supported by intelligence on adversary preferences and thresholds; credibility depends on employable means and plausible pathways, not declaratory policy alone (Schelling, 1966; Nakasone, 2019). Second, intelligence links strategy to execution and returns assessment to strategy; the quality and timeliness of intelligence condition lawful conduct and operational performance under uncertainty (Clark, 2019; Huskaj, 2024*c*). Third, offensive capability requires explicit authorities and anticipatory ethics so that tactical decisions advance strategic objectives while constraining unintended effects; governance is therefore integral to capability development and use (Huskaj and Wilson, 2021; Joint Chiefs of Staff, 2018).

The chapter proceeds in an essay structure that mirrors this integration. It first examines deterrence at the strategic level, specifying how credibility, signalling, and acceptable risk are maintained when capabilities and intentions are partly concealed. It then analyses intelligence at the operational level, describing how direction, collection, processing, analysis, and dissemination reduce uncertainty and inform decision-making under legal and ethical constraints. It next considers OCO at the tactical level, outlining how access, vulnerabilities, and payload behaviour condition feasibility and control, and how governance structures shape authorised use. The synthesis section integrates the three theoretical strands into a coherent framework and derives organisational implications. The concluding transition prepares Chapter 3, where the MLMD framework is formalised for planning, authorisation, and assessment (Huskaj, 2024*c*; Joint Chiefs of Staff, 2018).

2.2 Deterrence and the Strategic Grammar of Cyberspace

Deterrence is a form of power: the deliberate effort to alter an adversary's risk calculus by reshaping expected costs, benefits, and probabilities of success, based on the assumption that actors reason according to the principle of mathematical expectation (Snyder, 1960; Snyder, 1961). Under this principle, decision-makers compare alternative courses of action by weighting the value of possible outcomes against their estimated probabilities and selecting the option with the highest expected value. Deterrence influences behaviour only insofar as it modifies these expectations by increasing anticipated costs or reducing perceived benefits. The adversary's risk calculus therefore represents a structured evaluation of expected gains and losses derived from this decision rule.

As a form of political power, deterrence depends on resources that sustain credible capability, including forces, doctrine, and organisational means to apply or withhold them. Classical theory distinguishes deterrence by punishment, which threatens unacceptable costs following aggression, and deterrence by denial, which seeks to make aggression fail in practice. Both rely on credibility—the perceived likelihood that a threatened response will occur—and on signalling, which communicates capability, intent, and thresholds (Snyder, 1960; Schelling, 1966; Huskaj, 2024*c*). In Snyder's formulation, the calculus rests on four variables: valuation of the objective, expected costs of possible responses, the probability of each response (including restraint), and the probability of success for each response (Snyder, 1960).

During the Cold War, deterrence operated through visible forces, rehearsed planning, and formal declaratory policy. Deterrence by punishment imposed intolerable costs, while deterrence by denial promised that aggression would fail. Both required proven capability and a reputation for resolve (Snyder, 1960). Schelling's analysis of bargaining, salience, and the "power to hurt" explained how states communicated commitments and limits (Schelling, 1966). Credibility was sustained through observable capability, disciplined signalling, and stable governance arrangements. Because strategic forces were visible and their effects widely understood, adversaries could infer intent and capability with limited ambiguity. Proportionality was guided by shared expectations of damage, time, and scale, enabling calibrated responses without uncontrolled escalation.

The Cold War model remains analytically useful, but cyberspace alters its underlying conditions. OCOs unfold at machine speed, where observability is fragmented and effects may be reversible or deliberately concealed. These characteristics compress decision time, expand opportunities for action below the threshold of armed attack, and erode the visibility on which classical credibility and signalling depended. Deterrence in cyberspace therefore functions through continuous interaction aimed at shaping adversary behaviour, requiring persistent engagement to manage uncertainty and contest hostile activity (Fischerkeller and Harknett, 2017; Nakasone, 2019; Huskaj, 2024*c*).

Operations proceed through pre-positioning, lateral movement, and continual tool modification (Huskaj, 2024*c*; Joint Chiefs of Staff, 2018). Outcomes depend less on singular decisive moments than on sustained pressure that constrains adversary freedom of action over time (Fischerkeller and Harknett, 2017; USAF LeMay Center, 2023). The doctrines of Defend Forward and Persistent Engagement reflect this shift: cyber forces maintain forward presence in adversary infrastructure, impose repeated disruption, and shape behaviour through cumulative effects (USAF LeMay Center, 2023; Nakasone, 2019; Huskaj, 2024*c*). Deterrence thus acquires a campaign character defined by tempo, reach, and adaptation.

Credibility is more difficult to demonstrate in cyberspace because capabilities are temporary, protected by secrecy, and dependent on intelligence access. Employing an exploit to impose cost may expose methods and close valuable access, while withholding its use may generate doubt about capability or resolve (Huskaj, 2024*c*). States therefore sustain credibility through cumulative indicators rather than public demonstrations of specific tools. Whereas nuclear testing once served this function, cyber credibility is conveyed through attribution capacity, targeted sanctions, infrastructure seizures, cooperation with private and academic actors, and measured operations conducted under lawful authority that demonstrate competence without compromising sources or methods (Joint Chiefs of Staff, 2018). Over time, credibility rests on consistent execution of authorised missions, doctrinal coherence, and demonstrable operational results.

Signalling communicates intent and consequence to adversaries, allies, and domestic audiences. Attribution delays, evidentiary constraints, and audience heterogeneity complicate both timing and content (Rid and Buchanan, 2015; Buchanan, 2017; Schelling, 1966; Snyder, 1960). States therefore combine public attribution statements, coordinated indictments, targeted financial actions, diplomatic expulsions, and selective technical disclosures to demonstrate awareness without compromising intelligence collection (Joint Chiefs of Staff, 2018). NATO's acknowledgement that severe cyber operations may trigger Article 5 provides a collective signalling mechanism (Nakasone, 2019). Declaratory policy and curated demonstrations, including exercises, further shape adversary expectations while preserving operational security (Libicki, 2016; Huskaj, 2017).

Proportionality in cyberspace concerns the scale and effect of a response relative to the harm caused. Decision-makers must assess whether an operation achieves its purpose without producing excessive or unintended consequences. Relevant considerations include target type, duration of disruption, and potential spill-over to civilian systems (Joint Chiefs of Staff, 2018). Responses may combine legal, economic, informational, and military measures, but must remain consistent with domestic and international law, alliance commitments, and strategic intent (Huskaj, 2017; Snyder, 1960). Accurate intelligence and command review are therefore required to keep authorised actions within lawful and ethical limits.

Deterrence by denial in cyberspace seeks to make hostile operations difficult, costly, and uncertain. It relies on measures that constrain penetration, restrict lateral movement, and shorten intruder dwell time, including privilege control, network segmentation, intrusion monitoring, and rapid restoration (Huskaj, 2017; Huskaj, 2024*c*). Denial cannot prevent all intrusions, but consistent implementation increases detection probability, reduces adversary payoff, and undermines the value of persistence. The strategic requirement is to invest in defences that frustrate adversary objectives while preserving operational continuity and credibility.

Operationalising deterrence by denial in networked systems can be achieved through Saltzer and Schroeder's design principles for information protection. Applied consistently, these principles constrain access, authority propagation, and compromise recording, thereby altering the adversary's decision calculus by increasing cost, complexity, and detection risk (Saltzer and Schroeder, 1975).

Punishment in cyberspace alters adversary expectations by imposing concrete costs through law enforcement, administrative action, and tailored OCO (Fischerkeller and Harknett, 2017; Huskaj, 2024*c*). States indict operators, apply sanctions, expose infrastructure and methods, and conduct operations that disrupt services, degrade tools, or remove access at operationally relevant moments (Libicki, 2016; Huskaj, 2017). Legal reforms, including penalties for crimes against democratic processes, can further raise expected costs (Huskaj and Moradian, 2018). Under due-diligence norms, a state may incur responsibility if hostile cyber activity is attributable to it or if it knowingly fails to prevent harmful operations launched from its territory (Huskaj and Moradian, 2018). The implication is that visible, repeatable cost imposition—combined with due-diligence expectations—reduces anticipated benefit and constrains future operations.

Political direction defines expectations and authorises responses. National policy and international norms specify when OCO may generate authorised effects for deterrence and defence, while cabinet-level authority allocates legal powers and responsibility (Huskaj and Axelsson, 2023; Huskaj, 2024*c*; Huskaj et al., 2024). Clear authorities reduce hesitation costs, enable timely action, and integrate non-kinetic instruments such as exposure and sanctions with technical measures (Huskaj and Moradian, 2018). Alliances extend deterrence by pooling attribution capacity, coordinating disclosure, and sharing operational lessons, thereby increasing credibility and reducing safe havens (Huskaj and Moradian, 2018). Persistent engagement then links daily operations to denial and punishment by imposing continuous friction and constraining adversary freedom of action (Fischerkeller and Harknett, 2017; Huskaj, 2023*b*).

2.3 Intelligence as the Ethical Core of Cyber Statecraft

While Chapter 1 defined cyber statecraft as the integration of national instruments of power, intelligence serves as the central mechanism enabling decision-makers to apply that power deliberately by understanding adversary intent and capabilities. It supports OCO primarily through targeting by generating access, identifying vulnerabilities, and enabling the development of payloads (Huskaj, 2024*c*; Huskaj et al., 2024; Joint Chiefs of Staff, 2018). Intelligence conducted in cyberspace also supports operations in other domains by informing cross-domain planning and coordination (Joint Chiefs of Staff, 2018). In this context, intelligence is defined as the organised process that reduces uncertainty and creates decision opportunities through planning and direction, collection, processing and exploitation, analysis and production, and dissemination and integration (Huskaj, 2024*c*). In cyberspace, this process additionally informs the interpretation of international law and assessments of proportionality when offensive actions are considered (USAF LeMay Center, 2023).

The intelligence cycle constitutes the conceptual foundation of intelligence theory within the MLMD framework (Huskaj, 2024*c*). In the cyber domain, the cycle must be executed at increased speed because targets change rapidly, infrastructures are interdependent, and effects may materialise with limited warning, including cascading failures (Huskaj and Blix, 2022). Intelligence frameworks must therefore support faster iteration without altering the core structure of the cycle (Military Intelligence and Security Service, 2024). This requirement creates operational pressure on planning, collection, analysis, and dissemination during the preparation and execution of OCO (Huskaj, 2024*a*).

Planning and direction are continuous rather than discrete activities. Intelligence requirements evolve as collection identifies vulnerabilities (Huskaj, Iftimie and Wilson, 2020) and as adversaries modify their infrastructure. Collection combines reconnaissance with Cyberspace Exploitation (CE), defined as intelligence-gathering activities using non-destructive payloads intended to remain undetected over extended periods. These activities support future operations by collecting information, discovering vulnerabilities, and enabling target development. Processing and exploitation prioritise triage because data volumes—such as packet captures, logs, and artefacts—exceed the capacity of manual analysis. Automation and advanced computational techniques, including artificial intelligence, are therefore required to support timely exploitation while retaining human judgement for assessing relevance and source reliability (Granåsen, Huskaj and Varga, 2019; Huskaj, 2024*a*; Military Intelligence and Security Service, 2024).

Analysis and production rely on the fusion of classified and open information across multiple intelligence disciplines, including HUMINT, SIGINT, Open Source Intelligence, Technical Intelligence, and Cyber ISR. This fusion generates assessments that provide Cyber Situational Awareness (CSA) as an input to operational decision-making (Huskaj and Blix, 2022). Dissemination and integration emphasise precision and timing rather than volume, ensuring intelligence products reach operators and policy-makers in formats aligned with operational and decision cycles (USAF LeMay Center, 2023).

Intelligence activities are constrained by ethical and legal considerations that govern how information is collected, analysed, and used in support of offensive operations (Huskaj, 2024*c*). A central challenge concerns vulnerability management, including the Vulnerability Equities Process (VEP), which structures decisions on whether zero-day vulnerabilities should be disclosed to enable remediation or retained for intelligence or offensive purposes (Huskaj, 2019). These constraints shape both operational choice and strategic credibility.

Within the MLMD framework, intelligence provides the operational rationale linking the Strategic Level—where deterrence objectives and policy intent are defined—to the Tactical Level, where OCO are executed through specific technical actions (Huskaj, 2024*c*). The compression of the intelligence cycle does not remove its constituent disciplines; it requires their application at a higher operational tempo. This condition necessitates that legal constraints and Rules of Engagement (ROE) are established in advance to reduce friction in decision-making under time pressure (Huskaj and Blix, 2022). Predefined constraints enable informed action while mitigating risks associated with increased speed, including unintended cascading effects and the loss of operational capabilities.

Integration of Intelligence Disciplines

CSA cannot be produced by a single intelligence source because no individual discipline can account simultaneously for adversary intent, technical capability, and operational context. Technical observation can describe system behaviour, but it does not explain why actions occur or who directs them. Situational awareness in cyberspace therefore requires information derived from multiple intelligence activities rather than reliance on source primacy.

CSA refers to the current and forward-looking understanding of cyberspace and the surrounding operational environment upon which cyberspace operations rely (Joint Chiefs of Staff, 2018). CSA is produced by combining intelligence reporting, observations from ongoing operations, and continuous technical monitoring, because activity in cyberspace evolves at a pace that compresses decision cycles. Within the United States doctrine, Department of Defense Information Network (DODIN) operations sustain this awareness by maintaining visibility over friendly networks, preserving data availability, and controlling access conditions required for cyberspace operations (Joint Chiefs of Staff, 2018). Intelligence reporting, including SIGINT and indications and warnings, contributes information about adversary behaviour, while parallel assessment of friendly networks identifies degradation or compromise that may constrain operations. Decision-makers can act within compressed timeframes only when CSA is continuously maintained as adversaries adapt their behaviour.

Empirical research shows that CSA cannot be explained at the level of individual cognition alone because awareness in cyber defence operations emerges through interaction between people, organisational arrangements, and technical systems. Granåsen, Huskaj, and Varga conceptualise CSA as arising from the combined activity of personnel, organisational roles, technical artefacts, and communication channels within cyber defence teams (Granåsen et al., 2019). Using Endsley's three-tier model of situational awareness—perception, comprehension, and projection—their analysis demonstrates that these functions are distributed across human and technical components, including sub-teams, reporting mechanisms, and monitoring systems, rather than residing in individual operators. Awareness is produced through structured information exchange and artefact-supported assessment under operational time pressure. This aligns with doctrinal approaches that treat situational awareness as a command-and-control requirement sustained through coordinated intelligence processes and human–machine interaction.

The intelligence disciplines are operationally interdependent because collection and analysis occur iteratively rather than as discrete stages. Information derived from HUMINT can initiate or refine SIGINT activities by identifying relevant actors or communication nodes. OSINT constrains interpretation by exposing publicly observable technical or behavioural indicators that inform analytic hypotheses. Cyber ISR supports the validation or falsification of assessments through technical observation and, where authorised, access to adversary systems. Organisational processes that integrate intelligence outputs enable the construction of target system representations and the identification of feasible courses of action, thereby supporting proportional and operationally viable options (Huskaj, 2024*c*; USAF LeMay Center, 2023). Situational awareness therefore depends on coordination across intelligence activities, shared system understanding, and continuous testing of assumptions against observed behaviour.

HUMINT refers to the collection and use of information obtained from human sources to identify intent, motivation, and decision-making processes that cannot be derived from technical observation alone (Lenaerts-Bergmans, 2023; Group-IB Threat Intelligence Team, 2025; DiMaggio, 2024). In cyberspace, HUMINT extends established tradecraft into digital environments such as encrypted communication platforms, criminal marketplaces, and online forums. Operators adopt assumed identities and sustain interaction with targets to obtain information on planned activities, changes in tactics, and attribution-relevant indicators (DiMaggio, 2024). HUMINT addresses an analytic limitation of technical collection by linking observed activity to human agency, thereby supporting early warning, attribution assessment, and coordination with law-enforcement authorities (Lenaerts-Bergmans, 2023; Group-IB Threat Intelligence Team, 2025).

SIGINT is derived from the interception and analysis of electronic signals associated with communications systems and other emitters. In the cyber domain, SIGINT supports identification of command-and-control relationships, communication patterns, and operational tempo through analysis of signal content and metadata across adversary infrastructures (National Security Agency, 2024; Joint Chiefs of Staff, 2018; Huskaj, 2024*c*). United States doctrine treats SIGINT as part of the all-source intelligence enterprise and distinguishes Communications Intelligence (COMINT), Electronic Intelligence (ELINT), and Foreign Instrumentation Signals Intelligence (FISINT) according to signal type (TONEX, 2024; Spriet, 2024). Encryption and distributed cloud services constrain direct content access, shifting analytic emphasis towards traffic analysis and large-scale processing. SIGINT thus provides sustained visibility into adversary activity under legal and technical constraints that shape collection practice (National Security Agency, 2024).

National institutional arrangements for SIGINT vary across states and are treated in the empirical chapters where country context is analysed. Protective measures such as encryption and signals security constitute the defensive counterpart to collection. Across many cyberliterate states, this creates a dual responsibility for interception and protection consistent with established intelligence practice.

OSINT involves the systematic collection and analysis of lawfully accessible public information relevant to security-related decision-making (Säberg and Huskaj, 2024; Lindemulder and Forrest, 2023; Gill, 2023; Group-IB, 2025; Joint Chiefs of Staff, 2018). In cyberspace, exposed code repositories, configuration errors, and online discussion forums may disclose information relevant to both defensive and offensive activity (Jefferies, 2025). United States doctrine places OSINT within the cyber-persona layer, linking observable human behaviour to logical and physical network structures (Joint Chiefs of Staff, 2018). When assessed alongside classified or proprietary sources, OSINT provides contextual information for early warning, incident analysis, and attribution (Group-IB, 2025). Its operational value depends on explicit methodology and legal constraints (Gill, 2023).

Cyber ISR refers to authorised activities that observe, monitor, and analyse adversary networks in support of tactical and operational planning (Wunder, 2016; North Atlantic Treaty Organization, 2025*a*; Joint Chiefs of Staff, 2018). Joint doctrine defines cyberspace ISR as an intelligence activity conducted under formal authorisation and directed towards specific operational requirements, including network discovery and vulnerability identification (Joint Chiefs of Staff, 2018). Cyber ISR integrates information from human sources, intercepted signals, and open sources within the operational environment, enabling planners to assess system structure and use. It therefore functions as a coordinating activity within the all-source enterprise rather than as a separate discipline.

Together, these intelligence disciplines constitute the process through which cyber operations become possible. Political intent translates into deliberate action only when decision-makers possess intelligence that explains adversary systems, behaviour, and constraints. Proportionality, legality, and escalation management therefore, depend on intelligence that clarifies how cyber actions will affect adversaries. Intelligence is not an adjunct to cyberspace operations; it is the condition that permits their deliberate use.

The Ethical Dimension and Vulnerability Management

Ethical constraints condition intelligence and OCO by delimiting which actions are permissible across an operational sequence that begins with access development and extends to execution. The VEP specifies this constraint by requiring authorities to decide whether a discovered zero-day vulnerability should be retained for intelligence collection or offensive use, or disclosed to reduce systemic risk. Retention preserves access that may support intelligence requirements or planned operations but leaves domestic and allied systems exposed to the same vulnerability. Disclosure reduces this exposure while removing a means of access that could support operational objectives. The decision therefore requires explicit assessment of operational necessity, anticipated intelligence value, and foreseeable consequences beyond the intended target (Huskaj and Wilson, 2021; United States Government, 2017). Retention accepts known risk in exchange for access; disclosure prioritises defensive security and public confidence at the cost of foregone options.

The same ethical constraint governs planning and execution of OCO. Principles of necessity, distinction, and proportionality restrict cyber effects by requiring legitimate targets, effects limited to stated objectives, and constrained incidental harm (Mandsager et al., 2022). In cyberspace, where civilian and military functions rely on shared infrastructure, target distinction is difficult. Intelligence supports compliance by identifying system use, dependency chains, and effect propagation. Absent these constraints, OCO risk uncontrolled effects and erosion of the legal and normative commitments on which democratic justification depends.

Intelligence in the MLMD Framework

Intelligence theory explains how intelligence supports political decision-making by specifying information requirements and operational constraints rather than by transforming intent into action. At the strategic level, authorities define objectives such as deterrence or cost imposition, directing planning and collection towards relevant adversary activities. At the tactical level, OCO employ technical means—exploits and payloads—against specific systems. Intelligence identifies relevant systems, analyses their use, and assesses where access may be established within legal and operational limits (Huskaj, 2024*c*).

This process unfolds through targeting. Strategic guidance determines which adversary functions require attention; intelligence collection and analysis identify supporting systems, services, and dependencies; planners assess whether available technical means can produce the intended effect. When the objective is to constrain ransomware activity, intelligence identifies infrastructure used for command, control, and monetisation, and technical units act only against systems identified through this assessment. Without this sequence, action risks being driven by access opportunity rather than political direction.

OCO therefore depend on intelligence to constrain action rather than to justify it. Tactical activity is limited to targets examined for relevance, legality, and anticipated consequence. Intelligence determines where action is permitted and excludes options that cannot be defended against stated objectives.

Ethical dimension: legality, proportionality, privacy, oversight

Ethics in cyber intelligence concerns the structured balancing of means, ends, and foreseeable consequences (Omand, 2021; Brey, 2012). Sir David Omand argues that intelligence ethics cannot be reduced to compliance, because lawful authorisation alone does not resolve questions of legitimacy, proportionality, or public trust (Omand, 2021). Legality anchors judgement in domestic law and international obligations—including sovereignty, due diligence, and, where force thresholds may be approached, the law of armed conflict (LOAC)—but does not exhaust ethical evaluation (USAF LeMay Center, 2023). This position aligns with doctrinal guidance such as *FM 2-22.3 Human Intelligence Collector Operations*, which requires personnel to uphold high ethical standards in addition to legal compliance (Department of the Army, 2006). Operational credibility thus depends on sustained moral restraint as well as technical competence.

Proportionality requires weighing anticipated intelligence value or operational effect against foreseeable harm, including secondary effects arising from exploit persistence or unintended propagation (Huskaj, 2024*c*). Omand draws on *Just War* ethics to argue that intelligence activity must satisfy conditions analogous to right authority, intention, necessity, discrimination, and proportionality (Omand, 2021). In cyber operations, this reasoning extends to technical design and deployment choices shaping downstream risk to civilian systems and societal trust. Furrow's fourfold schema—agent, intention, act, and consequence—provides a complementary tool for operationalising judgement across the operation lifecycle (Huskaj and Wilson, 2020*a*, Furrow, 2005, as cited in). Cases such as the United States' cyber response to Iran's 2019 downing of a Global Hawk illustrate how anticipatory reasoning calibrates proportionality under escalation risk (Huskaj and Wilson, 2020*a*).

Privacy constrains cyber intelligence by limiting what authorities may collect, retain, and act upon. In liberal democracies, authorisation requires necessity, minimisation during collection, and purpose limitation during processing (Huskaj, 2024*a*). These constraints follow because intelligence intrudes on individual rights and unchecked collection undermines legitimacy and trust.

Constraints are implemented through concrete controls. Organisations restrict access through role-based permissions, record access and modification through differential logging, and separate raw holdings from processed intelligence to limit exposure and reuse (Säberg and Huskaj, 2024). These measures reduce the risk of unauthorised reuse or access beyond stated objectives.

Oversight bodies convert ethical requirements into enforceable limits. Judicial authorisation, independent review, and parliamentary scrutiny determine when collection may begin, which systems may be targeted, and when access must cease (Huskaj, 2024*c*). Democratic intelligence rests on the rule of law, regulation, and restraint because these conditions bind action in advance rather than justify it after execution.

Escalation management introduces a temporal dimension to ethical judgement because cyber actions unfold through rapid feedback loops that compress decision time and increase misperception risk. Philip Brey's concept of anticipatory ethics holds that evaluation should occur before deployment, when design choices still shape potential misuse (Brey, 2012). Applied to cyberspace, this directs attention to exploiting persistence, third-party reuse, and unintended propagation. Huskaj and Wilson distinguish between operator-controlled capabilities and those that continue to act once released, showing how loss of control—as in *WannaCry*—introduces moral risk beyond the initial target set (Huskaj and Wilson, 2021). Decisions on zero-day vulnerabilities fall squarely within this concern. The VEP evaluates whether retention outweighs security risk should vulnerabilities be independently discovered or leaked (Huskaj and Wilson, 2021). Anticipatory ethics therefore foregrounds delayed and systemic consequences often missed by assessments focused solely on immediate effects (Huskaj and Wilson, 2020*a*; Huskaj and Wilson, 2021).

Ethical judgement in cyber intelligence operates through prior authorisation and oversight rather than retrospective justification. Political authorities define purpose, scope, and duration, and organisations implement these mandates by constraining collection, access, and release from the outset (USAF LeMay Center, 2023). When legality, proportionality, privacy, and anticipatory reasoning are applied together, intelligence practice narrows the range of permissible operational choices by excluding actions irreconcilable with stated objectives or foreseeable consequences.

Intelligence Aligns Deterrence with OCO

Projecting state power in cyberspace is realised through a dynamic relationship between intelligence, deterrence, and OCO. Intelligence functions as the operational interlocutor linking deterrence policy with the tactical planning and execution of OCO, ensuring that threats remain credible and legally compliant (Huskaj, 2024*c*). Within the parameters of the previously outlined MLMD framework, this relationship translates strategic intent into coordinated political, ethical, and technical action (Huskaj, 2024*c*).

The progressive argument demonstrates that intelligence initiates the deterrence cycle by defining the adversary and its vulnerabilities (Strategic Level), transitions to guiding operational preparation and governance (Operational Level), and finally closes the loop by providing post-execution assessment (Tactical Level). However, first a note on the concept of "the deterrence cycle."

Cyberspace is dynamic, with new services being added and others removed, as well as hardware being added and removed. The adversary is also dynamic, constantly looking for ways to penetrate systems supported by attack infrastructure. When the adversary is detected and defensive measures are taken, the adversary takes counter-actions by pivoting to other infrastructure, continuing the cyber attacks. This continuous engagement demands that deterrence be considered as a cycle. This cyclical requirement is also evident in the formal modelling of deterrence, such as the risk calculus based on Snyder's (1961) mathematical approach. This method, rooted in utility theory, models deterrence as a sequence of move-and-response estimations between the aggressor and the deterrer (Huskaj and Moradian, 2018; Huskaj, 2017). The deterrer must continuously assess the adversary's estimated gains and costs to determine the likelihood of an attack, with this probability acting as a direct measurement of the deterrer's posture (Huskaj and Moradian, 2018; Huskaj, 2017). Consequently, policy documents and strategic planning must undergo continual adjustment to address the fluid environment and sustain credibility.

At the strategic level, intelligence fundamentally underpins Deterrence Theory and resides predominantly in the Political Dimension (Huskaj, 2024*c*). Deterrence strategies, whether by punishment or denial, depend on conveying a credible threat to the adversary (Snyder, 1960). Intelligence provides the situational awareness necessary to determine the feasibility and consequences of such threats (Huskaj and Moradian, 2018).

The crucial role of intelligence here is two-fold. First, it identifies the adversary's object values—the critical assets, such as financial systems, electoral infrastructure, or military networks, that the adversary holds dear and which, if attacked, would impose costs greater than the benefits of aggression (Huskaj and Moradian, 2018; Huskaj, 2017). Second, intelligence facilitates the risk calculus by furnishing decision-makers with information on threat actor capabilities, intent, and opportunity. This quantification of risk is paramount for policy officials to measure their deterrent posture and anticipate potential enemy courses of action (Huskaj and Moradian, 2018). The strategic policy outcome, based on this fused intelligence, is the decision to develop offensive cyber capabilities as a deterrence measure and to authorise OCO as a tool of national policy, often intended to send a signal (Huskaj, 2024*c*). The governance surrounding this strategic authorisation is critical, as fragmented governance cripples the effectiveness and affects the credibility of deterrence.

At the Operational Level, governed by Intelligence Theory, serves as the bridge between strategic intent and tactical execution (Huskaj, 2024*c*). This level is where intelligence fully interplays with OCO planning, spanning the Ethical and Technical Dimensions.

Intelligence directs the entire process of designing, planning, and preparing OCO (Huskaj, 2024*c*). Because operational units often lack the full intelligence needed initially, they must conduct Cyber ISR—an intelligence activity itself—to satisfy requirements regarding targets, vulnerabilities, and exploits (Huskaj and Blix, 2022). This multidisciplinary intelligence, combining HUMINT, SIGINT, OSINT, and Cyber ISR, is processed to provide target systems analysis on assets like financial or defence systems. This technical intelligence is then used by planners to assemble the OCO technical triad: access, vulnerability, and payload (Huskaj et al., 2024).

Critically, intelligence supports the Ethical Dimension by providing the data necessary for legal compliance and risk mitigation. Intelligence enables structured risk-modelling to assess the likelihood of cascading effects—unintended consequences that spread beyond the target system—which is essential for policy-makers concerned with maintaining proportionality (Huskaj and Iftimie, 2020). Furthermore, intelligence is central to the legal judgement process; it helps legal advisers interpret international law, such as the Law of Armed Conflict (LOAC), and translate that into ROE for cyberspace operations (Huskaj, 2024*c*; Huskaj and Blix, 2022). The ethical dilemma of the VEP—whether to disclose a zero-day vulnerability for defensive gain or retain it for offensive intelligence value—is primarily an intelligence-driven decision with strategic and ethical implications (Huskaj and Wilson, 2021).

At the Tactical Level, governed by OCO Theory, focuses on the execution of specific technical tools and tactics and ensures they align with operational strategies (Huskaj, 2024*c*). Intelligence informs every aspect of the OCO methodology, from identifying Indicators & Warnings to determining the desired end state (Huskaj and Iftimie, 2020).

During execution, OCO relies on intelligence to ensure its operations are precise. For example, the OCO model, such as the Ambidextrous Framework for Offensive Cyberspace

Operations (AF-OCO) (Huskaj and Iftimie, 2020), is designed to support the execution of offensive actions by guiding the tactical commander, although the framework's utility for detailed, real-time operator actions is limited (Huskaj and Blix, 2022). The OCO execution component of CE serves a dual function, not only achieving a tactical objective but also continuously collecting intelligence for forensic recovery and future planning (Huskaj et al., 2024).

Finally, intelligence supports deterrence by providing the necessary mechanism for post-action assessment. After an OCO is conducted, collection verifies whether the adversary's behaviour moved towards the intended deterrent baseline, effectively closing the cybernetic feedback loop that guides the refinement of national strategy and policy (Huskaj, 2024*c*; Huskaj and Wilson, 2020*a*). This validation is critical for maintaining the coherence and credibility of the nation's overall cyber strategy (Huskaj, 2024*c*).

In conclusion, the interplay among intelligence, deterrence, and OCO is inseparable and circular within the MLMD framework. Intelligence acts as the indispensable dynamic element, providing the strategic rationale (Political Dimension), defining the operational parameters (Ethical and Technical Dimensions), and ensuring tactical execution maintains fidelity to the strategic deterrence objective. Without intelligence, deterrence lacks credibility, and OCO lacks necessary governance and precision.

2.4 The Practice and Discipline of OCO

OCOs are evolving from predominantly clandestine technical activities into a formalised instrument of national power governed by doctrine, authority, and professional practice (Huskaj, 2024*c*). This evolution requires the systematic integration of technical capability, institutional governance, and ethical restraint so that strategic intent can be translated into controlled, policy-relevant effects. Within the MLMD framework, OCO is therefore situated as an operational capability that connects political objectives with disciplined execution under defined constraints (Huskaj, 2024*c*). Practising OCO entails addressing the inherent complexity of the cyber domain through structured procedures, professional training, and clearly defined lines of accountability (Huskaj and Axelsson, 2023). The result is that offensive cyber activity is organised as a governed military function rather than an improvised or purely technical undertaking (Huskaj, 2019).

The disciplinary character of OCO is expressed through its core functional distinctions and technical components, which enable policy-makers to select and authorise appropriate measures of force (Huskaj and Blix, 2022). OCO manifests primarily in two forms: CA and CE, distinguished by their operational purpose (Huskaj et al., 2024). CA consists of deliberate actions intended to alter, disrupt, or degrade computer systems, networks, or data in order to produce denial effects, which may in some cases extend beyond cyberspace (Joint Chiefs of Staff, 2018; Huskaj and Wilson, 2020*a*).

CE focuses on intelligence collection through non-destructive payloads designed to remain undetected and preserve access over time (Huskaj et al., 2024). Both forms rely on the technical triad of access, vulnerability, and payload, which together determine whether an intended effect can be generated within a target system (Huskaj et al., 2024; Huskaj, 2024*c*). Vulnerabilities—typically design flaws or implementation errors—are exploited by payloads engineered to produce specific effects under defined conditions (Huskaj, 2024*c*; Huskaj and Wilson, 2021). Sustaining these activities requires the continuous development of attack infrastructure that enables operators to move securely from friendly ("green") environments through neutral ("grey") space into adversary ("red") systems (Huskaj et al., 2020; Huskaj, 2024*c*).

Systematising OCO as a disciplined practice depends on doctrinal governance that aligns tactical choice with strategic political intent (Huskaj, 2024*c*). This governance is operationalised through planning models and frameworks, such as the AF-OCO, which structure the processes of planning, preparation, and formal order-giving (Huskaj and Blix, 2022; Huskaj and Iftimie, 2020). These frameworks integrate intelligence requirements, operational constraints, and policy considerations, translating abstract objectives into executable courses of action. Complementing this, the Cyberspace Operations Canvas—adapted from management theory—functions as a planning aid that organises indicators, target characteristics, and key operational activities prior to execution. Emphasis on structured processes rather than ad hoc action reduces uncertainty and supports deliberate decision-making throughout the operational lifecycle (Huskaj, 2019). In practice, this ensures that capabilities developed through software-centric cycles to exploit vulnerabilities are assessed and deployed within defined organisational and legal parameters.

The professional conduct of OCO is bounded by legal authority, ethical principles, and institutional accountability across strategic and operational levels (Huskaj, 2024*c*). Political authorities retain responsibility for authorising OCO and ensuring that its use conforms to national policy and international obligations (Huskaj and Axelsson, 2023). Legal compliance requires the continuous interpretation of applicable norms, including the LOAC, and their translation into ROE suitable for cyberspace operations (Huskaj, 2024*c*; Huskaj et al., 2024; Huskaj and Blix, 2022). These legal structures mitigate political risk by defining permissible action in advance rather than retroactively justifying outcomes (Huskaj, 2019). Proportionality further depends on intelligence-led assessment of system dependencies and potential cascading effects, which may propagate beyond the intended target set (Huskaj and Iftimie, 2020; Huskaj and Blix, 2022). Accountability is maintained through governance arrangements that render tactical decisions traceable and subject to review, thereby constraining operational discretion within authorised bounds (Huskaj and Axelsson, 2023; Huskaj, 2024*c*).

Sustaining OCO as a responsible capability also requires anticipatory ethics and continuous institutional learning (Huskaj and Wilson, 2020*a*). Anticipatory ethical analysis evaluates emerging technologies—such as zero-day vulnerabilities—by considering foreseeable consequences prior to deployment (Huskaj and Wilson, 2021). This approach addresses the policy dilemma of whether to retain vulnerabilities for intelligence or operational use or to disclose them to reduce systemic risk, a decision structured through the VEP (Huskaj and Wilson, 2021). The VEP signals institutional maturity by balancing intelligence requirements against broader security considerations and by establishing predictable disclosure practices that support trust between public authorities and private actors (Huskaj, 2019). Institutional learning is further supported through simulation and training environments, such as cyber ranges, which allow operators to test frameworks and refine procedures against realistic adversary systems (Huskaj and Blix, 2022). Post-action assessment feeds operational experience back into planning and doctrine, enabling adaptation while preserving ethical and legal restraint over time (Huskaj and Wilson, 2020*a*). Together, these practices position OCO as a disciplined professional activity embedded within a broader whole-of-society approach to defence (Huskaj and Axelsson, 2023).

2.5 Synthesising Strategy, Intelligence, and Operations

Projecting power in cyberspace depends on the deliberate integration of strategy, intelligence, and operations into a coherent system of action. Each component fulfils a distinct role: deterrence articulates strategic intent and establishes thresholds; intelligence converts intent into decision-relevant knowledge; and OCO provide the authorised means for generating effects (Snyder, 1960; Schelling, 1966; Huskaj, 2024*c*; Joint Chiefs of Staff, 2018). When aligned, these functions constitute cyber statecraft—the practice of employing digital capability to advance national objectives under legal and ethical constraints (Chas and Barrinha, 2024).

At the strategic level, deterrence supplies the grammar of purpose by shaping how states communicate resolve, manage escalation, and influence adversary behaviour (Fischerkeller and Harknett, 2017; Nakasone, 2019). In cyberspace, deterrence increasingly operates through persistent engagement that contests adversary activity below the threshold of armed conflict rather than through episodic signalling alone. This campaign logic relies on timely intelligence to sustain credibility and on disciplined OCO execution to demonstrate capability while protecting sources and methods (USAF LeMay Center, 2023; Huskaj, 2024*c*).

Intelligence functions as the operational bridge between strategic purpose and tactical action. By reducing uncertainty regarding adversary intent, capability, and vulnerability, intelligence supports decision-making while keeping legal and ethical constraints visible throughout planning and execution (Clark, 2019; Huskaj and Wilson, 2021). Within the MLMD framework, intelligence operates across political, ethical, and technical dimensions: politically, it informs deterrent signalling and coordination with partners; ethically, it enables proportionality and accountability assessments; technically, it supports target discovery, access maintenance, and post-operation evaluation (Huskaj, 2024*c*). Intelligence therefore both enables authorised action and constrains excess, ensuring that offensive decisions remain defensible and auditable.

OCO theory specifies how strategic intent and operational understanding are converted into concrete effects. Tactical action may take the form of exploitation to preserve access for intelligence purposes or attack to generate disruption, degradation, or manipulation within adversary systems (Joint Chiefs of Staff, 2018; Huskaj et al., 2024). In either case, the technical triad of access, vulnerability, and payload must be aligned to achieve proportional outcomes and limit unintended impact. OCO is thus characterised not by technical virtuosity alone but by its embedding within doctrine, legal authority, and ethical review (Huskaj and Axelsson, 2023). Its credibility as an instrument of power derives from repeatable governance and from learning processes that translate operational feedback into strategic adjustment (Huskaj and Wilson, 2020*a*).

The interaction among deterrence, intelligence, and OCO forms a continuous feedback loop. Intelligence identifies adversary values and vulnerabilities, enabling policy to define deterrent objectives and acceptable risk. These objectives are translated into authorised operational plans and executed within established constraints. Post-action assessment then generates new intelligence that informs subsequent deterrent posture, sustaining adaptation as technologies and political conditions evolve (Huskaj and Moradian, 2018; Huskaj and Wilson, 2020*a*; Huskaj, 2024*c*). This cyclical structure reflects the logic of both intelligence and deterrence, which require constant reassessment rather than static declarations.

Governance integrates the triad by defining authority, coordinating action, and enforcing restraint. Political leadership establishes legitimacy and thresholds; operational commands synchronise intelligence and execution; and technical specialists ensure feasibility and containment. Ethical oversight functions transversally, reinforcing legality, proportionality, and accountability at each stage (Omand, 2021; Huskaj and Wilson, 2021). Through this integration, cyber capability becomes an instrument of accountable statecraft rather than isolated expertise.

In sum, deterrence provides direction, intelligence supplies understanding, and OCO delivers action. Their synthesis transforms fragmented activities into a coherent capability governed by doctrine and informed by law. Within the MLMD framework, this integration aligns strategic, operational, and tactical levels across political, ethical, and technical dimensions, sustaining a cyber posture that is credible, adaptive, and legitimate (Huskaj, 2024*c*; USAF LeMay Center, 2023). The following section examines this synthesis in practice through selected cases illustrating how intelligence-enabled deterrence and controlled offensive action interact to produce strategic effect.

2.6 Illustrations of Integration in Practice

Stuxnet (2010)

Stuxnet illustrates how OCO can support strategic deterrence when guided by sustained intelligence. The operation depended on long-horizon collection, detailed engineering insight, and disciplined testing, which together translated abstract intent into executable options. Intelligence Preparation—conducted as cyber ISR—mapped industrial control pathways, validated programmable logic controller behaviour, and identified exploitable dependencies, thereby establishing feasibility and bounded risk. OCO then aligned access, vulnerability, and payload to produce precise manipulation rather than conspicuous destruction, which supported proportionality and constrained escalation. The resulting delay in nuclear progress communicated capability under conditions of limited disclosure, reinforcing credibility without overt signalling (Huskaj, 2024*c*).

The case demonstrates alignment across levels and dimensions. At the strategic level and political dimension, deterrence by punishment was advanced indirectly through demonstrated reach and effect, while declaratory policy remained sparse to preserve ambiguity. At the operational level and ethical dimension, planners balanced the intelligence gain–loss (IGL) dilemma by timing execution against longer-term collection value and constraining propagation through embedded payload safeguards. At the tactical level and technical dimension, access development and environment checks followed the doctrine on Operational Preparation of the Environment (OPE) and assessment-led execution. Conceptually, Stuxnet shows that tailored OCO, anchored in persistent intelligence and bounded by legal review, can support deterrence objectives while preserving strategic latency for subsequent options (USAF LeMay Center, 2023; Huskaj, 2024*c*).

APT10 (2013–2017)

APT10 illustrates how intelligence-enabled attribution underwrites deterrence by punishment and conditions OCO options against a campaigning adversary. The group's managed service provider intrusions generated broad supply-chain access, yielding sustained espionage returns. Intelligence fusion—combining technical forensics, infrastructure clustering, and liaison reporting—produced attribution assessments at policy-relevant confidence levels and exposed tradecraft at scale, enabling coordinated public attribution and legal measures. Deterrent signalling occurred through indictments, sanctions, and allied statements, while operational responses prioritised defence-in-depth and counter-intrusion consistent with doctrine. The case shows that punishment in cyberspace encompasses juridical and diplomatic instruments aligned with credible capacity for counter-operations (USAF LeMay Center, 2023; Huskaj, 2024*c*).

Within the MLMD perspective, the strategic–political layer centred on threshold-setting for economic espionage and alliance coordination. The operational–ethical layer prioritised stewardship of sources and methods during public disclosure, ensuring that signalling deterred repetition without compromising irreplaceable access. The tactical–technical layer focused on implant eviction, third-party hardening, and preparation of selective offensive options where authorised. Conceptually, APT10 demonstrates that attribution is an intelligence problem that, once resolved to policy standards, enables a calibrated mix of OCO and non-kinetic responses that raise adversary costs while strengthening collective defence (USAF LeMay Center, 2023; Huskaj, 2024*c*).

Estonia (2007)

The Estonia 2007 distributed denial-of-service (DDoS) campaign illustrates how attribution latency constrains deterrent leverage and limits OCO options during crises. The attacks stressed financial and governmental services, exploited commoditised botnets, and unfolded faster than investigative confidence could mature. Intelligence organisations prioritised triage and evidence preservation, yet decision-makers faced narrow near-term options because responsibility assessments remained preliminary during peak disruption. In this context, deterrence by denial became dominant: service restoration, traffic engineering, and content filtering mitigated harm while alliance consultations prepared subsequent signalling. The episode underscored the value of pre-negotiated data-sharing and shared operating pictures that shorten attribution timelines (Huskaj, 2024*c*).

Across levels and dimensions, the strategic–political layer advanced a collective posture—later reflected in alliance statements clarifying thresholds for severe cyber activity. The operational–ethical layer refined cross-border cooperation with private providers while preserving lawful process, evidentiary integrity, and proportional mitigation. The tactical–technical layer accelerated traffic characterisation, incident response rehearsal, and selective countermeasures consistent with doctrine on Defensive Cyberspace Operations and assessment-led recovery. Conceptually, Estonia shows that when punitive options are constrained by attribution latency, intelligence investment and resilience engineering can still generate a deterrent effect by limiting adversary utility and compressing recovery timelines (USAF LeMay Center, 2023; Huskaj, 2024*c*).

Taken together, these cases demonstrate the triad in practice. Intelligence establishes feasibility and responsibility, OCO delivers calibrated effects, and deterrence frames aims, thresholds, and messages. The interaction is iterative: assessment feeds back into policy and planning, sustaining coherence across strategic, operational, and tactical levels while engaging political, ethical, and technical dimensions (Huskaj, 2024*c*; Huskaj and Wilson, 2020*a*).

2.7 From Integration to the MLMD Framework

This section consolidates Chapter 2's integrated theory into a single organising perspective and prepares the transition to formal modelling in Chapter 3. The MLMD perspective emerges when deterrence, intelligence, and OCO are treated as mutually conditioning logics rather than parallel tracks. Deterrence supplies strategic purpose and thresholds; intelligence supplies the knowledge architecture that renders action discriminating; OCO supplies the means to project capability through networks. MLMD aggregates these functions across strategic, operational, and tactical levels while retaining political, ethical, and technical dimensions. The result is a coherent frame that reconciles persistent campaigning, attribution uncertainty, and legal constraint with practicable options (USAF LeMay Center, 2023; Huskaj, 2024*c*).

MLMD's analytical value lies in the disciplined linkage between strategy, ethics, and technology. Strategically, deterrence by punishment and deterrence by denial become assessable postures when anchored to observable adversary dependencies, declared thresholds, and authorised OCO menus. Ethically, the framework foregrounds proportionality, discrimination, and the IGL dilemma as recurring constraints that must be evaluated prior to authorisation. Technically, OCO is specified as missions that project power to create effects, supported by cyber ISR and assessment-led execution. This linkage ensures that declaratory posture remains tied to feasible access, vulnerability, and payload combinations and to defensible risk judgements (USAF LeMay Center, 2023; Huskaj, 2024*c*).

The perspective operationalises integration through level–dimension matrices that align aims, information requirements, and action types. At the strategic–political intersection, MLMD links deterrent aims to intelligence requirements concerning adversary valuation, escalation pathways, and audience perception. At the operational–ethical intersection, it schedules repeatable reviews of legal authority, collateral risk, and disclosure timing, including stewardship of sources and methods. At the tactical–technical intersection, it binds targeting to the OCO triad together with OPE and cyber ISR tasking. Persistent engagement is treated as a monitored campaign variable rather than an incidental outcome, preserving structure without foreclosing doctrinal choice (USAF LeMay Center, 2023; Huskaj, 2024*c*).

Methodologically, MLMD clarifies evidence standards and assessment pathways. Attribution confidence, vulnerability viability, and access persistence are explicitly graded and time-bounded. Deterrence claims are tied to indicators such as observed restraint near declared thresholds, changes in adversary hardening, or campaign re-tasking detectable through technical signatures. OCO performance is assessed against pre-agreed criteria: intended effect, containment of externalities, preservation of future options, and contribution to strategic latency. Residual uncertainty is recorded as managed risk with defined decision points and remediation routes, imposing analytic discipline on probabilistic judgement under incomplete observability (Huskaj, 2024*c*).

The framework also exposes recurrent doctrinal blind spots. First, declaratory posture often decouples from executable capability; MLMD requires auditable mapping from policy to authorised OCO families and intelligence pipelines. Second, campaign design frequently omits explicit ethical gates; MLMD inserts repeatable proportionality and necessity reviews prior to escalation. Third, assessments tend to undervalue cumulative effects; MLMD incorporates trend-based appraisal across incidents, episodes, and campaigns. These corrections translate theory into governance artefacts capable of withstanding institutional turnover and contested crises (USAF LeMay Center, 2023; Huskaj, 2024*c*).

Chapter 3 formalises MLMD as a working framework. It specifies level–dimension matrices, defines variables and measures, and presents planning and assessment templates linking deterrence aims, intelligence tasks, and OCO options. Process maps for requirement setting, targeting, authorisation, and post-action review are combined with criteria for lawful use and ethical sufficiency. In doing so, Chapter 3 translates the integrated foundation into a practical instrument for capability projection, risk control, and strategic communication in cyberspace (USAF LeMay Center, 2023; Huskaj, 2024*c*).

2.8 Conclusion: Towards a Coherent Theory of Cyber Power

This conclusion consolidates the triadic integration developed throughout the chapter. Deterrence provides strategic direction and threshold-setting; intelligence converts intent into situational knowledge; OCO supply the instrument for capability projection and effect creation. The chapter has shown that attribution challenges, escalation risk, and legal–ethical constraints are tractable when intelligence requirements are specified alongside deterrent aims and matched to executable OCO options. Cyber ISR links policy to operations by identifying adversary dependencies, viable attack surfaces, and indicators of behavioural change, enabling decision-makers to shape tempo while retaining policy control (USAF LeMay Center, 2023; Huskaj, 2024*c*; Huskaj and Blix, 2022).

The theoretical contribution is captured in four elements. First, tailored deterrence integrates punishment and denial with explicit signalling and confidence assessment. Second, intelligence is constitutive rather than auxiliary; it frames attribution, calibrates proportionality, and manages the IGL dilemma. Third, OCO is formalised through the triad of access, vulnerability, and payload, supported by OPE and assessment-led execution. Fourth, persistent engagement is rendered evaluable through thresholds, indicators, and repeatable review. Together these elements establish a disciplined linkage between strategy, ethics, and technology (USAF LeMay Center, 2023; Huskaj, 2024*c*; Huskaj and Wilson, 2021).

This synthesis provides the conceptual architecture for the MLMD framework formalised in Chapter 3. MLMD maps strategic, operational, and tactical tasks to political, ethical, and technical dimensions, turning declaratory posture into authorised, auditable, and ethically defensible action. By specifying intelligence requirements alongside OCO options and embedding governance checkpoints for legality and proportionality, MLMD offers a practicable basis for responsible national cyber strategy. Chapter 3 operationalises this architecture through matrices, processes, and use-cases that translate integrated theory into planning, authorisation, and assessment (USAF LeMay Center, 2023; Huskaj, 2024*c*; Huskaj and Blix, 2022).

Decision Exercise: Converting Cyber Power into Credible Influence

Scenario. Over the past eight weeks, an identified state-linked actor has conducted a sustained campaign against your country and two allies. The campaign combines (i) repeated intrusion attempts against election-adjacent services and managed service providers, (ii) theft of policy-relevant documents followed by selective leaks, and (iii) exploratory access activity in energy-sector networks. Technical indicators suggest that the adversary can shift infrastructure quickly. Public attribution is contested across domestic audiences, and an allied partner requests visible reassurance before an upcoming national vote. Your government asks for an authorised response option set within 72 hours that supports deterrence and preserves political control.

Analytical question 1—Deterrence purpose and credibility under partial observability. State the primary deterrence purpose you seek to achieve in the next 30 days (denial, punishment, reassurance, or a bounded combination). Specify (i) one observable behavioural indicator that would suggest movement towards the desired deterrence baseline, and (ii) why that indicator is credible given attribution frictions and adversary adaptation.

Analytical question 2—Intelligence requirements and time-compressed decision support. Specify three priority intelligence requirements that must be answered before authorisation (one about adversary intent, one about capability/feasibility, and one about escalation pathways). For each requirement, state (i) the minimum confidence level needed for decision, and (ii) what you would do if the requirement cannot be met inside the 72-hour window.

Analytical question 3—Action options and the IGL dilemma. Propose two distinct authorised response options:

- Option A: prioritises intelligence preservation and longer-term situational awareness.
- Option B: prioritises near-term cost imposition or disruption.

For each option, specify (i) the intended effect category (deny/manipulate or equivalent doctrinal framing), (ii) the principal IGL trade-off, and (iii) one constraint that limits reversibility or containment.

Analytical question 4—Governance, legality, and escalation exposure. Define the minimum governance conditions required to proceed: legal review standard, political approval threshold, oversight and logging requirements, and partner constraints. Explain how these conditions reduce escalation exposure while preserving timely action under operational tempo.

Short task—MLMD mapping (one page). Create a 3-row mapping (Strategic / Operational / Tactical) listing:

1. the decision to be made at each level,
2. the key dependency at that level (deterrence credibility, intelligence support, technical feasibility),
3. one failure mode where misalignment would cause technical action to diverge from political intent.

Optional extension—Signalling package. Draft a two-sentence declaratory statement that supports the chosen deterrence purpose without disclosing sources or methods. Specify which audiences it targets (adversary leadership, operators, allies, and the domestic public) and what misinterpretation risk it creates.

3

The MLMD Framework for Offensive Cyberspace Operations

Offensive cyberspace operations (OCO) have become a central component of national security, yet the field lacks an analytical model that links strategic intent to operational planning and tactical execution. Existing approaches often isolate a single level of analysis and thereby fail to show how political objectives, intelligence requirements, and technical actions interact. This limitation has both analytical and policy consequences. Offensive cyberspace actions generate outcomes shaped by the interaction of strategic guidance, operational design, and tactical decisions, meaning that partial models obscure how decisions at one level constrain or enable options at another.

The purpose of this chapter is to present the Multi-Level, Multi-Dimensional (MLMD) Framework as an analytical instrument for examining how authority, risk, feasibility, and oversight interact across strategic, operational, and tactical levels. It is not intended as procedural guidance for planning or executing offensive operations, and it does not specify techniques, targeting methods, or operational tradecraft. The intent is to support scholarly analysis and policy-level evaluation of governance, alignment, and constraint in state practice.

The MLMD Framework addresses this gap by examining offensive cyberspace actions across the strategic, operational, and tactical levels while incorporating cross-cutting political, ethical, and technological considerations (Huskaj et al., 2024). The MLMD Framework is grounded in deterrence theory, intelligence theory, and OCO theory. Figure 3.1 summarises the framework by mapping strategic, operational, and tactical levels against political, ethical, and technological dimensions.

The guiding analytical problem is how a MLMD framework can clarify how offensive cyberspace actions are designed, planned, and executed across the levels of war. Because offensive action unfolds in interconnected systems governed by political authority and normative constraints, analysis must link decision-making across levels to the political, ethical, and technological conditions that shape what can be done and what should be authorised.

The MLMD Framework is grounded in theory and military doctrine. It draws on deterrence theory to examine how cyber capabilities influence adversary decision-making, intelligence theory to capture the role of information collection and assessment, and OCO theory to explain how cyber effects are generated through access, exploitation, and payload execution. Together, these perspectives show that OCO require integrated attention to strategic objectives, operational planning processes, and tactical techniques. Military doctrine reinforces this integrated view. Joint Publication (JP) 3-12 defines OCO as activities "intended to project power in and through foreign cyberspace" and emphasises that cyber missions depend on timely intelligence and proper authorisation (Joint Chiefs of Staff, 2018, p. II-5).

The framework therefore incorporates political, ethical, and technological dimensions as cross-cutting conditions. Offensive cyberspace actions are shaped by political oversight and legal authority, ethical principles associated with responsible state behaviour, and the technical constraints inherent in capability development and vulnerability exploitation.

DOI: 10.1201/9781003655183-3

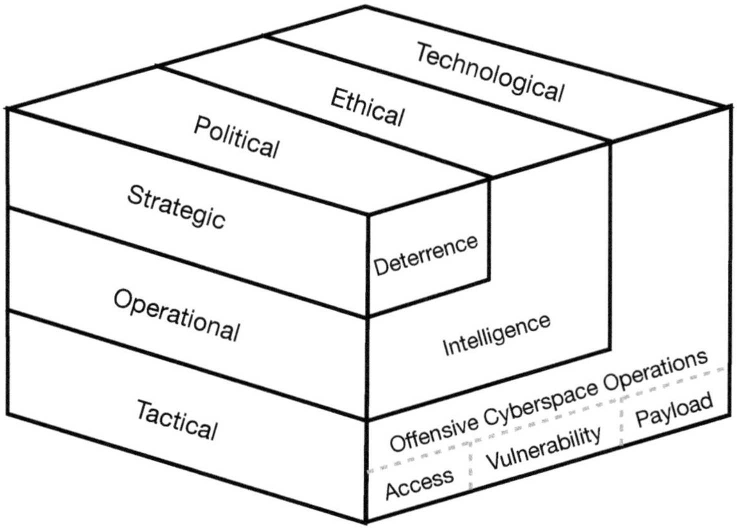

FIGURE 3.1
The MLMD Framework: a structured mapping of strategic, operational, and tactical levels and cross-cutting political, ethical, and technological dimensions linking deterrence, intelligence, and OCO considerations across decision-making levels.

This chapter proceeds as follows. Section 3.1 explains why single-level or single-discipline approaches are insufficient and motivates a MLMD framework. Section 3.2 outlines the theoretical foundations drawn from deterrence theory, intelligence theory, and OCO theory. Section 3.3 presents the structure of the MLMD Framework, showing how levels of warfare, functional lenses, and cross-cutting dimensions intersect. Section 3.4 examines how the framework is applied across the strategic, operational, and tactical levels. Section 3.5 analyses the cross-cutting political, ethical, and technological dimensions that condition decision-making at all levels. Section 3.6 concludes the chapter and prepares the transition to Chapter 4, where Sweden's cyber deterrence posture is examined as an empirical case.

3.1 Why a MLMD Framework?

Existing analytical models for OCO tend to isolate a single level of analysis or prioritise one disciplinary perspective. Strategic studies often emphasise adversary decision-making and high-level deterrence logic while offering limited insight into the technical feasibility of proposed actions. Conversely, technically oriented models often describe access, reconnaissance, and exploit development in detail but provide limited treatment of how these activities link to operational design or political guidance (Huskaj and Iftimie, 2020; Huskaj and Blix, 2022; Huskaj, 2024*c*). The result is fragmented guidance for practitioners and an analytical gap between strategic intent, operational planning, and tactical execution.

This fragmentation produces predictable blind spots. A strategy-centric approach may assert that a threat of retaliation will shape adversary behaviour, yet if the technical means to implement the threatened action are uncertain, or if the intelligence required to identify relevant targets is incomplete, the deterrent signal lacks credibility. Conversely, a technically successful intrusion may violate political thresholds or international norms if it is not aligned with national guidance or ROE. In both cases, the absence of vertical integration undermines the relationship between declared intent and executed action.

Past incidents illustrate this tension. Tactically limited actions, such as short-duration network disruptions, have at times generated disproportionate political consequences or escalatory dynamics. These outcomes were not necessarily the result of technical failure but of misalignment between tactical execution, operational context, and strategic intent. Such cases demonstrate that offensive cyberspace actions cannot be understood—or governed—through a single disciplinary lens.

A further rationale for an MLMD approach arises from the character of cyberspace itself. Offensive actions occur within an environment shaped by technology, institutions, and human behaviour. Because these elements are interdependent, even limited technical effects may propagate across systems and domains. A disruptive action against a single node may affect interconnected operational systems, trigger societal disruption, or prompt adversary retaliation (Mandsager et al., 2022). These cascading effects complicate prediction and control, particularly when actions are planned or assessed at only one level of decision-making.

This dynamic underscores the need for a framework that explicitly accounts for multiple levels of authority and action, as well as the contextual factors that condition them. Without such a structure, analysts and planners risk treating tactical feasibility, operational coherence, and strategic consequence as separable problems, rather than as interdependent components of the same decision process.

There is also a clear doctrinal basis for adopting a multi-level approach. Joint Publication 3-12 situates cyberspace operations within the joint planning process and recognises that cyberspace effects are generated at strategic, operational, and tactical levels (Joint Chiefs of Staff, 2018). NATO planning instruments, including AJP-5 (North Atlantic Treaty Organization, 2019) and the Comprehensive Operations Planning Directive, similarly require that cyber activities be synchronised with broader operational plans, subject to political direction, and informed by intelligence. Together, these documents mandate vertical coordination across command echelons and continuous interaction between intelligence functions, operational design, and strategic assessment.

Empirical work applying OCO models supports this doctrinal position. Tactical outcomes and intelligence findings routinely influence operational options and strategic expectations, particularly when access conditions change, vulnerabilities are disclosed, or adversary responses alter the operating environment (Huskaj et al., 2024). A structured multi-level framework therefore reduces the risk of misalignment and missed deconfliction opportunities, while avoiding claims of systemic over-centralisation or pervasive coordination failure.

Clarifying terminology, the "multi-level" element refers to the strategic, operational, and tactical levels traditionally used in military planning. The strategic level encompasses national policy, high-level decision-making, and doctrinal guidance that determine when and how OCO may be used. The operational level links strategy to action through campaign design and coordination, integrating cyberspace activities with other instruments of military power and with intelligence functions. The tactical level comprises mission execution, including the exploits, payloads, and technical engagements conducted by operators.

Although cyberspace operations may blur these boundaries in practice, the levels remain analytically useful. The 2021 Colonial Pipeline incident illustrates this point: a tactically limited compromise of a single credential produced operational-level disruption and strategic-level political response (Kerner, 2022). Such cases show that small-scale technical actions can generate effects far beyond their immediate scope, reinforcing the value of level-based analysis even in a fluid operational environment.

The "multi-dimensional" component captures the political, ethical, and technological conditions that constrain and enable OCO at every level. The political dimension concerns legal authority, legitimacy, sovereignty, alliance commitments, and policy oversight (Mandsager et al., 2022). The ethical dimension reflects principles such as necessity, proportionality, distinction, and precaution derived from the law of armed conflict (LOAC) and applicable to state-conducted cyberspace operations (Huskaj and Wilson, 2020*a*). The technological dimension addresses feasibility, reliability, and lifecycle considerations associated with offensive capabilities, including the risks of exploiting or revealing vulnerabilities (Huskaj et al., 2024).

These dimensions function as required filters rather than supplemental considerations. At each level, planners must confirm legal authority, obtain political approval, adhere to ROE, and ensure that available capabilities can generate the intended effect (Joint Chiefs of Staff, 2018; Kehler, Lin and Sulmeyer, 2017). Technological factors such as exploit reliability or the risk of revealing an intelligence access shape tactical decisions and influence strategic choices about whether to employ, preserve, or disclose a vulnerability (Huskaj and Wilson, 2021). The MLMD Framework makes these conditions explicit by requiring that political constraints, ethical obligations, and technical feasibility be assessed together when designing and conducting OCO (Mandsager et al., 2022).

In summary, a MLMD Framework is necessary because single-level or single-discipline approaches cannot capture the interdependencies that shape OCO. By linking strategic objectives, operational design, and tactical execution through political, ethical, and technological dimensions, the framework provides a structured method for analysing and planning offensive action. This rationale aligns with contemporary scholarship advocating a multilevel, multidisciplinary approach (Huskaj et al., 2024) and is consistent with military doctrine integrating cyberspace capabilities into broader strategic and operational structures (USAF LeMay Center, 2023). The following sections develop this logic by outlining the relevant theoretical foundations (Section 3.2), presenting the structure of the MLMD Framework (Section 3.3), and applying it across the strategic, operational, and tactical levels (Section 3.4 onwards).

3.2 Theoretical Foundations of the MLMD Framework

The MLMD Framework rests on three theoretical pillars: Deterrence Theory, Intelligence Theory, and OCO Theory. Each pillar captures a distinct requirement that states must address when they develop, authorise, and employ offensive cyber capability. Deterrence theory explains the strategic purpose of offensive capabilities and how they are expected to influence adversary behaviour. Intelligence theory explains how knowledge enables action and constrains choice across planning and execution. OCO theory explains how cyber effects are generated through specific technical and operational processes. When considered together, these perspectives explain how OCO are conceived, planned, and conducted within political, informational, and technical limits. Examining each in turn establishes the conceptual foundation for the integrated framework.

Deterrence theory explains how states seek to influence adversary behaviour by shaping expectations about costs, benefits, and the likelihood of success. Classical deterrence distinguishes between deterrence by punishment, which seeks to raise the expected cost of hostile action through the prospect of retaliation, and deterrence by denial, which seeks to reduce confidence in achieving the intended effect. Both mechanisms apply in cyberspace. States may signal that malicious cyber activity will trigger responses that impose costs on the adversary, including cyber or non-cyber measures, thereby influencing strategic calculation (Huskaj and Wilson, 2020*a*). Denial is pursued through defensive measures such as hardened networks, detection capabilities, and recovery arrangements that limit the effectiveness of hostile action. In practice, cyber deterrence is shaped by the interaction of these mechanisms rather than by reliance on one alone.

A central requirement for deterrence is credibility. The adversary must assess that the deterring state possesses relevant capabilities and that these capabilities are available for use under stated conditions. As emphasised in Schelling's work, credibility is shaped by perception rather than by material capacity alone (Huskaj and Wilson, 2020*a*). In cyberspace, credibility is constrained by the secrecy surrounding offensive capabilities and by the difficulty of communicating intent without exposing operational methods. These constraints limit the clarity of signalling and place greater weight on observable behaviour, institutional posture, and consistency between declared policy and action. As a result, cyber deterrence depends on how states combine declaratory statements, defensive measures, and selective disclosure to convey intent and resolve.

Deterrence theory also draws attention to uncertainty as a persistent condition. Deterrence by punishment depends on attribution with sufficient confidence to support a response, yet attribution in cyberspace often remains contested at both technical and political levels. Deterrence by denial depends on the adversary's assessment of defensive capacity, including detection, resilience, and recovery (Mandsager et al., 2022). These uncertainties shape the limits of deterrence and help explain variation in deterrence outcomes. Within the MLMD Framework, deterrence theory therefore anchors analysis at the strategic level by clarifying how offensive cyber actions are evaluated in terms of their anticipated influence on adversary expectations, escalation dynamics, and longer-term strategic behaviour.

Intelligence theory explains how knowledge enables action in cyberspace and why intelligence connects strategic intent with operational planning and tactical execution. In doctrine, intelligence is defined as "knowledge and foreknowledge of the world around us" produced to support decision-making (Huskaj, 2025*c*). This definition captures both immediate situational awareness and anticipatory assessment. In OCO, these requirements translate into reconnaissance, vulnerability analysis, access validation, and assessment of operational effects. Activities such as mapping an adversary's network, identifying credentials, or confirming software configurations prior to payload deployment depend on intelligence and shape what actions are possible.

The intelligence cycle—collection, processing, analysis, and dissemination—applies directly to offensive cyber operations at all levels. At the strategic level, intelligence supports assessment of adversary intent, doctrine, and capability, including indications of coordinated cyber activity. At the operational level, it enables target development and preparation of the environment, including monitoring whether vulnerabilities remain exploitable or systems have been altered. At the tactical level, intelligence provides configuration-specific information required for execution, such as verifying system dependencies or software versions prior to exploitation (Joint Chiefs of Staff, 2018). Decisions at each level are therefore conditioned by what intelligence reveals about the target environment and by the limits of that knowledge.

A defining constraint in this context is the intelligence gain-loss (IGL) trade-off. Joint doctrine requires that potential intelligence loss be assessed before executing cyberspace operations, recognising that employing an access for disruptive or destructive effect may expose the intrusion and terminate an ongoing source of information (Joint Chiefs of Staff, 2018). This consideration shapes decisions about timing and sequencing, including whether access should be retained for continued collection or used to achieve an immediate operational effect. Within the MLMD Framework, intelligence theory clarifies how such considerations influence planning and execution across levels of decision-making.

OCO theory explains how cyber intrusions and attacks are planned and executed, and under what conditions they can produce effects in and through cyberspace. U.S. doctrine defines OCO as "missions intended to project power in and through foreign cyberspace" (Joint Chiefs of Staff, 2018, p. II-5). This definition aligns offensive cyber activity with established concepts of offensive action in other domains and encompasses activities ranging from network disruption to data manipulation and infrastructure degradation.

Recent scholarship describes offensive cyber capability through the access, vulnerability, payload (AVP) triad (Huskaj et al., 2024). Any offensive cyber action requires access to the target system, a vulnerability that permits manipulation, and a payload that produces the intended effect. Access may be obtained remotely, locally, or through supply-chain compromise. Vulnerabilities may involve software flaws, configuration weaknesses, or human behaviour. Payloads may alter data, disrupt processes, or disable system functions. The AVP triad provides a structured way to account for how a specific effect is expected to be generated.

OCO theory also distinguishes between cyberspace exploitation (CE) and cyberspace attack (CA) (Huskaj et al., 2024). CE focuses on information collection and preparation of the environment, while CA seeks to produce a discrete disruptive or destructive effect. Although both rely on similar technical mechanisms, their purposes differ. Access established for exploitation may later be used for attack if authorised, illustrating how the same technical condition can support different objectives depending on strategic intent.

Beyond individual actions, OCO theory incorporates operational design in cyberspace. This includes the coordination and sequencing of multiple actions over time to achieve a cumulative effect. Activities such as reconnaissance, access maintenance, and timing of payload execution are planned in relation to broader operational objectives. Concepts such as persistent engagement reflect this approach, emphasising continuous interaction with adversary networks to shape the operational environment (Huskaj et al., 2024). Doctrine further recognises that cyberspace actions are integrated with operations in other domains. AFDP 3-12 notes that cyber activities often support or are supported by air, land, maritime, or space operations (USAF LeMay Center, 2023). This integration explains why OCO theory spans strategic, operational, and tactical concerns.

Taken together, the three theories provide a structured basis for analysing OCO. Deterrence theory explains the strategic purpose of offensive capability and how states seek to influence adversary behaviour (Huskaj and Wilson, 2020*a*). Intelligence theory explains how knowledge enables planning and execution while constraining choice through considerations such as the IGL trade-off (Joint Chiefs of Staff, 2018). OCO theory explains how effects are generated through specific technical and operational processes (Huskaj et al., 2024). Within the MLMD Framework, these perspectives clarify how strategic intent, available knowledge, and operational capability are examined together when planning and conducting OCO.

3.3 Structure of the MLMD Framework

Having established the theoretical foundations, this section presents the structure of the MLMD Framework. The framework organises analysis along three elements: levels of action (strategic, operational, and tactical), functional perspectives derived from deterrence, intelligence, and OCO theory; and cross-cutting political, ethical, and technological dimensions. Each analytical position within the framework reflects a specific combination of level, function, and constraint. This structure provides a systematic method for examining how OCO are designed, authorised, and executed across levels of decision-making.

The framework allows analysis to proceed in several directions. Examination across levels clarifies how tactical actions relate to operational design and strategic intent. Examination across functional perspectives integrates deterrence logic, intelligence requirements, and offensive capability considerations. Examination across political, ethical, and technological dimensions situates action within its legal, normative, and technical conditions. Together, these perspectives support structured analysis of OCO without isolating individual decisions from their broader context.

The structure can be illustrated through a simplified planning scenario. Consider a cyber operation intended to disrupt an adversary's air-defence system in support of an allied airstrike. At the tactical level, OCO theory directs attention to access, vulnerability, and payload selection, consistent with the access–vulnerability–payload (AVP) triad (Huskaj et al., 2024). Intelligence provides the configuration-specific information required to identify exploitable weaknesses and develop the payload, including network topology and system dependencies (Joint Chiefs of Staff, 2018; US Joint Chiefs of Staff, 2013). Tactical execution is constrained by ROE and legal principles that require discrimination between military and civilian systems and proportionality of effect (Kehler et al., 2017; Schmitt, 2017; Mandsager et al., 2022).

At the operational level, intelligence and offensive cyberspace functions are coordinated to align the cyber action with the timing and objectives of the air operation (USAF LeMay Center, 2023). Planners must address deconfliction, including IGL considerations when an access originally established for intelligence collection may be converted into an attack (Joint Chiefs of Staff, 2018). Operational planning also accounts for adversary resilience, redundancy, and recovery mechanisms, which may require persistent access or repeated action to maintain the intended effect (U.S. Cyber Command Public Affairs Office, 2022). Although deterrence considerations are determined primarily at the strategic level, operational actions may still generate observable effects that influence higher-level signalling and posture.

At the strategic level, deterrence and political considerations dominate. Political authorities determine whether the operation aligns with domestic legal authority, international obligations, and broader strategic objectives (Schmitt, 2017; Mandsager et al., 2022). Strategic intelligence assesses how the adversary is likely to interpret the action, including the probability of attribution and the risk of escalation or retaliation (US Joint Chiefs of Staff, 2013; Warner, 2014). Strategic decision-making also incorporates technological risk, particularly whether employing a capability exposes sensitive exploits or compromises long-term intelligence access (Huskaj and Wilson, 2021).

By examining these intersections systematically, the MLMD Framework makes explicit how constraints and opportunities propagate across levels. Strategic legal or political constraints may eliminate otherwise viable tactical options. Tactical intelligence findings may require modification of operational design or strategic signalling. The framework's structure ensures that such dependencies are identified and assessed explicitly rather than implicitly.

A defining feature of the MLMD Framework is its mapping of theoretical perspectives across the levels of warfare. Each theory applies at all levels, but with a different analytical emphasis. At the strategic level, deterrence theory concerns national posture, signalling, and articulation of thresholds, including how cyber operations are integrated into broader deterrence strategies (Nye, 2017; Valeriano et al., 2018). At the operational level, deterrence logic informs choices about how cyber actions are employed to manage escalation and shape adversary responses during campaigns (Fischerkeller, 2017; Healey, 2019). At the tactical level, deterrence is not formulated as policy, but operational conduct may still influence adversary perception through the manner and timing of execution (Snyder, 1960; Nye, 2017).

Intelligence theory maps across levels in a complementary manner. Strategically, intelligence supports understanding of adversary intent, doctrine, and capability, informing policy and long-term planning (US Joint Chiefs of Staff, 2013; Warner, 2014).

Operationally, intelligence enables target development, OPE, and continuous assessment of adversary defences (Joint Chiefs of Staff, 2018; Clark, 2019). Tactically, intelligence provides time-sensitive technical detail required for execution and assessment, including credentials, configuration data, and indicators of effect (Joint Chiefs of Staff, 2018; US Joint Chiefs of Staff, 2013).

OCO theory likewise spans all levels. Strategically, it appears in doctrine and capability development decisions regarding CE and attack, and their relationship to concepts such as persistent engagement (Lynn, 2010; Libicki, 2016; Nakasone, 2019). Operationally, it informs campaign design, sequencing, and integration with other instruments of power (Joint Chiefs of Staff, 2018; USAF LeMay Center, 2023). Tactically, it specifies the technical actions required to achieve an effect, including gaining access, exploiting vulnerabilities, delivering payloads, and conducting supporting network operations (Huskaj et al., 2024).

The framework's cross-cutting dimensions apply at every intersection of level and function. The political dimension ensures that legality, authority, and policy oversight are assessed throughout planning and execution (Joint Chiefs of Staff, 2018; Schmitt, 2017). The ethical dimension incorporates principles of necessity, proportionality, distinction, and precaution, shaping both strategic restraint and technical design choices (Mandsager et al., 2022). The technological dimension ensures that expectations remain aligned with capability reliability, adversary resilience, and vulnerability lifecycles (Joint Chiefs of Staff, 2018; Huskaj and Wilson, 2021).

Together, these dimensions ensure that OCO are assessed as legally authorised, ethically constrained, and technically feasible actions integrated across strategic, operational, and tactical levels. By making these conditions explicit, the MLMD Framework provides a structured analytical method for both retrospective assessment and prospective planning of OCO (Joint Chiefs of Staff, 2018; USAF LeMay Center, 2023; US Joint Chiefs of Staff, 2013).

3.4 The MLMD Framework Across Strategic, Operational, and Tactical Levels

Strategic Level

At the strategic level, OCOs are instruments of national power authorised and directed by political leadership and senior command structures (Joint Chiefs of Staff, 2018; USAF LeMay Center, 2023). Decisions at this level determine whether offensive cyber capabilities may be employed, for what purposes, and under what legal and political constraints. Because OCO can generate cross-border effects, affect diplomatic relations, and create escalation risk, their use is treated as a matter of national authority rather than as a technical or operational choice.

Table 3.1 provides a strategic-level MLMD matrix that situates deterrence, intelligence, and OCO within their political, ethical, and technological conditioning.

Strategic control is exercised through doctrine, legal frameworks, and policy guidance that specify who may conduct OCO and under what conditions (Joint Chiefs of Staff, 2018; Mandsager et al., 2022). These instruments define constraints such as targeting restrictions, requirements for interagency coordination, and the degree to which authority may be delegated to subordinate commands. The analytical implication is that operational planners and tactical operators do not determine the permissibility of offensive action; they operate within boundaries established by strategic decision-making.

TABLE 3.1
Strategic-Level MLMD Matrix: Authorisation, Purpose, and Constraint

Strategic Level	**Dimension**		
	Political	**Ethical**	**Technological**
Deterrence	Definition of national cyber posture, thresholds, declaratory policy, and alliance commitments shaping adversary expectations	Assessment of legitimacy, proportionality, and escalation risk associated with deterrence signalling	Credibility of deterrence claims given observable capability, resilience, and exposure to retaliation
Intelligence	Authorisation of intelligence priorities, target categories, and acceptable collection domains	Evaluation of IGL trade-offs and long-term consequences of capability exposure	Availability and sustainability of strategic access, sensing, and attribution capabilities
Offensive Cyberspace Operations	Political approval of OCO as an instrument of national power and integration with broader strategy	Determination of permissible effects and restraint consistent with national values and international law	Strategic management of vulnerabilities, capability investment, and long-term force sustainability

National arrangements differ, but they exhibit a common pattern of centralised political oversight. In the United States, authority over significant OCO resides with the President and Secretary of Defense, with execution delegated to U.S. Cyber Command under defined conditions (Joint Chiefs of Staff, 2018; USAF LeMay Center, 2023). Comparable governance structures exist in other states, where cabinet-level bodies or national security councils retain approval over offensive cyber activity (Huskaj and Iftimie, 2020; Huskaj et al., 2024). These arrangements illustrate a general principle of the MLMD Framework: strategic-level OCO are political decisions implemented through military or intelligence organisations, not autonomous technical actions.

Deterrence and strategic signalling are core functions of OCO at this level. Strategic leaders assess how offensive cyber capabilities influence adversary expectations and contribute to deterrence by punishment and denial (Huskaj and Wilson, 2020*a*; Nye, 2017). Because cyber capabilities are largely non-observable, signalling relies on declaratory policy, selective disclosure, and the visible integration of cyber capabilities into broader defence postures. Alliance-level statements, such as NATO's position that certain cyber operations may trigger collective defence commitments, function as strategic signals intended to shape adversary calculations (Mandsager et al., 2022). The implication is that OCOs at the strategic level are evaluated primarily for their political and deterrent effects rather than for their immediate operational impact.

Ethical and legal considerations are also determined at the strategic level. Principles derived from the LOAC—necessity, distinction, proportionality, and precautions—apply to state-conducted OCO (Schmitt, 2017; Mandsager et al., 2022). Strategic authorities must determine whether offensive cyber means are appropriate to achieve a legitimate military objective and whether their use is consistent with national and international legal obligations. In some cases, cyber options may be preferred to kinetic alternatives because they offer greater discrimination and reduced risk to civilians, which shapes strategic assessments of escalation and legitimacy (Huskaj and Wilson, 2020*a*).

The technological dimension at the strategic level concerns long-term capability development, vulnerability management, and national resilience (Huskaj et al., 2024). Decisions about whether to retain or disclose vulnerabilities, invest in specific offensive capabilities, or prioritise defensive resilience have strategic consequences that extend beyond individual operations (Huskaj and Wilson, 2021). Strategic leaders must also consider whether national infrastructure is sufficiently resilient to absorb retaliation, as the employment of OCO without adequate defensive capacity may expose the state to significant counter-action. These technological choices condition what is feasible at the operational and tactical levels.

In summary, the strategic level of the MLMD Framework treats OCO as politically authorised instruments governed by deterrence logic, legal and ethical constraints, and long-term technological considerations. Strategic decision-makers define the boundaries within which operational design and tactical execution occur by determining whether an operation aligns with national objectives, legal authority, and acceptable risk. These decisions establish the conditions under which OCO can be planned and executed at lower levels.

Operational Level

At the operational level, OCO are designed and synchronised as campaigns and major operations that connect strategic guidance to tactical execution (Joint Chiefs of Staff, 2018; USAF LeMay Center, 2023). This level is where joint force commanders and their staffs integrate cyberspace capabilities with other instruments of military power, determine how multiple cyber missions support the joint campaign, and translate political direction into executable plans. Joint doctrine characterises this function as operational art: the coordination and sequencing of actions in time and purpose to achieve strategic objectives (Joint Chiefs of Staff, 2018). Within the MLMD Framework, the operational level is where intelligence, deterrence logic, and OCO are combined under political, ethical, and technological constraints.

Table 3.2 presents an operational-level MLMD matrix that illustrates how deterrence, intelligence, and OCO are coordinated within political, ethical, and technological constraints during campaign planning.

A central operational task is the integration of intelligence and operations. Unlike the strategic level, where intelligence primarily informs posture and policy, at the operational level intelligence directly guides action. Target system characterisation, network mapping, and near-real-time assessments underpin target development and operational preparation of the environment (OPE) (US Joint Chiefs of Staff, 2013; Joint Chiefs of Staff, 2018; Clark, 2019). These activities determine which systems are accessible, which effects are feasible, and when action can be taken.

CE and CA frequently rely on the same accesses, infrastructure, and tooling (Huskaj et al., 2024). An access established through cyber espionage may function simultaneously as an intelligence source and as a potential attack vector. This overlap means that intelligence collection and offensive action are often operationally interdependent rather than distinct phases. Operational commanders must therefore coordinate closely with intelligence organisations to ensure that targets are correctly identified, prioritised, and deconflicted.

This requirement is formalised through the IGL assessment embedded in joint planning processes. Joint doctrine highlights the risk that uncoordinated cyberspace actions may expose or disrupt other intelligence activities operating in the same environment (Joint Chiefs of Staff, 2018). An IGL assessment evaluates how executing a proposed CA could compromise existing accesses or terminate ongoing collection. In practice, this involves coordination mechanisms in which operational planners, intelligence officers, and legal advisers assess whether employing a given access or exploit will forfeit intelligence value and

TABLE 3.2
Operational-Level MLMD Matrix: Campaign Design, Coordination, and Control

Operational Level	**Dimension**		
	Political	**Ethical**	**Technological**
Deterrence	Alignment of cyber actions with political intent, escalation management, and alliance coordination during campaigns	Selection of effects and timing to manage proportionality and avoid unintended escalation	Reliability and controllability of effects influencing credibility and persistence of operational signalling
Intelligence	Prioritisation and deconfliction of intelligence activities supporting operational objectives and joint planning	IGL assessment governing conversion of access from collection to action	Maintenance of access, sensing, and assessment capabilities under adversary adaptation
Offensive Cyberspace Operations	Operational approval and integration of OCO within joint and combined campaign plans	Control of scope, duration, and reversibility of effects to remain within authorised thresholds	Feasibility of access–vulnerability–payload combinations and sustainment of operational tempo

whether alternative collection paths remain available (Joint Chiefs of Staff, 2018; Huskaj et al., 2024).

Campaign design at the operational level therefore requires balancing immediate disruption against the preservation of longer-term access. Each use of a sensitive access or exploit increases the likelihood of detection, patching, and loss of capability. The requirement to conduct IGL assessments before execution institutionalises this trade-off (Joint Chiefs of Staff, 2018). For example, a covert foothold in an adversary's operational command network may be used to disrupt communications in support of a current operation or retained to provide continued insight into adversary planning (Huskaj et al., 2024). An MLMD-consistent operational plan may phase activities accordingly, prioritising CE for reconnaissance and OPE before authorising CA once intelligence requirements are satisfied and senior authorities judge the trade-off acceptable.

Operational planning also entails coordination with coalition partners and other national agencies. In multinational settings, cyberspace operations often involve multiple contributors: one state may provide access infrastructure, another supplies specific tooling, while others contribute intelligence or legal oversight. Allied planning doctrine emphasises that cyber activities must be integrated into the broader operational plan and aligned with political direction and intelligence support (North Atlantic Treaty Organization, 2019). This introduces operational constraints such as national caveats on targets and techniques, classification barriers to sharing intelligence, and the need for multinational deconfliction to avoid mutual interference in shared networks. Within the MLMD Framework, these alliance and interagency factors are treated as political constraints at the operational level.

Ethical considerations at the operational level focus on escalation management and control of effects. While strategic authorities establish overarching legal and ethical boundaries, operational planning applies those principles to specific courses of action. Doctrine distinguishes between different types of denial effects—degrade, disrupt, and destroy—each associated with different levels of persistence and reversibility (Huskaj and Wilson, 2020*a*). Operational planners therefore select effects that achieve the commander's intent while remaining within authorised thresholds and managing escalation risk (Mandsager et al., 2022). This may involve favouring temporary disruption over permanent destruction when consistent with mission objectives.

Collateral and cascading effects also require operational scrutiny. Joint doctrine notes that while first-order cyber effects may be technically bounded, second- and third-order consequences can be difficult to predict, particularly when critical infrastructure or dual-use systems are involved (Joint Chiefs of Staff, 2018). Operational planning staff assess whether disabling a logistics or communications network could affect civilian services and may mitigate risk through timing, scope limitation, or coordination with other authorities for consequence management.

The technological dimension at the operational level concerns feasibility, reliability, and control of effects. Operational plans must reflect a realistic assessment of available accesses, vulnerabilities, and payloads, as captured in the AVP triad (Huskaj et al., 2024). This includes understanding success probabilities, system dependencies, and indicators that may alert the adversary. OPE may involve maintaining implants over time, which requires disciplined access management to avoid premature detection (Joint Chiefs of Staff, 2018; Huskaj et al., 2024).

Planners must also ensure that payloads incorporate technical controls that confine effects to authorised targets and enable reversibility where required. Safeguards such as kill-switches, target verification checks, and propagation limits reduce the risk of unintended effects beyond the intended battlespace (Joint Chiefs of Staff, 2018; Huskaj and Wilson, 2021). Testing in representative environments and coordination with defensive and intelligence elements reduce technical uncertainty prior to execution.

In summary, at the operational level the MLMD Framework emphasises synchronisation and orchestration. OCO are designed as components of a coherent campaign in which intelligence integration, IGL assessments, alliance coordination, ethical constraints, and technological feasibility are treated as integral planning considerations (Joint Chiefs of Staff, 2018; USAF LeMay Center, 2023; Huskaj et al., 2024). This approach links strategic direction to tactical execution while reducing the risk of mutual interference, unintended escalation, or misaligned effects.

Tactical Level

At the tactical level, OCOs are executed by mission teams and operators who conduct specific actions against designated targets to achieve the commander's immediate objectives. In joint doctrine, the tactical level concerns the execution of assigned tasks through discrete actions directed by higher authority; in cyberspace, this corresponds to individual missions and technical actions that implement authorised objectives within a defined scope and ROE (Joint Chiefs of Staff, 2018; USAF LeMay Center, 2023). Within the MLMD framework, the tactical level is where strategic and operational intent is realised through the concrete application of access, vulnerabilities, and payloads under the political, ethical, and technological constraints set at higher levels (Huskaj et al., 2024).

Table 3.3 presents a tactical-level MLMD matrix that captures how deterrence, intelligence, and offensive cyberspace operations are executed under binding political authority, ethical restraint, and technical feasibility.

A core tactical consideration is the relationship between CE and CA. Joint doctrine distinguishes CA, which generates denial or manipulation effects, from CE, which gains and maintains access to collect information or prepare future operations (Joint Chiefs of

TABLE 3.3
Tactical-Level MLMD Matrix: Execution, Control, and Assessment

Tactical Level	**Dimension**		
	Political	**Ethical**	**Technological**
Deterrence	Execution of authorised actions within defined rules of engagement and delegated authority	Conduct of operations in a manner that avoids unnecessary escalation or norm violation	Observable effects, timing, and signatures influencing adversary perception
Intelligence	Use of authorised accesses strictly within mission scope and command direction	Protection of intelligence sources through disciplined tradecraft and gain/loss awareness	Validation of target configuration, system state, and indicators of effect in real time
Offensive Cyberspace Operations	Compliance with mission orders specifying targets, scope, and duration of action	Selection of the least-severe effect consistent with mission intent and proportionality	Execution of access–vulnerability–payload actions with precision, reliability, and effect control

Staff, 2018). In practice, this distinction is often technical rather than structural. The same access and many of the same techniques may support both functions, depending on intent and authorisation.

An operator who has established a foothold on an adversary system may use that access to exfiltrate data as part of CE or, if authorised, to deliver a payload that degrades, disrupts, or destroys specific functions as part of CA (Huskaj et al., 2024). Tactical tradecraft therefore commonly involves CE as a precursor: mapping the network, validating target characteristics, and confirming that the intended effect can be generated without affecting non-designated systems. Only once these conditions are met does execution proceed in accordance with the operational plan.

Transitions between CE and CA may also occur as a result of changes in political or operational direction. Where a mission has initially been authorised as CE, higher authority may later direct a transition to CA, for example, during crisis escalation. In such cases, existing accesses may be repurposed to deliver disruptive payloads, provided that mission authorities and ROE explicitly permit this shift (Joint Chiefs of Staff, 2018; Huskaj et al., 2024). Within the MLMD Framework, this illustrates that at the tactical level the technical distinction between CE and CA lies primarily in payload and intent, while the legal and policy distinction is governed by authority and ROE.

Tactical execution is tightly constrained by ROE and mission authorities. Cyber mission teams operate under detailed orders specifying authorised targets, permitted actions, and limits on scope, duration, or intensity of effects (Joint Chiefs of Staff, 2018; Kehler et al., 2017). These constraints may include defined IP ranges, restrictions on data manipulation, or maximum durations for service disruption. Because cyberspace actions can propagate rapidly and produce effects that are difficult to predict, operator discretion is typically more narrowly bounded than in many kinetic contexts (Kehler et al., 2017; Mandsager et al., 2022).

Operators are expected to halt execution and seek higher guidance if they encounter unanticipated systems or indications that effects are extending beyond the authorised scope, such as the involvement of civilian critical infrastructure. The Newport ROE Handbook highlights that attribution uncertainty, escalation risk, and potential second-order effects complicate ROE formulation in cyberspace and require clear command-and-control arrangements even at the tactical level (Kehler et al., 2017). In MLMD terms, this reflects how political and ethical dimensions exert direct pressure on tactical choices rather than remaining abstract constraints.

Ethical requirements at the tactical level translate into concrete technical and procedural practices. Principles of distinction and proportionality require that cyber capabilities be designed and employed to affect only legitimate military objectives and to minimise collateral effects (Schmitt, 2017; Mandsager et al., 2022). For operators, this entails verifying target identity, confirming host characteristics, and tailoring payloads to specific software versions or configurations before execution (Huskaj and Wilson, 2020*a*).

Proportionality considerations are implemented through effect selection. Doctrine distinguishes between denial effects such as degrade, disrupt, and destroy, each associated with different levels of persistence and reversibility (Huskaj and Wilson, 2020*a*; Joint Chiefs of Staff, 2018). Tactical planners and operators favour the least severe effect consistent with the commander's intent, particularly where reversible or time-limited effects can achieve the required objective. Accountability is maintained through detailed mission logging and reporting. Operators record actions taken, system responses observed, and deviations from expected behaviour, enabling legal review, after-action assessment, and investigation where necessary (Joint Chiefs of Staff, 2018; Mandsager et al., 2022). Within the MLMD Framework, the ethical dimension at the tactical level is realised through payload design, ROE adherence, and disciplined execution.

The technological dimension at the tactical level focuses on precision, stealth, reliability, and control of effects. Operators must navigate adversary defensive measures such as intrusion detection systems, endpoint protection, and network segmentation while maintaining access and avoiding premature detection (Joint Chiefs of Staff, 2018; Huskaj et al., 2024). This may involve the use of valid credentials, traffic pattern mimicry, or routing activity through pre-compromised infrastructure to blend with expected network behaviour (Huskaj et al., 2024).

Tactical tooling is rarely a single capability. Operators employ a toolkit of exploits, implants, and support utilities and select among them based on observed target configurations and defensive posture. Reliability concerns arise from configuration differences, patch levels, or hidden dependencies that may cause payloads to fail or behave unpredictably. To mitigate this risk, doctrine and practice emphasise testing in representative environments and the inclusion of technical controls such as environment checks, kill-switches, and mechanisms to halt or reverse effects where feasible (Joint Chiefs of Staff, 2018; Huskaj and Wilson, 2021; Mandsager et al., 2022). These controls are central to the MLMD technological dimension at the tactical level, as they confine effects to the authorised battlespace.

Tactical actions also generate essential feedback to higher levels of analysis. Joint doctrine emphasises that cyberspace assessment requires both measures of performance (MOPs) and measures of effectiveness (MOEs), and that second- and third-order effects may emerge over time (Joint Chiefs of Staff, 2018). Operators contribute to this process by reporting whether accesses were gained or maintained, whether payloads executed as intended, and what observable changes occurred in target systems or adversary behaviour (Huskaj et al., 2024). This information feeds operational-level assessment and strategic evaluation of capability value, risk exposure, and deterrence signalling.

In summary, at the tactical level the MLMD Framework views OCO as the execution of CE and CA through specific accesses, vulnerabilities, and payloads, conducted under clearly defined authorities and ROE and shaped by ethical and technological constraints. Tactical operators implement strategic and operational decisions at the level of code, network paths, and system interactions, while their actions and observations provide empirical input that informs assessment and adaptation across all levels of the framework (Joint Chiefs of Staff, 2018; USAF LeMay Center, 2023; Huskaj et al., 2024).

3.5 Cross-Cutting Dimensions

Beyond the hierarchy of levels and functional theories, the MLMD Framework identifies three cross-cutting dimensions—political, ethical, and technological—that condition OCO at all stages. These dimensions do not constitute additional levels of analysis; rather, they define persistent constraints and enabling conditions that shape how operations are authorised, designed, and executed. Addressing these dimensions continuously is necessary to ensure that OCO remain politically legitimate, legally grounded, and sustainable over time. Although analytically distinct, the dimensions interact in practice and frequently reinforce or constrain one another.

Political Dimension

The political dimension encompasses legitimacy, legal and policy oversight, statecraft, and alliance politics. Any employment of offensive cyberspace capabilities must align with national legal obligations, constitutional arrangements, and foreign policy objectives (Joint Chiefs of Staff, 2018; Mandsager et al., 2022). Political legitimacy is therefore central. Operations perceived as unlawful, disproportionate, or misaligned with declared policy can impose diplomatic costs, erode trust among partners, and weaken long-term deterrence credibility (Nye, 2017; Mandsager et al., 2022). For this reason, democratic states establish political and legal oversight mechanisms for OCO, including civilian control over authorisation, interagency coordination procedures, and—in some cases—briefings to selected legislative bodies (Joint Chiefs of Staff, 2018; Mandsager et al., 2022). Because many cyberspace operations occur below the threshold of public visibility, transparency and accountability are primarily internal and rely on documented chains of authorisation, legal vetting, and interagency consultation rather than public disclosure (Mandsager et al., 2022).

The political dimension also includes signalling and perception management. States seek to shape adversary expectations through deterrence by punishment and deterrence by denial, using declaratory policy, public strategic documents, and selective disclosure of capabilities or operations (Nye, 2017; Fischerkeller and Harknett, 2017; Huskaj and Wilson, 2020*a*). Public attribution of significant malicious cyberspace activity—such as coordinated statements by the United States and its allies attributing an incident to a specific state—can function as strategic signalling by implying the availability of offensive cyberspace responses, even when operational details remain classified (Nye, 2017; Mandsager et al., 2022). Political authorities must therefore balance visibility, which sustains deterrence credibility, against secrecy, which protects sensitive accesses and methods (Fischerkeller and Harknett, 2017). This balance is inherently political and cannot be resolved through technical or military considerations alone.

Alliance and coalition politics further shape the political dimension. Within NATO, Allies have affirmed that a cyber attack may, in certain circumstances, lead the North Atlantic Council to decide that Article 5 collective defence obligations apply (Mandsager et al., 2022). As a result, strategic discussions about offensive cyberspace options may occur in collective settings when an Ally is subject to significant malicious cyberspace activity. Differences in capabilities, legal frameworks, and risk tolerance among Allies can generate friction, with some states favouring assertive cyberspace responses and others preferring diplomatic or economic measures. Political coordination mechanisms—such as alliance consultations and agreed crisis-response frameworks—are therefore necessary to ensure unity of effort, understood here in plain terms as different national authorities acting towards shared objectives without a single chain of command (Mandsager et al., 2022). Similar dynamics arise in other coalitions or ad hoc partnerships, where states with more advanced offensive cyberspace capabilities may support partners under mutually agreed political mandates (U.S. Cyber Command Public Affairs Office, 2022; Huskaj et al., 2024).

Norm development and precedent-setting constitute an additional component of the political dimension. Early and repeated uses of OCO contribute, intentionally or otherwise, to shaping expectations about acceptable state behaviour in cyberspace (Schmitt, 2017; Mandsager et al., 2022). Decision-makers must therefore assess whether conducting—or refraining from—specific operations supports the evolution of norms they regard as desirable. For example, many Western states have argued that certain categories of critical infrastructure, such as hospitals or power grids, should be off-limits to CA in peacetime. Maintaining credibility for this position requires corresponding restraint in their own targeting practices (Schmitt, 2017; Mandsager et al., 2022). Smaller states often rely on intelligence sharing, capacity-building, and operational support from larger partners to develop offensive cyberspace capabilities, which in turn requires political alignment, trust, and agreed frameworks for supported operations (Huskaj and Moradian, 2018; U.S. Cyber Command Public Affairs Office, 2022; Huskaj et al., 2024). Within the MLMD Framework, these factors underscore that OCO are expressions of political choice embedded in broader structures of governance, alliances, and norm-building rather than isolated technical acts.

Ethical Dimension

The ethical dimension concerns the requirement that OCO comply with legal and moral principles and do not undermine the values the state seeks to protect. Although cyberspace operations often appear comparatively bloodless because their immediate effects target data or system availability rather than physical harm, they raise substantive ethical challenges. These challenges intersect with the principles of distinction, proportionality, necessity, and precautions under the LOAC (Schmitt, 2017; Mandsager et al., 2022). Ethical analysis therefore applies across planning, authorisation, and execution rather than being confined to post hoc assessment.

A central concept in this dimension is anticipatory ethics. Because offensive cyberspace capabilities evolve rapidly and lack stable historical analogues, ethical assessment must consider potential second- and third-order effects before irreversible harm occurs (Huskaj and Wilson, 2020*a*). An operation intended to disrupt an adversary regime's financial flows by accessing a civilian banking network may achieve a strategic objective while simultaneously imposing disproportionate burdens on uninvolved civilians. Such cases illustrate why ethical constraints must be evaluated prior to authorisation. Comparative analyses of cyber and kinetic options in crisis scenarios further indicate that proportionality judgements vary when effects are reversible, geographically bounded, or temporally limited, reinforcing the need for structured ethical assessment during planning (Huskaj and Wilson, 2020*a*).

Proportionality in cyberspace requires assessing whether the anticipated military advantage justifies the scale, scope, and duration of foreseeable harm (Schmitt, 2017). In practical terms, this involves designing effects that achieve the required operational outcome while avoiding excessive collateral disruption. Where an operation serves a signalling purpose, planners should prefer narrowly scoped and time-bound effects rather than actions that risk widespread or persistent outages. Distinction remains equally fundamental. Even when a cyber capability does not directly cause physical injury, it may affect systems supporting essential civilian services. Ethical application therefore requires restricting payload execution to the intended military system, for example, by embedding environment checks to prevent propagation from a military satellite control node to civilian infrastructure or the wider Internet (Mandsager et al., 2022; Huskaj et al., 2024).

Accountability is a further ethical requirement. The opacity of cyberspace and the difficulty of attribution create incentives for states to operate without public acknowledgement, yet such practices risk eroding internal accountability and weakening norms of responsible state behaviour. Democratic states therefore maintain internal mechanisms to document authorisation chains, preserve records of operator actions, and conduct post-operation review, even when operational details remain classified (Mandsager et al., 2022). If an operation unintentionally affects a protected civilian system, such as a hospital network connected to a targeted logistics node, an ethical approach requires mitigation and internal acknowledgement rather than treating the effect as an acceptable by-product of secrecy. This practice reinforces restraint and prevents the emergence of permissive precedents in covert cyberspace operations.

Transparency dilemmas arise because states must demonstrate adherence to legal and ethical frameworks without exposing sensitive methods. Partial transparency—through limited public attribution, publication of national cyber strategies, and participation in norm-development processes—provides assurance of responsible conduct while preserving operational security (Nye, 2017; Mandsager et al., 2022). The ethical dimension also extends to the human element of OCO. Military organisations increasingly incorporate ethical reasoning into the training of cyber operators, emphasising that technical feasibility does not justify use unless an action conforms to authorised purpose, legal requirements, and ethical constraints (Huskaj et al., 2024). Within the MLMD Framework, these considerations ensure that OCO remain aligned with national values and legal obligations.

An additional ethical issue concerns the use of automation and artificial intelligence in OCO. Although automation can accelerate defensive responses, delegating decisions to employ offensive force—including CA—raises questions about whether autonomous systems can reliably apply distinction, proportionality, and precaution in accordance with LOAC (Schmitt, 2017; Mandsager et al., 2022). Most analyses therefore stress that a human decision-maker must remain responsible for authorising offensive effects, since moral agency and legal accountability cannot be transferred to automated processes (Schmitt, 2017). For example, an automated system configured to trigger a CA based on detected hostile network behaviour may misclassify benign activity and generate unintended effects on civilian infrastructure. Within the MLMD Framework, this reinforces the requirement that OCO incorporate human judgement at the point of authorisation and avoid purely technical execution divorced from political, legal, and ethical review (Huskaj et al., 2024).

The Technological Dimension

The technological dimension concerns the material properties and constraints of technology that condition what OCO can and cannot achieve. Not all desired effects are technically attainable given the characteristics of specific target systems. Certain environments, such as isolated or air-gapped networks or systems built on bespoke architectures, may present no viable exploit path within the available time horizon (Joint Chiefs of Staff, 2018). Strategic and operational decision-making therefore depends on an accurate understanding of technical viability, expected success rates, and observable indicators of compromise in order to avoid assumptions about effects that cannot be generated in practice (Joint Chiefs of Staff, 2018; Huskaj et al., 2024). Personnel responsible for capability development and technical operations provide assessments of what effects can be produced against specific targets using existing accesses, vulnerabilities, and payloads (Joint Chiefs of Staff, 2018). These assessments limit the range of operational options available to commanders and inform how strategic intent is translated into executable plans. Within the MLMD Framework, technological constraints condition strategic choice rather than following from it.

The technological dimension also reflects the continuous interaction between offensive and defensive capabilities. Cyber tools typically lose effectiveness as vulnerabilities are patched, system configurations change, or defensive monitoring improves (Joint Chiefs of Staff, 2018; Huskaj et al., 2024). Developments in encryption, authentication, and anomaly detection restrict exploitation and payload delivery, while advances in computing may, over time, weaken existing protective measures (Huskaj et al., 2024). Offensive and defensive capabilities, therefore co-evolve, with each constraining the operational lifespan of the other. Exploits and tools that are not updated lose operational value, while the accumulation of offensive capabilities without corresponding defensive investment can introduce systemic risk. Capabilities intended to affect core Internet services or strategic command-and-control systems may generate cascading effects beyond the intended target, which has prompted concerns about stability and restraint (Huskaj and Wilson, 2021). These technological properties link directly to political deliberation over acceptable use.

Management of software vulnerabilities constitutes a further element of the technological dimension. Decisions to retain or disclose previously unknown vulnerabilities are taken at strategic and operational levels but depend on technical evaluation. When a state identifies a vulnerability in widely deployed software, it must decide whether to preserve that vulnerability for potential operational use or to disclose it for remediation (Huskaj and Wilson, 2021). Retention provides potential access, while disclosure strengthens overall system security. These choices involve explicit trade-offs. Retaining a vulnerability may support intelligence collection or offensive action, but increases the risk that the same weakness will be exploited by others. Disclosure reduces offensive opportunity but mitigates long-term exposure across civilian and governmental systems (Huskaj and Wilson, 2021). Many states address this dilemma through formal Vulnerabilities Equities Processes (VEP), which assess technical prevalence, likelihood of independent discovery, criticality of affected systems, and potential collateral consequences should an exploit escape control (Huskaj and Wilson, 2021). Within the MLMD Framework, vulnerability stewardship demonstrates how technical characteristics constrain strategic discretion.

Reliability and controllability of cyber capabilities represent additional technological constraints. Cyber effects are sensitive to configuration details and to changes in the operational environment. JP 3-12 emphasises that assessment of cyberspace operations must account for uncertainty regarding second- and third-order effects, which may diverge from initial intent (Joint Chiefs of Staff, 2018). Testing is limited by the absence of fully representative target environments, even when test ranges or simulated systems are available. As a result, offensive capability development requires detailed system knowledge in addition to exploit development. Operators and planners must account for interdependencies between systems and incorporate technical safeguards into payload design (Huskaj et al., 2024). Where effects are intended to be temporary or reversible, additional engineering is required. Denial effects may, for example, rely on cryptographic mechanisms or timed controls that permit restoration after a defined period, which constrains both payload design and operational use (Huskaj et al., 2024).

Attribution capabilities also form part of the technological dimension. States invest in sensors, logging, and analytic methods to correlate indicators across incidents and improve technical attribution (Joint Chiefs of Staff, 2018; US Joint Chiefs of Staff, 2013). In response, offensive operations employ layered infrastructure and anti-forensic techniques to delay attribution (Joint Chiefs of Staff, 2018). As technical attribution improves through data fusion and international cooperation, sustained campaigns become increasingly likely to be detected and linked to responsible actors over time (Joint Chiefs of Staff, 2018; Mandsager et al., 2022). This reality constrains operational design. Single, limited actions may remain difficult to attribute with confidence, but repeated use of similar tools or infrastructure produces patterns that can be recognised. Within the MLMD Framework, technological constraints therefore limit assumptions about concealment, persistence, and deniability.

Taken together, the technological dimension situates OCO within limits imposed by feasibility, reliability, vulnerability management, and attribution. It anchors strategic and operational decision-making in the material properties of technology rather than in abstract expectations of cyber capability (Joint Chiefs of Staff, 2018; Huskaj et al., 2024; Huskaj and Wilson, 2021).

3.6 Conclusion

This chapter has shown that OCO emerge from the interaction of strategic intent, operational design, and tactical execution, each conditioned by political authority, ethical constraint, and technological feasibility. The MLMD Framework captures this interaction by integrating deterrence theory, intelligence theory, and OCO theory into a single analytical construct.

At the strategic level, the framework clarifies how political authority, legal mandate, and deterrence logic define the scope and purpose of OCO. At the operational level, it shows how campaign design and intelligence integration condition which courses of action remain viable over time. At the tactical level, it explains how authorised intent is translated into concrete effects through access, vulnerability exploitation, and payload execution under defined ROE. Across all levels, the political, ethical, and technological dimensions function as conditioning constraints rather than as considerations applied after execution.

Taken together, the MLMD Framework provides a structured means of tracing how OCO are authorised, prepared, executed, and assessed across levels of decision-making. It enables analysis of how dependencies and frictions at one level propagate to others. Chapter 4 applies the framework to Sweden's cyber deterrence posture using publicly available policy and doctrinal material to examine authority, governance, and authorisation arrangements.

Decision Exercise: Using the MLMD Framework Under Time Compression

Scenario. Over the past eight weeks, an identified state-linked actor has conducted a sustained campaign against your country and two allies. The campaign combines (i) intrusion attempts against election-adjacent services and managed service providers, (ii) theft and timed release of policy-relevant documents, and (iii) exploratory access activity in energy-sector networks. Attribution is contested across domestic audiences. An ally requests visible reassurance before its national vote. Your government asks for an authorised response option set within 72 hours that supports deterrence while preserving political control.

Analytical question 1—MLMD problem definition. State the strategic objective for the next 30 days (denial, punishment, reassurance, or a bounded combination). Then write one sentence for each level:

- **Strategic:** what is being authorised and what is explicitly excluded?
- **Operational:** what must be synchronised and deconflicted?
- **Tactical:** what effect category is permitted and what control property is mandatory (time-boundedness, reversibility, containment)?

Analytical question 2—Intelligence readiness and the gain/loss dilemma. Specify three priority intelligence requirements (adversary intent; feasibility and access persistence; escalation pathways and audience interpretation). For each, state (i) the minimum confidence level required for decision, and (ii) what action you take if it remains unresolved inside 72 hours. Then decide: *retain* sensitive access for collection, or *convert* it for action. Provide one trigger for switching your choice.

Analytical question 3—Two response options with explicit constraints. Propose two distinct authorised options:

- **Option A (denial-oriented):** specify the intended effect (degrade/disrupt) and one containment constraint.
- **Option B (punishment-oriented):** specify the intended effect (cost imposition against adversary capability-support functions) and one auditability constraint.

For each option, specify one failure mode where misalignment causes technical action to diverge from political intent.

Analytical question 4—Minimum governance conditions. Define the minimum governance conditions required to proceed: political approval threshold, legal review standard, oversight and logging requirements, and partner constraints. State one way these conditions reduce escalation exposure under time compression.

Short task—MLMD mapping (three lines). Write three lines in the form:

- **Strategic.** decision → dependency → constraint.
- **Operational.** decision → dependency → constraint.
- **Tactical.** decision → dependency → constraint.

Optional extension—Signalling package. Draft a two-sentence declaratory statement that supports the chosen objective without disclosing sources or methods. Identify the primary audience and one misinterpretation risk.

Part II

Organising for Cyber Power

4

Threats, Policy, and Practice in Sweden's Cyber Deterrence

Chapter 3 defined the Multi-Level, Multi-Dimensional (MLMD) Framework as an analytical instrument for tracing how OCO (OCO) are authorised, designed, and executed across strategic, operational, and tactical levels under political, ethical, and technological constraints. This chapter applies MLMD to a national case to examine how a cyberliterate state frames threats, translates policy into institutional mandates, and positions OCO within a deterrence posture, based on what open sources permit.

The purpose is to analyse how publicly stated threat perceptions, policy choices, and organisational arrangements interact to enable or constrain a credible offensive cyber posture. Sweden is treated as an empirical case of a digitally advanced, highly network-dependent small or medium-sized state. The analytical intent is to draw theory-informed inferences about governance and alignment problems that recur across comparable states, rather than to provide a country descriptions for their own sake.

The analysis relies on publicly available policy documents, institutional mandates, doctrine, and open-source reporting. It does not describe operational methods, targeting practices, capability inventories, classified thresholds for use, or planning tradecraft for OCO. Where public material is incomplete, the chapter avoids inference beyond what the sources support.

Methodologically, the chapter uses MLMD as a structured coding scheme. At the strategic level, it examines threat framing, the articulation of deterrence intent, and how legal and political oversight is described in policy and doctrine. At the operational level, it examines how authority and coordination are organised across institutions and how intelligence and operational functions are positioned relative to deterrence objectives. At the tactical level, the chapter remains bounded by open sources and therefore analyses publicly observable indicators of posture and response rather than technical tradecraft.

The chapter proceeds as follows. Section 4.1 introduces Sweden as an analytical case and specifies how the *Smart State* concept is used to link structural exposure, stated policy intent, and institutional design. Section 4.2 analyses Sweden's cyber threat environment as described in intelligence assessments and public security discourse. Section 4.3 examines governance and institutional structures relevant to deterrence, intelligence integration, and the positioning of offensive capability within the national security architecture.

Section 4.4 examines strategic objectives and policy frameworks, including legal authorities, oversight arrangements, and the role of EU and NATO commitments in shaping response options. Section 4.5 applies the MLMD Framework to derive strategic and organisational implications and clarifies how these implications inform Chapter 5's analysis of offensive tools and vulnerability policy processes. Section 4.6 examines how declared intent, legal authority, and institutional arrangements translate into an operationally usable deterrence posture within the limits of open sources.

Section 4.7 presents illustrative foresight scenarios that specify deterrence-relevant requirements in electorally sensitive administration, digital financial services, and hybrid

DOI: 10.1201/9781003655183-4

influence activity. Section 4.8 synthesises the interaction between strategy and practice by identifying how coordination across state, private, and societal functions conditions deterrence posture. Section 4.9 provides a chapter-level synthesis and implications. Section 4.10 concludes by restating the case-based findings and the resulting boundary conditions for analysing Sweden's cyber deterrence posture using open sources.

4.1 Sweden as a Smart State in Cyberspace

This section specifies why Sweden is analytically useful for examining cyber deterrence posture in a digitally dependent, small or medium-sized state. The purpose is to introduce the *Smart State* concept as the lens for linking structural exposure, stated policy intent, and institutional design within the evidentiary limits of open sources. The section proceeds in four steps. It defines how *Smart State* is used in this chapter, specifies how extensive digitalisation creates exposure to hostile cyber activity, outlines the mobilisation problem created by limited kinetic mass and distributed societal resources, and identifies the governance tensions that make the case suitable for analysis through the MLMD Framework.

The *Smart State* Concept and Offensive Integration

Open-source Swedish civil–military security discourse has used the concept of a "Smart State" to describe how national security is pursued through coordinated use of state capabilities and societal resources (Sundelius, 1995). In this chapter, the concept is used as an analytical lens for examining how a digitally dependent small or medium-sized state links resilience claims, governance design, and the publicly stated option to employ cyberspace capabilities for national-security purposes. The purpose is to assess how strategic self-description and institutional design shape political justification and oversight within the evidentiary limits of open sources.

The concept is operationalised by tracing three linkages in public material. First, it examines how dependence and exposure are translated into threat narratives and prioritised risks. Second, it examines how those narratives are translated into mandates, coordination arrangements, and oversight structures across relevant institutions. Third, it examines how OCO is positioned relative to deterrence objectives, including how intelligence functions and inter-agency coordination are described in relation to offensive integration (Joint Chiefs of Staff, 2018).

Strategic Exposure and the Threat Landscape

High digitalisation increases national dependence on networked systems and therefore increases exposure to intrusion, coercion, and disruption. National security and intelligence reporting frames cyber threats as a central concern and describes state-linked intrusions as recurring and increasingly sophisticated (Security Service, 2025; National Defence Radio Establishment, 2024). In a region marked by heightened geopolitical tension—and following NATO accession—open reporting describes activity spanning espionage, pre-positioning, influence, and other hybrid threats. It describes persistent campaigns by Russian actors targeting military and governmental infrastructure, Chinese operations aimed at intellectual property theft, and Iranian activities directed against media and public institutions (Army Technology, 2024; Security Service, 2025; Hellerstedt, 2023; Euractiv, 2024).

The implication is that Sweden faces a threat environment similar in scope to that faced by larger powers while operating with the constraints of a small or medium-sized state. This makes the governance problem central: deterrence posture and offensive integration depend on how the state mobilises expertise, coordinates institutions, and converts policy intent into implementable mandates. In this chapter, the mobilisation problem is analysed through the *Smart State* lens.

Mobilising the Smart State

Sundelius associates the "Smart State" with compensating for material limitations through ideas, technical solutions, and competent leadership that shape outcomes beyond what scale alone would suggest (Sundelius, 1995; Eriksson, 2019). In cyberspace, the mechanism is organisational: technical expertise and institutional credibility can generate strategic value only if they are translated into mandates, coordination arrangements, and oversight that support sustained capability development and controlled use.

Sweden's potential cyber power is shaped by the interaction between widespread ICT dependence and its governance model. Extensive domestic ICT use creates sustained demand for advanced cybersecurity services and a population with high digital literacy (Edquist and Henrekson, 2017). Universities and research institutes supply specialised competence, while agencies operate within a tradition of rule-of-law governance and transparency (Sundelius, 1995; Eriksson, 2019). These conditions can support claims of restraint and democratic oversight in how offensive capabilities are governed, which in turn can shape political authorisation and international signalling.

Interview-based material reports a perception among policy-makers that no single public actor can sustain the full spectrum of cyber defence and offensive capability development with its own resources (Huskaj and Axelsson, 2023). On that basis, the study develops an interpretive division-of-labour model in which commercial firms contribute infrastructure and tools, academia contributes methods and human capital, and defence and intelligence organisations contribute legal authority and strategic direction (Huskaj and Axelsson, 2023). Within this chapter, this model is treated as a research-based proposition about mobilisation constraints, not as a description of institutional practice.

Institutional Arrangements and Declared Direction

Policy decisions for 2021–2025 and 2025–2030 state an intent to strengthen the Armed Forces' capability for defensive and OCO and associate this intent with deterrence-related aims (Government, 2020; Government, 2024*b*). Open descriptions of the establishment of a dedicated Cyber Defence Regiment in 2025 present it as an organisational development linked to cyber-defence tasks and capability development within the Total Defence framework (The Armed Forces, 2025). Taken together, these sources permit analysis of declared direction and institutional design, while remaining bounded by what open material can substantiate.

Sweden as an Analytical Case for the MLMD Framework

From an analytical perspective, Sweden provides a useful lens through which to examine the broader arguments of this book. It is a state that may need to balance the imperatives of an "active and independent" security policy with adherence to international law and democratic norms (Huskaj, 2025*d*). This creates observable tensions that are central to the study of OCO: the trade-off between the secrecy required for offensive operations and the transparency expected in a democracy; the dilemma of disclosing vulnerabilities versus retaining them for national security purposes; and the potential challenge of aligning national priorities with alliance commitments in NATO (Huskaj and Wilson, 2021; Henriksén, Lexert, Dahn, and Hacks, 2025).

Therefore, this case functions as the primary empirical basis for applying the Multi-Level Multi-Dimensional (MLMD) framework across the manuscript. The case material allows tracing how strategic objectives (deterrence and influence) are translated into operational planning (institutional cooperation and legal mandates) and tactical execution (capability development and intelligence integration) (Huskaj et al., 2024). By examining how a cyberliterate democratic state organises for offence under legal and political constraint, the analysis yields inferences about the governance conditions under which offensive cyber capabilities can be developed and employed lawfully and under political control.

Sweden's position as a highly digitalised state with advanced information infrastructure generates both operational advantages and structural exposure, a duality consistently identified in national security, intelligence, and security assessments and research (Bengtsson and Huskaj, 2021; Huskaj et al., 2021; Security Service, 2025; Military Intelligence and Security Service, 2024; National Defence Radio Establishment, 2024). High connectivity enables economic efficiency and rapid information flows, but it also expands the range of systems and societal functions that may be targeted in or through cyberspace. As a result, hostile activity directed at Swedish interests increasingly exploits the technical and organisational characteristics of a digitally integrated society, rather than relying on isolated or overtly escalatory actions. Because such activity is conducted predominantly below the threshold of armed conflict and often embedded within long-term campaigns, its full scope and sequencing cannot be reconstructed from open sources alone. Any assessment based on publicly available material must therefore proceed with partial visibility and inferential caution.

4.2 Sweden's Cyber Threat Environment

The case faces a sustained cyber threat environment shaped by the activities of Russia, China, and Iran, each employing OCO to obtain strategic advantage through espionage, preparatory intrusions, and cyber-enabled influence activities (Security Service, 2025; Military Intelligence and Security Service, 2024; National Defence Radio Establishment, 2024; Henriksén et al., 2025). Although these operations vary in scale, tempo, and technical sophistication, they collectively target government agencies, critical infrastructure, research environments, and private organisations, thereby exerting pressure across political, economic, and technological domains. Activity directed at national interests is conducted predominantly below the threshold of armed conflict, where legal ambiguity, attribution challenges, and operational deniability enable persistent probing over extended periods. The resulting environment is characterised less by isolated incidents than by cumulative campaigns designed to create strategic leverage without triggering overt escalation (Security Service, 2025; Military Intelligence and Security Service, 2024; National Defence Radio Establishment, 2024).

Russian activity illustrates an integrated approach to information confrontation in which cyber intrusions, electronic warfare, and coordinated influence operations are combined to weaken adversaries, map vulnerabilities, and prepare options for coercive action (Huskaj et al., 2021; Military Intelligence and Security Service, 2024). Swedish intelligence reporting confirms that Russian intelligence services, including the FSB, SVR, and GRU, conduct espionage, reconnaissance, and influence operations targeting defence, government, and research sectors (Security Service, 2025; National Defence Radio Establishment, 2024; Military Intelligence and Security Service, 2024). While some elements of Russia's broader operational ecosystem—such as expendable intermediaries and specialised units—are more visible in other theatres, their relevance for Sweden lies in the logic they reveal: the generation of deniable capabilities that can be activated or escalated in response to political developments or crisis conditions (Military Intelligence and Security Service, 2024; Security Service, 2025). Russian activity must therefore be understood as a continuous campaign that seeks to exploit both technical vulnerabilities and societal vulnerabilities.

Chinese activity is characterised by long-term intelligence collection, technology acquisition, and cyber espionage intended to support strategic economic and military objectives (Security Service, 2025; Military Intelligence and Security Service, 2024; Huskaj et al., 2021). The Security Service assesses that Chinese state-linked actors employ a combination of legal and illicit methods, including research collaboration, investment strategies, and computer-network exploitation, to obtain dual-use technology, sensitive research data, and information related to diaspora communities (Security Service, 2025). Empirical cases, such as the Cloud Hopper campaign attributed to APT10, demonstrate how supply-chain compromises targeting managed service providers in Europe, including firms operating in Sweden, enabled large-scale exfiltration of industrial and defence-relevant information (Bengtsson and Huskaj, 2021). This pattern indicates that Chinese OCO are embedded within broader strategies of technological accumulation, creating long-term risks that incremental losses of sensitive knowledge undermine Sweden's competitiveness and defence capability (Security Service, 2025; Military Intelligence and Security Service, 2024).

Iranian activity reflects a model in which OCO, intelligence collection, and information operations are integrated to compensate for conventional asymmetries and to reinforce regime security (Huskaj et al., 2021). Iranian cyber units conduct espionage and disruptive operations against government institutions, academia, and private companies, and Swedish assessments confirm that Tehran systematically targets opposition figures in exile, universities, and selected firms for intelligence collection purposes (Security Service, 2025; Military Intelligence and Security Service, 2024). The 2023 SMS incident illustrates this approach: an Iranian state-linked actor compromised a Swedish messaging service and disseminated large volumes of messages intended to inflame social tensions and reinforce narratives portraying Sweden as hostile to Islam (Security Service, 2025). Such operations demonstrate how technical intrusion and psychological effects are combined to generate impact beyond the immediate cyber domain, testing societal resilience and crisis-response mechanisms (Huskaj et al., 2021; Military Intelligence and Security Service, 2024).

Taken together, the activities of Russia, China, and Iran produce a multi-vector threat environment characterised by sustained espionage, reconnaissance for potential sabotage, and cyber-enabled influence operations (Security Service, 2025; Military Intelligence and Security Service, 2024; National Defence Radio Establishment, 2024). Swedish intelligence services emphasise that foreign actors systematically probe for vulnerabilities in systems supporting essential societal functions, exploit periods of political or social stress to shape perceptions, and maintain long-running campaigns intended to constrain Sweden's strategic freedom of action (Security Service, 2025; Military Intelligence and Security Service, 2024). The defining feature of this environment is continuity rather than episodic escalation: adversaries seek advantage through the accumulation of access, knowledge, and influence over time rather than through singular, decisive cyber actions (National Defence Radio Establishment, 2024; Military Intelligence and Security Service, 2024; Security Service, 2025).

4.3 Governance and Institutional Structures

National cyber governance in a cyberliterate state is commonly organised through legally separate public authorities operating under statutory mandates and rule-of-law oversight (Huskaj and Axelsson, 2023). This design supports continuity and specialisation, yet it may create a coordination constraint because cyber incidents routinely cross administrative jurisdictions and combine technical intrusion with societal effects. The analytical purpose of this section is to specify how distributed authority conditions the conversion of warning into decision support for political leaders under evidentiary uncertainty and compressed decision windows.

This governance setting interacts with the principle of responsibility, under which the authority responsible for an activity in peacetime retains that responsibility during heightened alert or war (Huskaj and Axelsson, 2023). The implication is that incidents with cross-sectoral effects can activate parallel responsibilities rather than a single command relationship. Deterrence posture is conditioned by whether assessment, public communication, and continuity management can be coordinated across mandates without exceeding legal authority or compromising oversight obligations.

Open material describes a national coordination arrangement for joint threat analysis and structured information exchange among relevant civilian, security, and military actors and places this arrangement within the SIGINT function (The Riksdag, 2025; National Cybersecurity Centre, 2025*b*; National Cybersecurity Centre, 2025*a*). At the mandate level, this permits analysis of an institutional mechanism intended to support shared situational awareness. Open sources do not, however, substantiate how analytic outputs are operationalised across agencies or how rapidly they translate into government-level decision support.

Within this institutional landscape, government documents describe a military cyber function responsible for protecting and restoring military information systems and, under lawful political authorisation, conducting cyberspace activity intended to restrict an adversary's use of information systems (Government, 2024*a*). Analytically, the coupling of defensive continuity with an authorised option for cost imposition matters because it places deterrence-relevant action inside a governance chain that is political by design. Open sources do not permit inference about internal readiness cycles or decision timelines; the observable point is the boundary condition created by declared authority and oversight.

Public reporting further describes a SIGINT function producing technical reporting relevant to warning, threat characterisation, and attribution-oriented assessment (National Defence Radio Establishment, 2024; National Defence Radio Establishment, 2022). This function conditions deterrence posture because below-threshold activity is often interpreted through cumulative patterns rather than single-event attribution. The policy relevance of technical reporting follows from its role in shaping confidence judgements that inform whether political leaders treat activity as coercive, preparatory, or nuisance-level.

Open material also describes a domestic security and counterintelligence function responsible for detecting, investigating, and countering foreign intelligence activity within national jurisdiction, including cyber-enabled espionage and preparatory activity, and for contributing to threat assessment and information exchange (Government, 2024*a*; Security Service, 2025; National Cybersecurity Centre, 2025*a*). In deterrence terms, this function shapes what forms of disruption, public attribution, and legal response are feasible because evidentiary standards and mandate boundaries condition how activity can be characterised and acted upon.

Civil cyber preparedness is described in public material as currently organised through the Civil Defence Authority (formerly the Swedish Civil Contingencies Agency) and a national CSIRT function responsible for coordination support, incident-management elements, technical advisories, and vulnerability-management support across public and private sectors (Ministry of Defence, 2024; Government, 2024*a*; National Cybersecurity Centre, 2025*a*). Note, however, that a structural transition is underway: while the authority has been renamed to emphasise civil defence, the operational CSIRT elements are scheduled to transfer to the National Cybersecurity Center by mid-2026. This function remains deterrence-relevant because denial is partly produced through baseline resilience and continuity in essential services, which reduces the likelihood that hostile activity yields visible disruption that can be politically exploited.

Finally, public material describes a psychological-defence function addressing hostile influence activity and crisis communication support (Psychological Defence Agency, 2024). The analytical point is that hybrid activity can synchronise technical compromise with confidence effects. Deterrence by denial, therefore depends on whether authoritative communication and societal resilience can limit the secondary impact of cyber incidents without relying on escalation-prone signalling.

Taken together, the open-source record supports an account of distributed governance with a formal coordination mechanism intended to support shared situational awareness across functions separated by mandate and oversight (National Cybersecurity Centre, 2025*b*). The MLMD implication is that credibility depends on alignment across intelligence production, civilian preparedness, domestic security assessment, sector regulation, and military cyber authority, because the availability of time-sensitive options is conditioned by coordination latency and legal constraint rather than by technical capability alone.

4.4 Strategic Objectives and Policy Frameworks

The national cybersecurity and deterrence posture is articulated through policy direction that treats cyberspace as an operational domain requiring explicit authority, legal constraint, and coordinated institutional action. Government policy frames cyber defence as part of total defence and states an intent to maintain capability for both defensive and OCO to protect sovereignty and freedom of action (Government, 2024*a*). The same proposition describes cyberspace operations as a natural component of warfare alongside land, sea, air, and space operations and indicates that government-authorised OCO may contribute to deterrence-related aims (Government, 2024*a*). Analytically, these claims matter because they position cost-imposition options inside a political authorisation chain, which shapes credibility through governance rather than through technical capacity alone.

The legal and normative framework structures this posture through centralised political authority. On the basis of open material, the Whole-of-Society study treats legal authority for cyberspace operations as centralised at the Cabinet Office level and as translated into operational guidance comparable to Rules of Engagement (ROE) for the use of force in cyberspace (Huskaj and Axelsson, 2023). Analytically, this model implies concentrated political oversight, a basis for compliance with the Law of Armed Conflict (LOAC), and an authorisation pathway for OCO under civilian control.

At the same time, national policy recognises that hostile states frequently disregard voluntary norms of responsible state behaviour (Huskaj et al., 2021). The implication is that commitment to international norms is paired with the maintenance of capabilities for detection, attribution, and, when authorised, OCO (Government, 2024*a*). Taken together, these policy foundations articulate Sweden's strategic objectives in cyberspace:

1. To reduce adversaries' ability to generate effects through systematic, risk-based improvements in civil and military cybersecurity (Government, 2024*a*).
2. To sustain government-level situational awareness through continuous foreign cyber intelligence reporting delivered to national decision-makers (National Defence Radio Establishment, 2024).
3. To retain the option of government-authorised OCO conducted by the Armed Forces and enabled by supporting intelligence and technical access (Government, 2024*a*).
4. To embed national cyber defence within EU and NATO frameworks that expand collective resilience and coordinated response options (Government, 2024*a*).

These objectives define the strategic boundary conditions within which Sweden operationalises cyber deterrence.

Threshold, Attribution, and Response Calibration

The policy framework further specifies requirements for strengthening national capacity to detect, analyse, and attribute hostile cyber activity. Government documents emphasise investments in technical intelligence capabilities and early-warning mechanisms designed to support politically directed response options (National Defence Radio Establishment, 2024). Policy guidance also underscores the need to preserve readiness for OCO when authorised, subject to international law and proportionality (Government, 2024*a*). The absence of fixed international thresholds for what constitutes an armed attack in cyberspace, as reflected in the Newport Rules of Engagement Handbook (Mandsager et al., 2022), introduces calibrated ambiguity into national decision-making. This ambiguity complicates adversary assessments of response conditions and thereby conditions the strategic environment in which deterrence operates.

Domestic and International Legal Constraints on Use and Preparation

National policy further establishes that cyber defence is an integrated component of total defence, requiring both defensive and offensive capabilities to protect national sovereignty (Government, 2024*a*). These offensive operations are intended to prevent adversary system usage or compel the cessation of attacks, thereby generating deterrent effects (Government, 2024*a*). Structurally, the Cabinet Office retains ultimate strategic authority—establishing legal frameworks and authorising execution—while the Armed Forces are responsible for operational execution with key planning and technical support from the National Defence Radio Establishment (Government, 2024*a*; Huskaj and Axelsson, 2023). This arrangement reflects established doctrinal principles where political authority is exercised at the strategic level, military command at the operational level, and specialised technical functions at the tactical level (Huskaj and Axelsson, 2023).

ROE constitute the mechanism through which legal authority is translated into operational guidance. The Newport Rules of Engagement Handbook underscores the absence of international consensus on what constitutes a use of force or an armed attack in cyberspace, which compels states to define national thresholds for when functional disruption, even without physical destruction, may qualify as an attack under self-defence provisions (Mandsager et al., 2022). Sweden does not publish national thresholds; open sources, therefore do not permit inference beyond general legal principles. In general terms, states may rely on diplomatic and law-enforcement measures for lower-severity incidents while reserving military involvement for situations where cyber effects rise towards the level of serious functional disruption, including against critical infrastructure (Mandsager et al., 2022). This uncertainty shapes adversary assessments of response conditions and conditions the deterrence environment.

Domestic law further conditions the strategic environment by raising the threshold for successful foreign cyberspace operations. The Security Protection Act (2018:585) obliges operators of security-sensitive activities to conduct documented security-protection analyses, implement information-, personnel-, and physical-security measures, and report incidents with potential national-security implications (The Riksdag, 2018; Bengtsson and Huskaj, 2021). These obligations apply to public and private actors whose systems underpin essential functions. By mandating risk-based measures and enabling administrative sanctions for non-compliance, the Act reduces systemic vulnerabilities and limits adversaries' ability to generate effects through cyber activity (Bengtsson and Huskaj, 2021).

International law further constrains how national cyber capabilities may be employed. Government documents affirm that the UN Charter and the LOAC apply fully to cyberspace and that OCO require political authorisation and must be conducted within these legal bounds (Government, 2024*a*). This framework combines adherence to the rules-based order with the preservation of national options for discriminate, necessary, and proportional action. Because authorisation rests at the Cabinet level, OCO remain subject to democratic oversight, reinforcing the credibility of state action (Huskaj and Axelsson, 2023).

EU and NATO Frameworks as Collective Constraint and Multiplier

Sweden's alignment with the European Union constitutes a central pillar of its cybersecurity posture and embeds national cyber defence within a collective political framework. The Total Defence Proposition identifies the EU as the primary cooperation arena, highlighting legislation such as NIS2, coordinated crisis-management arrangements, ENISA, and the Union's mechanisms for diplomatic responses to cyber threats (Government, 2024*a*). These instruments enable coordinated political measures, including restrictive measures and sanctions, that extend the consequences of hostile cyber activity beyond the bilateral relationship between attacker and target state. Empirical evidence illustrates this dynamic. The Manifestation study documents that the EU imposed its first cyber-related sanctions in July 2020 against actors associated with major cyber incidents, including Operation Cloud Hopper (Bengtsson and Huskaj, 2021). Participation in EU frameworks therefore raises the potential political costs of hostile cyber activity, as actions directed at Sweden may elicit a Union-wide response rather than remaining confined to a national level.

Within EU cybersecurity governance, coordinated vulnerability disclosure (CVD) practices function as a complementary resilience mechanism by structuring how vulnerabilities are reported, coordinated, and remediated across affected stakeholders (Pupillo, Ferreira, Varisco and Zarra, 2018).

The proposition further emphasises that Sweden's NATO membership entails expanded opportunities and obligations in cybersecurity and cyber resilience, reflecting the Alliance's increasing strategic focus on cyber and emerging technologies (Government, 2024*a*). It also stresses that EU–NATO cooperation should be complementary and mutually reinforcing, as duplication could impede capability development and undermine efficiency (Government, 2024*a*). Through these arrangements, the country integrates into collective deterrence structures that combine political signalling, shared situational awareness, and coordinated response options. EU and NATO partnerships thus function as strategic force multipliers by extending the nation's ability to impose political and operational costs while distributing risk and responsibility across allied frameworks.

NATO membership represents a structural shift in Sweden's defence posture, including in the cyber domain, by embedding national capabilities within the Alliance's collective defence system. Government documents affirm that, as a NATO ally, Sweden participates in collective defence across all operational domains, including cyberspace, and that cyberspace operations are regarded as a natural part of warfare on par with land, sea, air, and space operations (Government, 2024*a*). The Total Defence Proposition (2025–2030) further states that cyber defence encompasses both defensive and offensive activities conducted to protect national sovereignty and freedom of action, situating Swedish cyber capabilities within a broader military and strategic context (Government, 2024*a*). These policy statements establish that Sweden's cyber deterrence posture is no longer defined solely by national considerations but is integrated into an alliance-based conception of defence and response.

Intelligence reporting reinforces this assessment. MUST's 2024 annual overview observes that Swedish defence is now part of NATO's collective defence and that membership provides access to additional capabilities, information, and cooperation forums, while simultaneously increasing foreign intelligence collection directed at NATO planning processes (Military Intelligence and Security Service, 2024). This combination of expanded access and increased exposure conditions Sweden's deterrence posture within an allied context characterised by both enhanced capability integration and heightened strategic scrutiny. The proposition further specifies that NATO must maintain deterrence and collective defence in all domains, including cyberspace, and identifies the Alliance as the primary multilateral platform for cyber-defence cooperation (Government, 2024*a*). Sweden's contribution to NATO's operational and capability-development activities, including support for cyber research and development at the Alliance's cyber defence centre in Estonia, reflects this integration and conditions future coordination of cyber responses with allies possessing advanced offensive cyberspace capabilities (Government, 2024*a*).

International Cooperation and Normative Framing

Official SIGINT reporting describes bilateral and multilateral cooperation as a recurring feature of Sweden's intelligence posture and as relevant for situational awareness and the interpretation of complex threat environments (National Defence Radio Establishment, 2024). The official public record does not identify partner services, cooperation mechanisms, or division of labour. Some open sources discuss possible historical arrangements, but their contemporary relevance cannot be established on the basis of current official reporting. This section therefore treats international cooperation only as a stated enabling condition for analysis and warning and avoids specification beyond what official material supports (National Defence Radio Establishment, 2024).

Taken together, the open-source record permits only a limited conclusion: Swedish authorities describe international intelligence cooperation as relevant for analysis and warning, while the official public record does not specify partner configurations, mechanisms, or operational interfaces (National Defence Radio Establishment, 2024).

Engagement with international norms and confidence-building measures is anchored in the United Nations process on responsible state behaviour in cyberspace. Public policy material indicates consistent support for the 2014/2015 UN agreement on eleven voluntary norms intended to guide state conduct, reduce misperception, and mitigate escalation risks. The study on *unspoken norms* documents that the norms address responsible behaviour, cooperation, capacity-building, and confidence-building measures, while emphasising that their voluntary character permits selective compliance and continued offensive practice (Huskaj et al., 2021). This duality conditions the state's normative posture and limits expectations regarding adversary compliance.

The study further argues that interpreting state behaviour requires attention to both declared and undeclared norms, because observable actions can diverge from official commitments (Huskaj et al., 2021). In this reading, norms function primarily as political reference points that enable assessment and framing of conduct in an environment characterised by ambiguity and persistent below-threshold activity.

Endorsement of UN norms serves strategic purposes. Public alignment with a rules-based order signals restraint and legal consistency and generates diplomatic legitimacy that can be mobilised when norms are violated. Because the UN framework includes expectations regarding the protection of critical infrastructure in peacetime, these norms can be invoked to characterise hostile cyberspace operations as norm-deviant and to justify coordinated political responses. This function is salient in multilateral settings, where shared normative language enables attribution, condemnation, and collective measures even when legal thresholds for armed conflict are not met.

These commitments operate alongside statutory and policy constraints on the use of force in cyberspace. National policy establishes that OCO are subject to political authorisation and conducted within defined legal boundaries, while intelligence collection and international cooperation supply situational awareness for potential responses (Government, 2024*a*; Huskaj and Axelsson, 2023; National Defence Radio Establishment, 2024). Normative alignment complements these arrangements by shaping how response options are considered, communicated, and legitimised, thereby supporting deterrence-related practice without relying on declaratory threats alone.

4.5 Applying the MLMD Framework: Strategic and Organisational Implications

This section applies the MLMD Framework to the preceding case material in order to derive strategic and organisational implications for a cyber deterrence posture that includes the option of government-authorised OCO. The purpose is to translate the chapter's descriptive findings into an MLMD-coded account of how political intent, institutional design, intelligence dependencies, and technical prerequisites condition one another across levels and dimensions.

The analysis remains bounded by open sources and therefore specifies alignment requirements and plausible dependencies rather than internal procedures, readiness cycles, or decision timelines. The section proceeds by examining implications at the strategic, operational, and tactical levels, followed by cross-cutting dimensions that shape feasibility and sustainment across levels. The resulting propositions provide the analytical bridge to Chapter 5's focus on offensive tools and vulnerability policy as enabling and constraining conditions for political usability.

Analytical Starting Point and Case Constraints

Having established the MLMD Framework in the preceding chapter, this section applies the framework to the case's cyber-deterrence posture in order to identify strategic, organisational, and capability implications (Huskaj et al., 2024). The purpose is not to restate the threat environment or to infer operational practice, but to show how the framework structures analysis of how political intent, institutional design, intelligence dependencies, and technical capability interact across levels and dimensions.

The case is analytically useful because high dependence on networked systems combines with limited scale relative to major cyber powers, which sharpens recurring design problems: how deterrence concepts are translated into politically authorisable options; how intelligence and operational functions are integrated without eroding legal constraint and oversight; and how technical capabilities are sustained under resource constraints (Huskaj and Moradian, 2018). The section remains bounded by open sources and by research-based inference. It therefore treats the implications below as analytical propositions about alignment requirements, rather than as claims about classified arrangements or as operational guidance for planning and execution.

Strategic Level: Deterrence Design, Authority, and Constraint

At the strategic level, an MLMD reading directs attention to how OCO are positioned within deterrence design and how political authority and restraint delimit their plausible use. Earlier open-source scholarship noted that public articulation of cyber-deterrence concepts and decision authority was, at the time, limited and at points ambiguous, particularly for below-threshold contingencies (Huskaj and Moradian, 2018). Because subsequent policy and organisational developments may have altered internal arrangements in ways not visible in open sources, the analytical issue in this chapter is framed more narrowly: where public doctrine and decision pathways remain indistinct, cross-government alignment becomes harder because planners, intelligence producers, and oversight actors lack a shared public reference for what OCO is intended to achieve and under what conditions it is politically usable.

The MLMD framework further clarifies that strategic design choices can be placed on a spectrum between deterrence by punishment and deterrence by denial and that these logics impose different governance requirements (Nye, 2017). A punishment-oriented posture places weight on signalling capacity and political resolve, which makes the credibility problem partly communicative: a state needs a way to convey that it can impose costs and that political authority is prepared to do so under defined conditions (Nye, 2017). A denial-oriented posture places weight on resilience, continuity, and rapid recovery, which shifts the credibility problem towards institutional preparedness and sustained defensive performance. An MLMD interpretation treats these as complementary logics whose relative emphasis conditions what kinds of intelligence support, authorisation pathways, and oversight routines are needed for coherence across levels (Huskaj, 2024*c*).

Strategic constraint is equally central. Prior research treats politically endorsed legal authority and authorisation mechanisms as boundary conditions that delimit when and how OCO could be employed while remaining consistent with international law and domestic constitutional requirements (Huskaj and Moradian, 2018). In addition, ethical parameters, including restraint concerning civilian critical infrastructure in peacetime, can function as strategic-level constraints that shape operational feasibility and international signalling (Huskaj and Wilson, 2020*a*). A doctoral study on OCO argues that credibility depends on alignment across levels, linking strategic intent, operational organisation supported by policy and intelligence functions, and a tactical emphasis on tailored capability and access development (Huskaj, 2024*c*). Within the MLMD framework, this claim is treated as an analytical proposition about integration requirements rather than as a description of institutional practice.

Operational Level: Integration, Coordination, and Campaign Logic

At the operational level, the MLMD framework directs attention to an integration problem: deterrence-relevant options are typically conditioned by sustained interaction between operational planning, intelligence support, legal review, and political oversight. In resource-constrained settings, research suggests that large, autonomous command constructs comparable to those of major cyber powers may be less plausible than organisational designs that consolidate scarce expertise and reduce coordination latency across functions (Huskaj, 2024*c*). Within MLMD, this is treated as an organisational inference: where scale is limited, coherence often becomes a central determinant of whether options remain politically and operationally usable.

Operational planning for OCO is intelligence-dependent, and the framework treats intelligence support as an operational precondition rather than as an end in itself. Planning commonly presupposes access to intelligence products used for target development, intelligence gain–loss (IGL) assessment, and preparation of the operational environment (Joint Chiefs of Staff, 2018). The operational issue, as framed here, concerns how intelligence equities, oversight constraints, and operational timelines are aligned in planning and execution without fragmenting responsibility or diluting command authority (Huskaj, 2024*c*).

The political–organisational dimension of the MLMD framework further implies that cross-institutional coordination can shape whether time-sensitive options remain usable under time compression. Empirical studies discuss coordination challenges where military activity intersects with intelligence collection, legal oversight, and foreign policy considerations (Huskaj and Moradian, 2018; Huskaj, 2024*c*). One organisational response discussed in the literature is the use of standing interagency mechanisms in which proposed operations are assessed against strategic objectives and external constraints within a shared planning environment (Huskaj, 2024*c*). Analytically, such mechanisms are relevant because they allow deconfliction and risk assessment to be treated as planning inputs rather than as late-stage coordination problems.

Finally, the operational dimension of MLMD aligns OCO with campaign logic rather than discrete intrusions. Joint and allied doctrine describe cyberspace operations as activities that may be sequenced over time, integrating exploitation, disruption, and supporting actions such as attribution-related signalling when politically appropriate (Joint Chiefs of Staff, 2018; USAF LeMay Center, 2023). Within this logic, operational art concerns prioritisation, deconfliction, and risk management across intelligence collection, offensive action, and political signalling. The MLMD contribution is to treat these as interdependent design problems that are difficult to handle in isolation if alignment with strategic intent is to be maintained under external constraints (Joint Chiefs of Staff, 2018; USAF LeMay Center, 2023).

Tactical Level: Capability Sustainment Under Technical Volatility

At the tactical level, open literature commonly treats specialised technical competence as a prerequisite for generating selective advantage in settings where scale is limited. Because many details relevant to exploitation capability are classified, open sources rarely permit confident assessment of how any specific state organises, sustains, or prioritises such capabilities. The analysis therefore remains at the level of general dependencies: where offensive options exist, they tend to rely on technically perishable access, vulnerability knowledge, and specialist skills that degrade without sustained investment and disciplined oversight (Huskaj, 2024*c*).

Within this analytical boundary, the literature treats capability sustainment as a recurring problem. Tactical preparedness depends on maintaining competence for access development, persistence management, and controlled effect generation in environments characterised by patch cycles, defensive adaptation, and target volatility (Huskaj, 2024*c*). A further dependency concerns training and organisational learning. Empirical research on ambidextrous capability development indicates that recurring exercises in controlled environments contribute to technical proficiency, organisational memory, and trust relationships among operators and supporting functions, including legal and intelligence roles (Huskaj et al., 2024). Within MLMD, these sustainment mechanisms matter because tactical reliability conditions whether politically authorised options remain usable within compressed decision windows.

Cross-Cutting Dimensions: Partnerships, Human Capital, and Adaptation

Cross-cutting dimensions condition feasibility and sustainability across all levels. In small- and medium-sized state settings, the literature commonly treats external partnerships as enabling conditions for access to intelligence products, technical indicators, and interoperability routines, while noting that open sources rarely permit specification of partner configurations or division of labour (Huskaj and Moradian, 2018). Within an MLMD interpretation, the analytical point is that partnership constraints can shape planning timelines, consultation requirements, and evidentiary standards, thereby affecting the usability of response options without implying specific operational arrangements.

Human-capital strategy is also conditioned by scale and resource allocation. Earlier open-source scholarship on the case argued that limited scale constrains the ability to build extensive personnel pipelines and tool inventories comparable to major cyber powers, which increases the importance of prioritisation and selective capability development (Huskaj and Moradian, 2018). At the same time, a highly digitalised economy can supply specialised competence that may be mobilised through organisational arrangements that avoid permanent expansion of the standing force structure. One feasible option discussed in the literature is the use of temporary secondments or crisis mobilisation of industry-based specialists to augment capacity while preserving the distinction between civilian expertise and military command responsibility (Huskaj and Moradian, 2018). In MLMD terms, such arrangements are cross-cutting because they affect tactical sustainment, operational planning capacity, and strategic credibility.

MLMD also highlights adaptation as a continuing requirement that complements initial design choices. Empirical analysis of activity directed at national interests indicates variation between prolonged intelligence collection, preparatory access, and episodic disruption, each implying different demands on offensive and defensive capabilities (Huskaj, 2024*c*). An MLMD reading therefore treats reassessment and recalibration as elements of posture maintenance: shifts in adversary behaviour can alter which options are feasible, which intelligence dependencies are binding, and which legal and political constraints become salient under time compression (Huskaj and Moradian, 2018).

Synthesis: MLMD Implications for Posture Coherence

An MLMD reading suggests four coherence requirements that condition when offensive options can be rendered politically usable under legal and political constraint.

Strategic level: Posture coherence is conditioned by a publicly legible strategic framing that positions OCO within deterrence design, clarifies the relationship between cost-imposition logic and denial-oriented measures, and specifies how legal authority, decision competence, and boundaries for use operate as strategic constraints (Huskaj and Moradian, 2018; Huskaj, 2024*c*; Nye, 2017).

Operational level: Option usability is conditioned by planning structures that connect operational design to intelligence dependencies, legal review, and political oversight, and that support campaign-oriented sequencing and deconfliction across activities that interact over time (Joint Chiefs of Staff, 2018; USAF LeMay Center, 2023; Huskaj, 2024*c*).

Tactical level: Option usability is conditioned by sustainment of technically perishable access and specialist competence through disciplined readiness and recurring training and exercises that integrate operators with intelligence and legal functions under time pressure (Huskaj, 2024*c*; Huskaj et al., 2024).

Cross-cutting dimensions: Coherence is conditioned by how partnership constraints, human-capital mobilisation, and continuous reassessment routines are organised so that time-sensitive options remain politically usable while oversight obligations, legitimacy claims, and alignment with international obligations are preserved (Huskaj and Moradian, 2018; Huskaj and Wilson, 2020*a*).

4.6 Operationalising Cyber Deterrence

This section examines how the state's publicly stated strategic intent, legal authority, and institutional arrangements translate into an operationally usable deterrence posture. The analytical focus is on the interaction between political direction, intelligence inputs, and defensive and—when authorised—offensive cyberspace functions as described in policy and public reporting (Government, 2024*a*; National Defence Radio Establishment, 2024; Military Intelligence and Security Service, 2024; Security Service, 2025). The central claim is conditional: strategic documents articulate objectives, yet deterrence-relevant credibility depends on whether mandates, coordination routines, and decision-support processes can connect warning to planning and, where authorised, execution within compressed time windows (Joint Chiefs of Staff, 2018; USAF LeMay Center, 2023; Huskaj, 2024*c*). The analysis remains bounded by open sources and therefore treats operationalisation as an institutional and procedural problem rather than as an account of operational sequences or classified decision pathways.

Sweden's political and legal frameworks distribute responsibilities across agencies in ways that shape how defensive and, when authorised, offensive cyberspace activities may be organised. Public material states that OCO are conducted by the Armed Forces following government authorisation and within applicable international-law constraints (Government, 2024*a*; Mandsager et al., 2022). The mandate for SIGINT and technical cyber-intelligence collection is described as supporting warnings, indicators, and analysis relevant to preparedness and planning (National Defence Radio Establishment, 2024; National Defence Radio Establishment, 2022). The Security Service provides assessments of foreign intelligence activity, cyber intrusion, and influence operations affecting Swedish institutions, thereby contributing to the multi-source assessment picture that informs operational decision-making (Security Service, 2025). Taken together, these mandates describe an institutional setting for deterrence-oriented planning and response without allowing inference about operational sequences or classified procedures.

From an analytical perspective, operationalising deterrence presupposes that capabilities and decision arrangements are sustained over time and aligned with political direction. In cyberspace, credibility is commonly discussed in terms of whether a state can maintain options that are usable under legal and political constraints, rather than in terms of declaratory signalling alone (Huskaj, 2017; Huskaj, 2023*b*). U.S. doctrinal concepts such as persistent engagement and defend forward illustrate one approach to sustained activity below the threshold of armed conflict (U.S. Cyber Command Public Affairs Office, 2022; Nakasone, 2019). Sweden does not publicly adopt these doctrines as national doctrine; however, official descriptions of mandates for defensive and OCO, together with intelligence-support functions, indicate a general requirement to maintain preparedness and viable options across time-sensitive contingencies (National Defence Radio Establishment, 2024; The Armed Forces, 2024).

Detection and attribution are further requirements for managing thresholds and calibrating responses. Swedish intelligence assessments describe hostile activity as campaign-like and persistent, which places emphasis on attribution practices that consider cumulative patterns and multi-source indicators (Military Intelligence and Security Service, 2024). Threat reporting also highlights challenges associated with distinguishing state-linked activity from criminal operations in technical terms (National Defence Radio Establishment, 2024). The Security Service's assessments describe how cyber intrusion and influence activity may be combined in ways that shape institutional and political conditions (Security Service, 2025). In this framing, attribution is treated as an institutional process that integrates technical indicators and security assessments to inform political judgement, rather than as a single technical determination. Operationalising deterrence therefore implies the existence of structured mechanisms for cross-agency intelligence integration that can support timely threshold assessments, while recognising that open sources do not specify the internal procedures through which such judgements are reached (Huskaj, 2024*a*).

Decision processes further condition how deterrence can be operationalised. Joint doctrine and the academic literature emphasise that certain offensive options may depend on preparatory work conducted in advance of a political decision, which creates a need for coordination between political authority, intelligence functions, and operational planning (Joint Chiefs of Staff, 2018; Mandsager et al., 2022). Considerations such as acceptable risk, potential secondary effects, and requirements for allied consultation are therefore treated in the literature as planning problems that cannot be addressed only at the moment of execution (Huskaj et al., 2024). Consistent with the MLMD framework, the implication is that deterrence-oriented posture depends on legal and procedural arrangements that permit transition from warning to planning and, where authorised, execution within compressed decision windows, while remaining bounded by the limits of open evidence concerning Swedish internal processes (Huskaj, 2024*c*).

NATO membership provides an additional context for how cyber deterrence is discussed at an operational level, because national defence planning is conducted within an alliance framework for multi-domain operations (Joint Chiefs of Staff, 2022). NATO doctrine emphasises coordination across intelligence, operational, and legal functions, and alliance consultation can place weight on attribution quality and evidentiary standards. Public descriptions by the Armed Forces present cyber defence as including contributions to allied situational awareness and the ability to integrate national capabilities into joint activity when required (The Armed Forces, 2024). In analytical terms, this implies a requirement for national processes that can generate assessments and decision support suitable for alliance dialogue within time-constrained situations, without implying particular internal procedures beyond what open sources describe.

Institutional arrangements within Sweden's cybersecurity architecture also shape how preparedness and coordination are organised. The placement of the National Cybersecurity Centre within the National Defence Radio Establishment is described in public material as providing a platform for technical collaboration, information exchange, and joint analysis among relevant actors (National Cybersecurity Centre, 2025*b*; The Riksdag, 2025). The establishment of the Authority for Civil Defence is presented as extending coordination across prevention, incident management, and continuity planning in the civilian domain (Ministry of Defence, 2024). In this framing, such arrangements support a deterrence-oriented posture by strengthening shared situational awareness and enabling coordinated risk management, while preserving distinct mandates and lines of authority.

Intelligence support is commonly treated as enabling conditions for such a posture. FRA reporting describes SIGINT as contributing to technical indications, warnings, and analysis relevant to understanding hostile activity (National Defence Radio Establishment, 2024). MUST provides strategic and operational assessments of foreign intentions and preparatory activity (Military Intelligence and Security Service, 2024). The Security Service contributes counterintelligence analysis of domestic targeting and influence efforts (Security

Service, 2025). These inputs serve different analytical purposes and, as described in doctrine, can require structured integration to support planning and political decision-making, while noting that open sources do not specify how such integration is conducted in practice in the Swedish case (US Joint Chiefs of Staff, 2013; Wunder, 2016).

A further analytical issue concerns how protective measures relate to the option of cost-imposition. Public reporting and policy material emphasise resilience, protective security, and measures intended to reduce adversary opportunities for access and prepositioning (National Defence Radio Establishment, 2024; The Swedish Civil Contingencies Agency, 2024). Policy also states that OCO may be available as an option when politically authorised and used in combination with other instruments, such as diplomatic or legal measures (Government, 2024*a*; Valeriano et al., 2018). Because Sweden does not publish an explicit offensive doctrine, analysis at the open-source level is best limited to the proposition that deterrence-related credibility depends on sustained preparedness and lawful authorisation, rather than on claims about operational practice or the content of specific response options (Schmitt, 2017; Lindsay, 2020*b*).

In summary, open sources support treating Sweden's cyber deterrence posture as grounded in the interaction of political authority, intelligence assessment, and defensive and, when authorised, offensive capabilities within institutional and alliance contexts. The emphasis in this chapter remains on preparedness and coordination as described in policy and public reporting, rather than on claims about operational chains or execution practice. Under conditions of persistent hostile activity, this framing highlights the relevance of continuous situational awareness, cross-agency coordination, and the ability to align national assessments with collective frameworks when required.

4.7 Case Studies in Swedish Cyber Deterrence Practice

This section develops three illustrative foresight scenarios to clarify how the chapter's analytical claims about cyber deterrence apply to high-trust societal functions. The scenarios cover electoral administration, digital financial services, and hybrid influence activity affecting societal trust. They are not empirical reconstructions of observed Swedish operations. Their purpose is to provide a structured way to examine how technical dependency, distributed responsibility, and public legitimacy can shape deterrence-relevant requirements under conditions of sustained hostile activity. The emphasis remains on governance, preparedness, and decision conditions within political and legal constraints, rather than on operational methods or execution practice.

Case 1—Electoral Integrity as an Operational Deterrence Environment

This scenario is a constructed foresight vignette, adapted from the author's earlier graduate work, and is used to illustrate how cyber-deterrence concepts may be applied to electoral administration under conditions of increased digital dependence. It is not presented as observed Swedish practice. It does not describe operational methods, technical procedures, or classified arrangements. Its purpose is to clarify how institutional responsibilities, decision constraints, and cross-agency coordination requirements could interact when electoral administration becomes more reliant on networked information systems.

The scenario assumes that core electoral safeguards remain anchored in paper ballots and decentralised counting. At the same time, it assumes that surrounding administrative functions become more digitally supported, including voter-information services, coordination platforms for logistics and staffing, and partial electronic reporting of preliminary results. This combination would create interdependencies where disruption of peripheral systems could affect public confidence even if the integrity of ballots and final counts remains intact. Under these conditions, electoral protection becomes an operational environment where continuity planning, attribution assessment, and crisis communication intersect.

Expanded digitalisation of electoral administration would imply a governance setting in which the Election Authority, municipalities, and relevant ministries depend on interconnected systems to sustain routine processes under compressed timelines. The operational sensitivity arises because adversary activity could focus on plausibly deniable interference intended to create uncertainty, delays, or reputational damage, rather than on altering vote totals. In such a setting, the relevant problem is the management of confidence effects generated through disruption or ambiguity in the administrative layer. Deterrence, understood operationally, would therefore depend on the capacity to sustain continuity, to assess hostile activity with sufficient confidence to inform political direction, and to communicate in a manner that reduces opportunities for escalation.

Within this hypothetical environment, early indicators of foreign interest could be expressed through anomalies directed at externally exposed administrative services, irregular access attempts against supporting accounts, and probing of interfaces used for coordination and preliminary reporting. In parallel, influence narratives could circulate that question voter-roll integrity or procedural fairness, potentially aligning with technical disturbances in timing or theme. The analytic challenge is that each signal is individually ambiguous, while their combination can be interpreted as a pattern of activity directed at institutional trust. The scenario therefore treats deterrence as a sustained posture grounded in cumulative assessment rather than as a response triggered by a single incident.

A first operational requirement concerns deterrence by denial. In this vignette, denial is pursued through strengthened access control, segmentation of supporting systems, continuous monitoring, and redundancy for time-sensitive reporting functions. The intent is to ensure that interference attempts are detected, contained, and managed without generating visible disruption that can be amplified through messaging. Verification practices and fallback procedures, including manual cross-checks and alternative reporting routines, further reduce the probability that administrative anomalies translate into perceived loss of control. The operational implication is that technical resilience and organisational preparedness jointly shape adversary expectations regarding achievable effects.

A second operational requirement concerns calibrated signalling. Political and administrative communication could state that interference with electoral administration is treated as a sovereignty-relevant activity and that repeated anomalies are assessed collectively rather than as isolated incidents. Such communication can be paired with restrained statements indicating that technical disturbances are being investigated and managed without disclosing investigative methods or response options. The deterrence logic here is limited and procedural: signalling aims to reduce adversary confidence that ambiguity will persist, while preserving discretion for authorities to manage escalation pathways under legal and political oversight.

A third operational requirement concerns preparedness for proportionate response options. Where legal frameworks permit, response planning may include a spectrum of measures across diplomatic, legal, informational, and—if authorised—cyberspace instruments. The scenario treats this as an internal planning condition rather than as an external threat posture. In practice, maintaining viable options under electoral time compression requires prior coordination between responsible authorities, risk assessment regarding secondary effects, and consideration of deconfliction with parallel intelligence activities and alliance obligations. The vignette therefore frames preparedness as an organisational requirement that can shape deterrence credibility, without specifying the technical content of any option.

During an electoral period conducted under such conditions, attempted interference against supporting administrative interfaces combined with messaging that questions procedural integrity would test the operational posture. Monitoring and incident-handling functions would focus on continuity: isolating affected services, restoring availability, and validating data integrity against authoritative records. Parallel assessment would integrate technical reporting with counter-interference and influence analysis to support attribution judgements calibrated to available evidence. Communication would focus on limiting uncertainty among voters and stakeholders by clarifying what is known, what is being done, and which functions remain stable, thereby reducing the informational space in which adversaries seek to create confusion.

Taken together, the scenario illustrates how cyber deterrence concepts could be applied to an electoral setting where the principal strategic objective is to prevent interference from producing durable confidence effects. The posture described links continuity measures, cross-agency assessment, and decision support under political authority. The analytical contribution is to specify dependencies and constraints that condition deterrence in practice, rather than to describe operational execution. Electoral protection is therefore treated as a national-level function that connects legal frameworks, operational readiness, and interagency coordination, with deterrence embedded in institutional routines that sustain continuity and manage ambiguity.

Case 2—Cyber Deterrence in Sweden's Financial Sector: A Foresight Scenario

This foresight scenario considers how a highly digitalised financial system could shape the practical requirements of cyber deterrence. In a context where payment, authentication, and settlement functions are tightly coupled across institutions and service providers, adversaries may seek to generate strategic effects by disrupting confidence and continuity rather than by producing direct physical damage. The analytical purpose is to illustrate how deterrence considerations may emerge from the interaction of sectoral governance, technical dependencies, and decision-making under uncertainty, rather than to describe Swedish operational procedures or specific response arrangements.

Progressive digitalisation of financial services can create systemic exposure where outsourced ICT, cloud services, and shared authentication components introduce concentration points. Because day-to-day transactions rely on continuous availability, even short-lived disturbances may generate perceptions of fragility, particularly if technical disruption coincides with messaging intended to amplify uncertainty. Illustrative stressors include denial-of-service pressure against major service providers or anomalous activity affecting shared third-party dependencies. Under such conditions, deterrence would depend primarily on the capacity to reduce the probability of service interruption, to support timely situational awareness across responsible actors, and to maintain decision processes that allow proportionate responses within established legal and political constraints.

Within this scenario, early warning would rely on the detection of patterns consistent with hostile interest in financial-sector dependencies, such as anomalous traffic against externally exposed interfaces or irregularities affecting common service providers. In parallel, influence-oriented activity might frame digital payment systems as unreliable, indicating a potential linkage between technical disturbance and cognitive effects. Reports from supervisory and sectoral coordination mechanisms could provide additional indications of clustering across institutions, suggesting that activity is oriented towards systemic leverage rather than isolated compromise. These signals would increase the need for structured information exchange and cross-organisational assessment to support decisions on continuity measures and public communication.

A first requirement concerns deterrence by denial, pursued through measures that sustain continuity under pressure. This includes enhanced monitoring for anomalous traffic, absorption capacity for denial-of-service activity, segmentation of critical functions, and redundancy across authentication and settlement pathways. Sectoral crisis-preparedness arrangements and manual contingency procedures would further reduce the likelihood that technical disruption translates into visible loss of service. The deterrence implication is that adversaries face higher uncertainty about whether interference attempts will produce observable effects.

A second requirement concerns calibrated signalling through public and supervisory communication. In this scenario, messaging would emphasise that interference with core financial functions is treated as a serious matter and will be addressed through coordinated national measures. Supervisory guidance could clarify reporting expectations and sector-wide coordination routines, while public statements could prioritise transparency about continuity without amplifying uncertainty. Where attribution remains uncertain, communication would remain cautious and avoid claims exceeding available evidence. The deterrence purpose is to shape adversary expectations without disclosing sensitive capacities or decision thresholds.

A third requirement concerns the maintenance of response options appropriate to escalation beyond nuisance-level disruption. These options may include legal, regulatory, diplomatic, and economic measures, and—where lawful and authorised—technical measures that constrain hostile activity. The analytical point is that response credibility depends on prior planning across institutions, since time compression and systemic dependencies limit the feasibility of purely improvised measures during a fast-moving incident.

As activity subsides, review processes would focus on continuity performance, third-party dependency risk, and information-sharing routines. Lessons learned could feed into revised supervisory guidance, expanded joint exercising, and clarified decision pathways for degraded-service scenarios. In this way, the vignette positions financial-sector protection as a recurrent governance and preparedness problem in which deterrence effects are produced through continuity, coordination, and disciplined communication rather than through isolated technical actions.

Case 3—Cyber Deterrence Against Hybrid Influence Operations–Illustrative Scenario (SMS Incident, 2023)

The purpose of this scenario is to illustrate how cyber deterrence considerations may arise when hostile influence activity combines unauthorised use of communication services with messaging intended to amplify societal tension. In settings where public communication and mass-notification functions depend on commercial platforms and outsourced service providers, auxiliary channels may be exploited to create ambiguity about source and intent. The 2023 SMS incident, described in Swedish public reporting as involving large-scale dissemination of hostile messages during a period of heightened societal tension, provides an empirical reference point for this type of hybrid activity. The scenario treats the incident as illustrative of how technical compromise and psychological effect can be synchronised to generate impact beyond the immediate digital vector.

Mass-messaging and alerting functions typically rely on third-party services, delegated administration, and authentication arrangements that create dependencies outside core government systems. Public accounts of the 2023 incident indicate that a commercial messaging service was misused to distribute messages formatted to resemble trusted communication and calibrated to an ongoing societal controversy. In deterrence terms, the key analytical point is that the intended effect can be cognitive and political—provoking reaction, reducing trust in authorities, and increasing perceptions of disorder—rather than focused on long-duration service disruption. This convergence implies requirements for continuity arrangements, disciplined public communication, and attribution practices that avoid claims exceeding available evidence.

Within this scenario, early warning would depend on the capacity of responsible actors to detect and assess anomalies consistent with attempted misuse of third-party communication services, alongside monitoring for coordinated messaging intended to exploit existing tensions. Where large-scale dissemination occurs, assessment processes would aim to clarify whether the exploitation is confined to an auxiliary service dependency or reflects broader exposure. Under such conditions, deterrence functions as an institutional requirement shaped by the speed of situational awareness, the quality of cross-organisational assessment, and the ability to communicate publicly in ways that reduce ambiguity and limit opportunities for escalation.

A first requirement concerns deterrence by denial. In this setting, denial is pursued through the capacity to contain misuse of the affected service, sustain continuity of authoritative communication channels, and issue timely clarification that reduces uncertainty among recipients. The operational objective is to limit the adversary's ability to convert technical access into behavioural mobilisation or reputational damage. Coordinated communication involving public authorities and, where appropriate, civil-society intermediaries can reinforce clarification without amplifying the adversary's messaging.

A second requirement concerns calibrated signalling. Where attribution is supported by authoritative assessment, signalling may include public identification of the activity as malign interference and diplomatic messaging that frames such interference as unacceptable. Where attribution remains uncertain or partial, signalling would remain cautious, emphasising observed behaviour and the state's intent to address interference through lawful measures. The deterrence purpose is to shape expectations about consequences without disclosing sensitive capabilities or decision thresholds.

A third requirement concerns preparedness for proportionate responses appropriate to the influence domain. In this scenario, emphasis rests on legal, diplomatic, regulatory, and coordinated international measures, complemented by protective and resilience-building actions that reduce the utility of similar attempts. The analytic point is that hybrid operations derive advantage from deniability and narrative manipulation; therefore, response credibility depends on prior arrangements that enable coordinated action and disciplined communication rather than on a single retaliatory instrument.

Analytically, the vignette foregrounds MLMD dependencies between strategic authority for public communication and escalation management, operational coordination across mandates for attribution-oriented assessment, and tactical continuity measures that limit visible disruption. The deterrence-relevant effect follows from alignment: when continuity, assessment, and communication are integrated under lawful authority, adversary opportunities for durable confidence effects are narrowed.

4.8 Synthesising Strategy and Practice: Towards a Whole-of-Society Approach

This section synthesises how the state translates strategic intent into deterrence-relevant practice through alignment of institutional structures, technical functions, and societal dependencies. National strategy articulates objectives related to resilience and deterrence, yet the preceding scenarios indicate that deterrence conditions depend on sustained coordination among public authorities, private operators, and societal actors and are weakened when measures remain sector-bound (Huskaj and Axelsson, 2023; National Defence Radio Establishment, 2024; Security Service, 2025).

The synthesis focuses on five integration mechanisms visible in open sources and research-based analysis: governance arrangements that structure authority and coordination, organisational proximity among cyber-relevant functions, pooled human-capital models, structured interaction between intelligence production and planning, and psychological-defence functions that constrain hybrid effects.

A movement towards more integrated governance and institutional coordination has emerged in response to the requirement for coherent decision structures and defined authority under sustained hostile activity (Government, 2024*b*). The establishment of a national cybersecurity centre reflects this development by consolidating joint threat analysis, technical coordination, and situational awareness across the SIGINT function, the domestic security service, the military, and civilian preparedness authorities, together with relevant partners (Government, 2024*b*). The deterrence implication is organisational: when information exchange and shared analytic baselines reduce coordination latency, political leaders can receive more consistent decision support within existing legal authority.

Organisational proximity and interface management further condition the plausibility of timely response, particularly where intelligence functions, defensive cyber functions, and—when mandated—offensive cyberspace functions operate in close organisational contact (Huskaj and Axelsson, 2023). This configuration corresponds to doctrinal claims in JP 3-12 and adjacent scholarship that emphasise deconfliction, shared situational awareness, and timely interaction between ISR, defensive monitoring, and operational planning. The analytical point is correspondence at the level of requirements; the open record does not substantiate specific national procedures. The deterrence implication follows from time compression: when assessment, planning, and legal-political interfaces are organised to reduce delay, response options remain more usable under constrained decision windows.

Public–private coordination constitutes an additional pillar because large portions of critical infrastructure and essential digital services are operated by private entities (The Swedish Civil Contingencies Agency, 2024). Public guidance associated with national coordination arrangements emphasises structured information flows, shared situational awareness, and mechanisms through which public authorities can support private operators during periods of elevated activity (The Swedish Civil Contingencies Agency, 2024). The deterrence implication concerns denial: when anomalies detected in one sector inform national assessment and continuity measures elsewhere, adversaries face fewer exploitable seams across outsourced ICT dependencies.

Constraints on specialised human capital further motivate pooling and sharing of expertise across institutional boundaries (Huskaj and Axelsson, 2023). Models discussed in the literature include secondments, co-location, and joint employment of personnel with scarce competencies, concentrating expertise where operational demand is highest while keeping it accessible across relevant authorities. The deterrence implication is capacity preservation: when scarce competence is organised as a shared national resource, sustained monitoring, incident handling, and option preparation become more plausible without requiring permanent expansion of a single organisation.

The interaction between intelligence, operations, and decision-making is a recurrent prerequisite for attribution-oriented assessment and response preparation (National Defence Radio Establishment, 2024; Military Intelligence and Security Service, 2024; Joint Chiefs of Staff, 2018). Public reporting and doctrine indicate that cyber intelligence, defensive monitoring, ISR, and planning functions shape each other through cumulative pattern assessment and risk-informed preparation. In the Swedish context, open sources support treating this interaction as enabled through cross-agency analytic processes and decision chains that translate assessment into policy-relevant options within established authority. The deterrence implication is procedural: when assessment pathways are structured, threshold judgements and response calibration can be handled with greater consistency under evidentiary uncertainty.

Psychological defence and societal resilience extend deterrence-relevant coordination into the cognitive domain (Security Service, 2025). The establishment of a dedicated psychological-defence function reflects recognition that foreign actors can combine technical intrusion with influence activity aimed at undermining trust in public institutions or amplifying societal tension. The deterrence implication concerns effect limitation: when authoritative communication and behavioural assessment integrate with technical incident management, hybrid operations are less likely to convert ambiguity into durable confidence effects.

Taken together, this whole-of-society coordination model treats deterrence conditions as an emergent property of governance cohesion, organisational alignment, shared human resources, structured intelligence–planning interaction, and societal resilience. Deterrence-relevant capacity is embedded in institutional arrangements that narrow adversary opportunity by strengthening continuity, attribution-oriented assessment, and escalation management. Under these conditions, deterrence is treated as a national-level function grounded in institutional coherence and cross-societal coordination.

Within the MLMD Framework, this synthesis shows how strategic authority and oversight delimit which deterrence objectives are politically usable, how operational-level coordination determines whether intelligence and planning can be integrated under time compression, and how tactical-level continuity and technical readiness condition whether options can be executed within legal and ethical bounds. The implication is that posture credibility is produced by alignment across these levels and dimensions, because governance latency, intelligence dependencies, and technically perishable access jointly shape whether offensive and defensive measures can be translated from intent into controlled practice.

4.9 Synthesis and Implications

This chapter has treated OCO as a class of state activity shaped by interaction across levels and dimensions. Strategic intent, intelligence insight, and operational execution interact under political authority, legal frameworks, ethical considerations, and technological conditions (Joint Chiefs of Staff, 2018; Joint Chiefs of Staff, 2022). The MLMD Framework structures analysis of these interactions by linking deterrence objectives to the organisational, procedural, and technical conditions associated with authorised cyberspace operations, thereby connecting strategic purpose with operational design choices.

From a theoretical perspective, the framework responds to fragmentation in the literature in which deterrence theory, technical analyses of cyberspace operations, and organisational studies of intelligence–operations integration often proceed along separate tracks (Libicki, 2021; Nye, 2017). By placing deterrence logic, intelligence practice, and OCO inside a single analytical structure, MLMD contributes to the development of a coherent account of how states design, authorise, and employ offensive cyber capabilities under constraint (Huskaj et al., 2024). This synthesis aligns with work that links technical capability to organisational control in information operations (Denning, 1999) and with strategic analyses that treat offensive cyber activity as an instrument of statecraft embedded in wider policy processes (Fischerkeller and Harknett, 2018).

A further theoretical implication concerns operational design in cyberspace. Doctrine and scholarship continue to develop concepts for campaign-level planning in this domain (Joint Chiefs of Staff, 2022; Joint Chiefs of Staff, 2018). MLMD supports analysis of how individual actions can be sequenced and integrated in pursuit of strategic objectives, including how access, vulnerabilities, and payloads are connected to intended effects over time and coordinated with other instruments of state power where relevant. In this respect, the framework functions as an analytical bridge between strategic objectives and tactical execution, paralleling the role attributed to operational art in broader military theory.

This logic corresponds with strategic concepts such as persistent engagement and defend forward, which emphasise sustained activity below the threshold of armed conflict oriented towards shaping adversary behaviour through intelligence-informed targeting and continuous interaction (Fischerkeller and Harknett, 2018; Fischerkeller and Harknett, 2019). The MLMD contribution lies in specifying the organisational and analytical conditions associated with such approaches, including intelligence integration, campaign-level planning capacity, and political oversight across levels.

The framework's multi-dimensional structure implies an interdisciplinary character of cyberspace operations. OCO draws on political judgement, legal and ethical reasoning, and technical expertise in a shared decision space. This implication supports arguments for interdisciplinary approaches in education, policy development, and planning practice while leaving institutional form open to national variation.

From a practical standpoint, MLMD provides a structured basis for policy development and organisational design by specifying alignment conditions across strategic, operational, and tactical levels when OCO are intended to support deterrence objectives (Joint Chiefs of Staff, 2018; US Joint Chiefs of Staff, 2013). Applied to national contexts, the framework foregrounds interaction between declaratory strategy, legal authority, intelligence processes, planning mechanisms, and specialised technical competence. This focus supports analysis of how decisions in one domain propagate constraints and dependencies across others, including tensions between intelligence equities, signalling objectives, and escalation management.

The framework also informs analysis of international cooperation and norm development by treating political and ethical dimensions as integral alongside technical and operational considerations. Used as an internal decision-support structure, it can help states articulate consistent positions in multilateral processes on responsible state behaviour in cyberspace despite continuing ambiguity in legal thresholds and obligations (Schmitt, 2017; Huskaj et al., 2021). Over time, consistent practice under political oversight and legal compliance can contribute to the emergence of shared expectations reflected in doctrinal and normative instruments (Mandsager et al., 2022; Huskaj and Wilson, 2020*a*).

MLMD further supports capability diagnosis by mapping how prerequisites are distributed across levels. Tactical proficiency in exploitation and access development, operational capacity for campaign planning and intelligence integration, and strategic clarity regarding authority and oversight condition one another (Joint Chiefs of Staff, 2018; USAF LeMay Center, 2023). The framework enables analysis of how concentration of capability in one area can coexist with gaps in enabling structures elsewhere, which provides a basis for prioritisation discussions grounded in identified dependencies (Nye, 2017; Fischerkeller, 2017; Valeriano et al., 2018).

Finally, the framework foregrounds responsibility and restraint as conditions for credibility. Political authorisation, legal bases, ethical constraints, and oversight shape legitimacy, coalition cohesion, and escalation risk (Huskaj and Wilson, 2020*a*; Maschmeyer, 2021; Omand, 2021). By embedding these considerations as explicit analytical dimensions, MLMD supports analysis of how offensive cyber capability can remain politically usable while remaining aligned with domestic and international constraints (Schmitt, 2017; Huskaj and Wilson, 2021). This integration of capability with disciplined employment aligns with classical deterrence reasoning and contemporary cyber deterrence analyses that treat credibility as a function of both capacity and controlled use (Schelling, 1966; Gartzke and Lindsay, 2017).

The chapter establishes an analytical foundation for examining a state's cyber deterrence posture in the subsequent chapter. The case analysis uses the framework to assess how publicly observable policy direction, institutional arrangements, and declared authorities correspond with the alignment conditions specified here, under the evidentiary limits of open sources (Huskaj and Moradian, 2018; Huskaj, 2024*c*).

4.10 Conclusion

This chapter has analysed Sweden's cyber deterrence posture as an interaction between strategic intent, institutional arrangements, operational capacity, and societal resilience. Within the limits of open sources, the chapter treats deterrence as a posture shaped by denial-oriented measures, calibrated communication, and the availability of government-authorised offensive cyberspace options within established political and legal parameters (Huskaj, 2024*c*). This framing reflects the character of contemporary hostile activity, where actors pursue intelligence collection, preparatory access, disruption, and influence activity across a spectrum of intensity.

The analysis further indicates that Sweden's governance architecture, characterised by legally independent agencies operating within defined mandates, conditions how coordination and decision-making can be organised in practice. Coordination arrangements among the SIGINT function, the domestic security service, the armed forces, and civilian cybersecurity and preparedness authorities are described in the literature as mechanisms for reducing ambiguity and supporting timely government action when activity approaches policy-relevant thresholds (Huskaj and Axelsson, 2023). The analytical point is to identify how institutional design structures translation of assessment into response options under legal constraint, while avoiding inference about performance, internal timelines, or operational tempo beyond what open material supports (Mandsager et al., 2022).

The scenarios illustrate how deterrence-relevant effects may arise when detection, attribution-oriented assessment, and response mechanisms limit an adversary's ability to generate intended effects. The electoral, financial, and hybrid-influence vignettes show how denial-based measures can stabilise functions while political, diplomatic, regulatory, and communication measures shape the response environment without implying escalation control in any specific case. Across these settings, the capacity to manage continuity and coordinate assessment is distributed across public authorities, private operators, and societal actors, and its deterrence relevance follows from how such coordination can reduce exploitable seams and constrain the conversion of disruption into strategic effect (Huskaj and Axelsson, 2023).

Taken together, the chapter supports the analytical claim that the credibility of a cyber deterrence posture depends on combined functioning across institutional coherence, operational readiness, and societal resilience rather than on any single capability or organisation. Within an MLMD reading, this credibility depends on alignment between strategic authority and oversight, operational coordination linking intelligence production to planning, and tactical continuity measures that preserve usability under time compression and evidentiary uncertainty. This provides the bridge to Chapter 5, which examines how offensive cyberspace capabilities—including the discovery, retention, and use of zero-day vulnerabilities—shape the strategic, legal, and ethical conditions under which cyber deterrence is pursued (Huskaj and Wilson, 2021).

The chapter is intended to support institutional and policy-level evaluation rather than operational guidance, and it remains bounded by what can be substantiated in publicly available material.

Decision Exercise: Calibrating Cyber Deterrence Under Partial Visibility

Scenario. Over six weeks, a cluster of incidents spans (i) access attempts against election-adjacent services, (ii) suspected long-term collection against security-relevant research, and (iii) indicators of preparatory activity in a critical-infrastructure supply chain. Attribution is contested and agencies apply different evidentiary standards. A partner requests a coordinated posture statement before a near-term multilateral meeting. The government requests response options within 96 hours that preserve rule-of-law oversight and remain compatible with external obligations.

Analytical question 1—Purpose and success condition. State the posture for the next 30 days (denial, punishment, reassurance, or a bounded combination). Specify one observable success condition and why it is credible under partial attribution.

Analytical question 2—Threshold for action. Define the minimum evidentiary threshold to move from *incident handling* to *deterrence-relevant response*. Specify what must be true in (i) the technical assessment and (ii) the counterintelligence assessment, plus one uncertainty you accept under the 96-hour constraint.

Analytical question 3—Two response packages with constraints. Propose:

- **Package A (denial/continuity):** one technical–organisational measure and one public-communication measure; state one dependency on private operators.
- **Package B (cost/signalling):** one diplomatic/legal/economic measure and one constrained cyber-related measure that does not disclose sources or methods; state one constraint created by partner consultation.

For each package, state one failure mode that could amplify uncertainty or erode legitimacy.

Analytical question 4—Governance under time compression. Specify minimum governance conditions: political approval threshold, legal review standard, logging/audit requirement, and interagency coordination. Include one IGL trigger for deconfliction.

Short task—MLMD mapping (one page). Create a 3-row mapping (Strategic / Operational / Tactical): decision, key dependency, and one misalignment failure mode per row.

5

Vulnerability Exploitation and Ethical Implications

Offensive Cyberspace Operations (OCO) depend on the ability to generate access and produce effects against adversary information systems. In practice, this dependence makes software and hardware vulnerabilities—particularly rare and undisclosed flaws—central to how states project power in and through cyberspace. Exploiting such weaknesses can enable operations that compromise confidentiality, integrity, or availability and thereby create political and operational outcomes that resemble, and at times substitute for, conventional uses of force (Huskaj and Wilson, 2020*b*). Contemporary doctrine reinforces this link between cyber advantage and broader operational success by treating cyberspace as a prerequisite for manoeuvre, command and control, and mission assurance across domains (Joint Chiefs of Staff, 2018; USAF LeMay Center, 2023).

The purpose of this chapter is to examine vulnerability exploitation as a governance and ethics problem rather than as a technical practice. The central claim is that the discovery of a high-value vulnerability generates a strategic decision dilemma: disclosure reduces systemic exposure by enabling remediation, while retention preserves operational advantage by sustaining a privileged access vector. This dilemma is not resolved by technical assessment alone because the choice redistributes risk across civilian, governmental, and allied infrastructures and therefore carries ethical, legal, and strategic consequences (Huskaj and Wilson, 2021). The chapter analyses how states can reason about this trade-off under conditions where intelligence requirements, operational timelines, and uncertainty about cascading effects interact.

The scope and limits of the chapter are aligned with the manuscript's general stance. The analysis synthesises publicly available scholarship, open doctrine, and documented policy mechanisms for vulnerability handling. It does not provide operational instruction, technical exploitation procedures, target-selection guidance, or tradecraft. Technical terms are used to specify conceptual dependencies and governance constraints, not to describe how to conduct offensive operations.

Methodologically, the chapter adopts an anticipatory ethics perspective that evaluates foreseeable secondary and tertiary effects of retaining, deploying, or disclosing vulnerabilities before operational use (Huskaj and Wilson, 2021). It combines doctrinal sources, including Joint Publication 3-12 and the Newport Rules of Engagement Handbook, with case material such as Stuxnet, Heartbleed, and WannaCry, and with institutional processes such as the United States Vulnerabilities Equities Process, to specify how ethical criteria can be translated into decision procedures and oversight mechanisms.

The chapter proceeds as follows. Section 5.1 defines vulnerability categories and explains why zero-day flaws possess distinctive strategic value for offensive operations. Section 5.2 develops historical analogies and structured comparisons that situate vulnerability exploitation within broader debates on coercion, operational risk, and legal constraint. Section 5.3 examines ethical dilemmas in vulnerability exploitation through necessity, proportionality, distinction, and accountability. Section 5.4 analyses institutional approaches to vulnerability

DOI: 10.1201/9781003655183-5

management, including equities-style processes and disclosure-oriented models. Section 5.5 evaluates case material that illustrates tensions between stated policy and observed practice. Section 5.6 develops a normative vulnerability-management framework designed to institutionalise deliberation and periodic reassessment under uncertainty. Section 5.7 concludes by specifying governance requirements for integrating operational utility with legal constraint, ethical responsibility, and coordination needs relevant to deterrence and allied settings.

5.1 Vulnerabilities and Zero-Days as Strategic Resources

Vulnerabilities in hardware and software systems—particularly rare and undisclosed zero-day flaws—constitute a central mechanism by which states project power in and through cyberspace. OCO gain their operational utility from exploiting weaknesses that defenders neither expect nor can readily mitigate, enabling intrusions that compromise the confidentiality, integrity, or availability of critical systems and, in turn, create effects comparable to those generated through conventional kinetic means (Huskaj and Wilson, 2020*b*). Modern doctrine reinforces this logic by emphasising that all military operations depend on cyberspace and that advantage in this domain must be established and maintained to enable wider operational success (Joint Chiefs of Staff, 2018; USAF LeMay Center, 2023). Offensive cyberspace capabilities are commonly described as relying on access to exploitable vulnerabilities to deny, disrupt, degrade, destroy, or manipulate adversary systems (Huskaj and Wilson, 2021).

At the strategic level, the discovery of a critical vulnerability generates a persistent dilemma characterised by competing imperatives: disclosure contributes to collective security by reducing systemic risk, whereas retention preserves a unique operational advantage that can shape adversary behaviour and enable tailored effects in crisis or conflict. The resulting decision problem is therefore not merely technical but reflects a wider ethical and strategic calculus in which the anticipated benefits of exploiting a vulnerability must be assessed against potential geopolitical, legal, and normative consequences (Huskaj and Wilson, 2021). Historical cases illustrate these tensions; conventional pre-emptive strikes such as Israel's operations against nuclear facilities in Iraq (1981) and Syria (2007) demonstrate the risks associated with anticipatory action, while the Stuxnet operation achieved comparable delay of Iran's nuclear programme through covert manipulation rather than overt force (Huskaj and Wilson, 2020*b*). These examples highlight why decisions to weaponise or remediate vulnerabilities require a structured evaluation of consequences.

To navigate these considerations, this chapter adopts an anticipatory ethics perspective that evaluates the secondary and tertiary effects of deploying or withholding a cyber capability before its operational use (Huskaj and Wilson, 2021). This perspective requires decision-makers to integrate assessments of operational utility, legal constraints, proportionality, and potential cascading effects into a single evaluative framework. The analysis is grounded in a synthesis of doctrinal sources—including Joint Publication 3–12 and the Newport Rules of Engagement Handbook—combined with case material such as Stuxnet, Heartbleed, and WannaCry and with institutional processes such as the United States Vulnerabilities Equities Process. The intent is to derive a structured logic for understanding how states balance vulnerability retention and disclosure within OCO.

The sections that follow therefore proceed as an integrated analytical sequence. Section 5.2 defines categories of vulnerabilities and explains why zero-day flaws possess distinctive strategic value for offensive operations. Section 5.3 compares the operational, legal, and risk profiles of cyber exploitation and traditional kinetic strike options. Section 5.4

examines the ethical dilemmas inherent in vulnerability exploitation, drawing on principles such as necessity and discrimination. Section 5.5 analyses institutional approaches to vulnerability management, with attention to the design of the VEP. Section 5.6 evaluates real-world incidents that expose tensions between policy and practice. Section 5.7 proposes an ethical vulnerability management framework, Section 5.8 assesses the implications for deterrence and alliance structures, and Section 5.9 concludes by outlining the requirements for integrating operational utility with ethical responsibility.

A vulnerability refers to any weakness in an information system's design, implementation, or configuration that an adversary could exploit to undermine confidentiality, integrity, or availability (Huskaj and Wilson, 2020*b*). Such weaknesses may arise from coding errors, architectural flaws, or misconfigured settings that permit arbitrary code execution (Huskaj and Wilson, 2020*b*). Incidents such as the 1988 Morris Worm, which propagated through a buffer overflow in Unix's `fingerd` service (Huskaj and Wilson, 2020*b*), illustrate how a single overlooked flaw can enable widespread disruption. Managing these weaknesses therefore becomes a strategic requirement, because the presence of exploitable defects directly affects the ability of states to protect or project power in and through cyberspace. As a standard reference notes, "a vulnerability is a weakness ... that might be exploited to cause loss or harm" (Pfleeger and Pfleeger, 2012, p.10), and this functional definition underscores why vulnerability management is integral to national cyber capability development.

Within this broader category, zero-day vulnerabilities occupy a distinct operational role. A zero-day is a flaw unknown to the vendor and defenders at the moment of exploitation, meaning that no patch or countermeasure exists to mitigate its use (Huskaj and Wilson, 2020*b*). Because these vulnerabilities provide access to systems that are otherwise defended, they are "highly sought-after" by criminal syndicates, state-linked advanced persistent threat groups, and organisations conducting OCO (Huskaj and Wilson, 2020*b*). Stuxnet illustrates the strategic value of such vulnerabilities: the operation used four distinct zero-day exploits in Windows environments to penetrate secure facilities and manipulate centrifuge operations while avoiding detection (Huskaj and Wilson, 2020*b*; Huskaj and Wilson, 2020*b*). The use of multiple undisclosed flaws in a single campaign demonstrates how zero-days enable offensive action that bypasses conventional defensive mechanisms and thereby alter adversary risk calculations.

The pursuit and trading of zero-day vulnerabilities has generated a commercialised global marketplace, and external research demonstrates that discovery, acquisition, and resale occur through economically organised channels where exploit developers negotiate directly with surveillance firms, intelligence-linked buyers, and state customers (Anderson et al., 2017; Miller, 2007; Greenberg, 2012; Zetter, 2016). Independent security researchers, penetration testers, and black-hat actors routinely identify new vulnerabilities and may choose between coordinated disclosure or sale on the open market. Governments and defence contractors purchase functional exploits, sometimes at prices reaching hundreds of thousands or even millions of dollars, while exploit brokers specialise in acquiring and reselling vulnerabilities to agencies with offensive mandates. Conversely, technology companies operate bug bounty programmes to incentivise responsible disclosure, illustrating how vulnerabilities simultaneously constitute liabilities requiring mitigation and assets that underpin the operational utility of offensive cyberspace capabilities.

From a strategic perspective, vulnerabilities enable both persistent infiltration and overt disruption. Persistent exploitation provides long-term covert access for cyber espionage or pre-positioning of malware, functioning as an intelligence preparation mechanism inside an adversary's networks. In contrast, overt exploitation seeks immediate operational effects through disruption or destruction of targeted systems. Stuxnet demonstrates the latter approach, because activating the malware produced rapid physical effects on centrifuges and simultaneously revealed the underlying exploits once the operation became public (Huskaj and Wilson, 2021). The strategic calculus therefore concerns whether a vulnerability should be retained for sustained access or expended to generate immediate effects, recognising that overt use typically eliminates the future value of the exploit once defenders implement patches. Offensive planners must therefore assess whether a given vulnerability has greater utility as a one-time cyber munition or as an intelligence asset that supports persistent operations.

The centrality of vulnerabilities to cyber weaponisation follows from the functional requirement that every offensive cyberspace operation must identify a viable access vector before any effect can be generated. As noted in recent analysis, offensive capability development requires a "tactical emphasis on identifying and exploiting zero-day vulnerabilities" (Huskaj, 2024*c*), because these undisclosed flaws transform computer code into operational tools for projecting power in and through cyberspace. However, exploiting vulnerabilities raises questions concerning control, consequence, and strategic timing, which subsequent sections analyse through the lens of anticipatory ethics and comparative assessments of cyber and kinetic operations. Understanding these constraints is essential before evaluating how states should balance disclosure with exploitation or how vulnerability management affects broader policy, governance, and operational decision-making structures.

These issues arise in any state that combines foreign intelligence collection, cybersecurity, and national security decision-making. The chapter therefore treats vulnerability retention and disclosure as a comparative governance problem and does not draw inferences about specific national internal arrangements beyond what is explicitly documented in public sources. Country-specific institutional analysis is reserved for the empirical chapters, where the evidentiary basis and method are presented.

5.2 Historical Analogies and Comparisons

Kinetic precedents such as the 1981 Osirak strike illustrate how states have historically approached emerging nuclear threats through decisive preventive action. Israel assessed that Iraq's reactor could enable weapons-grade plutonium production and therefore conducted a surprise attack using F-16 aircraft supported by F-15 escorts, destroying the facility at Tuwaitha (Huskaj and Wilson, 2020*b*). Casualties included ten Iraqi soldiers and one French technician (Huskaj and Wilson, 2020*b*), and the operation generated a unanimous United Nations Security Council condemnation, with several governments, including the United States, criticising the infringement of Iraqi sovereignty (Huskaj and Wilson, 2021). U.S. intelligence assessments further noted that the strike adversely affected regional political interests (Huskaj and Wilson, 2020*b*). Nevertheless, Israeli policy-makers considered the action successful because it delayed Iraq's nuclear programme, consistent with the Begin Doctrine's intent to prevent adversaries from acquiring nuclear capabilities (Huskaj and Wilson, 2021).

A comparable logic informed Israel's 2007 operation against the Syrian al-Kibar facility, which intelligence indicated was a plutonium-producing reactor supported by external assistance. The Israeli Air Force penetrated Syrian airspace on 6 September 2007 using F-15 and F-16 aircraft to destroy the structure beyond repair (Huskaj and Wilson, 2020*b*). Unlike Osirak, this operation remained undisclosed for years; Israel acknowledged its role only in 2018, and Syria refrained from initiating formal complaints, resulting in a muted international response (Huskaj and Wilson, 2020*b*). Available reporting suggested no immediate civilian casualties. Strategically, the operation eliminated a potential nuclear capability without triggering regional escalation, demonstrating how secrecy and deniability can modulate geopolitical consequences. Although both strikes reflected similar preventive intent, al-Kibar generated less diplomatic friction, indicating how operational visibility influences state reactions and subsequent political dynamics.

A cyber parallel emerged when the United States and Israel employed Stuxnet (2007–2010) to impede Iran's nuclear programme. Stuxnet was engineered to infiltrate the Natanz enrichment facility and manipulate centrifuge operations, marking the first publicly known cyber weapon to cause physical destruction. The operation relied on multiple zero-day vulnerabilities (Huskaj and Wilson, 2020*b*), using four undisclosed Windows flaws and one previously patched issue to traverse networks and deliver tailored payloads to Siemens industrial controllers (Huskaj and Wilson, 2021; Huskaj and Wilson, 2020*b*). Approximately 1,000 centrifuges were damaged, with analysts estimating a delay of one to two years in enrichment activities (Huskaj and Wilson, 2020*b*). The operation required detailed preparation, including the use of infected removable media to cross air-gapped systems and mechanisms to present false telemetry to operators (Huskaj and Wilson, 2020*b*). The effect was achieved without kinetic force or casualties, and attribution remained ambiguous until independent analysis revealed its scope and sophistication.

These cases enable a comparative assessment of cost, risk, and collateral effects across kinetic and cyber operations. Israel's airstrikes required extensive planning, rehearsals, aerial refuelling coordination, and acceptance of pilot risk deep within hostile territory (Huskaj and Wilson, 2020*b*). By contrast, Stuxnet's execution exposed no personnel to physical danger, although it required considerable intelligence collection and software development efforts. The ambiguity surrounding attribution reduced the likelihood of immediate retaliation, thereby lowering the political threshold for the use of force. From a proportionality perspective, Osirak resulted in fatalities and international censure, while Stuxnet was designed to target specific centrifuge control logic and remain dormant elsewhere, limiting collateral harms (Huskaj and Wilson, 2021). However, cyber operations introduce distinct uncertainties, including potential cascade effects and risks of code propagation beyond intended environments.

Overall, these examples illustrate how states have utilised both kinetic and cyber instruments to disrupt emerging strategic threats. The airstrikes delivered visible and unequivocal results but carried higher diplomatic and operational risks, whereas Stuxnet achieved similar strategic objectives through covert means that limited immediate political fallout. The shared preventive logic underscores that both modalities function as tools for projecting power before threats mature. The differences in execution and transparency, however, highlight why evaluating the ethical and legal implications of exploiting hidden vulnerabilities is essential when cyber operations can approximate the effects of kinetic force. The next section therefore examines how these considerations shape the ethical assessment of zero-day exploitation.

The exploitation of undisclosed software vulnerabilities confronts states with a structural IGL dilemma, because retaining a vulnerability preserves access, operational optionality, and strategic leverage, while disclosure reduces systemic risk by enabling remediation across affected infrastructures. Retention allows intelligence services and offensive cyber units to maintain covert entry points into adversary systems, support long-term collection, pre-position capabilities, and preserve time-sensitive operational options. However, the same decision implies acceptance of continued exposure across all systems that depend on the vulnerable component, including domestic and allied infrastructures, thereby increasing the probability of independent discovery, criminal exploitation, or cascading failure. Disclosure, by contrast, diminishes intelligence and operational advantage by eliminating a unique access vector, but it simultaneously reduces collective exposure, reinforces norms of responsible state behaviour, and mitigates second- and third-order effects associated with unpatched vulnerabilities. The dilemma is therefore not technical but strategic and ethical: any decision to retain or disclose a vulnerability reallocates risk between intelligence advantage and societal protection, and this reallocation produces consequences that extend beyond the immediate operation to affect trust, escalation dynamics, and long-term cyber stability.

5.3 Ethical Dilemmas in Vulnerability Exploitation

Once vulnerability exploitation is recognised as an intelligence–operations interface rather than a purely technical practice, ethical evaluation becomes unavoidable. Decisions to retain, disclose, or operationalise undisclosed vulnerabilities are not neutral engineering judgements but intentional policy choices that redistribute risk between intelligence advantage and systemic exposure. Retention preserves access, operational optionality, and strategic leverage by maintaining covert entry points into adversary systems, while simultaneously accepting continued exposure across all infrastructures dependent on the affected component. Disclosure, by contrast, eliminates a unique access vector and constrains intelligence and operational advantage, yet reduces collective risk by enabling remediation and limiting second- and third-order effects. Ethical analysis is therefore required not to establish the existence of this dilemma—which has already been demonstrated—but to determine how such choices should be evaluated, constrained, and governed when their consequences extend beyond the immediate operation to affect trust, escalation dynamics, and long-term cyber stability.

This chapter approaches that task through an anticipatory ethics perspective, which evaluates the foreseeable secondary and tertiary consequences of action before operational deployment (Huskaj and Wilson, 2021). From this perspective, withholding a vulnerability constitutes an affirmative policy decision that preserves access and operational flexibility while accepting asymmetric risk distribution across civilian, governmental, and allied systems. Ethical responsibility therefore arises not only from the effects of exploit use, but from the deliberate deferral of remediation in highly interconnected environments. Existing national mechanisms such as the United States Vulnerabilities Equities Process and the United Kingdom's Equities Process reflect this logic by treating exploit retention as an exception requiring justification rather than as a default posture (United States Government, 2017; GCHQ and National Cyber Security Centre, 2021). These processes do not resolve ethical tensions automatically; instead, they institutionalise deliberation by embedding explicit reasoning about necessity, proportionality, control, and societal impact within governance structures. To operationalise this evaluation, the following subsections apply four criteria—necessity, proportionality, distinction, and accountability—which translate the IGL dilemma into concrete ethical constraints on state behaviour in cyberspace.

One way to structure this evaluation is by applying criteria that parallel the normative logic governing the use of force. The first criterion, *Necessity*, requires that exploitation constitute the least harmful means of achieving a legitimate objective and align with doctrinal principles specifying that cyber operations must serve an imperative purpose (Huskaj, 2024*c*). This assessment demands that decision-makers consider whether the intended effect could be achieved using already disclosed vulnerabilities, alternative tools, or non-cyber measures that carry fewer systemic risks. In operational terms, necessity also requires evaluating the relative importance of the target: disrupting an adversary's integrated air-defence system during a conflict may plausibly meet this threshold, whereas penetrating a lower-value diplomatic communication platform would not. VEP procedures operationalise this reasoning by requiring agencies to justify exploit retention in cases where disclosure would provide broader benefits to national and international cybersecurity (United States Government, 2017).

The second criterion, *Proportionality*, extends this logic by demanding that the anticipated intelligence or military advantage derived from deploying the exploit not be outweighed by the potential harm resulting from deferred patching. Proportionality in cyberspace must therefore account for both the direct consequences of an operation and the broader systemic risks created when vulnerabilities persist across interconnected infrastructures. In practice, decision-makers must evaluate the prevalence of the affected technology, the severity of exploitation if a malicious actor gains access, and the likelihood that adversaries may independently discover the same flaw (Huskaj and Wilson, 2021; United States Government, 2017). A vulnerability embedded in widely deployed software supporting hospital systems, financial networks, or industrial automation introduces externalities that extend far beyond the immediate target environment, implying that exploit retention becomes increasingly difficult to justify unless the operational gain is decisive. This expanded notion of proportionality therefore requires states to integrate intelligence requirements, operational timelines, patch-deployment dynamics, and systemic risk assessments into a single evaluative framework.

A third criterion, *Distinction*, mirrors the requirement under the Law of Armed Conflict (LOAC) that operations be directed only at legitimate military or intelligence targets. In the cyber domain, distinction translates into engineering exploits and payloads that activate solely under tightly specified conditions, thereby reducing the probability of unintended propagation or collateral effects. Historical cases, such as malware engineered to check for specific industrial control configurations before executing, illustrate how technical safeguards can constrain effects (Huskaj and Wilson, 2020*b*). Yet even carefully designed capabilities can escape their intended environment when deployed against complex, interconnected systems. VEP processes partially address this challenge by requiring agencies to assess whether exploit use can be controlled or whether the underlying vulnerability is so deeply embedded in global infrastructures that safe operationalisation is infeasible (United States Government, 2017). The implication is that distinction in cyberspace is not solely a matter of targeting precision but also a function of technical architecture, exploit design, and systemic interdependencies that can generate cascading effects if not properly contained.

The final criterion, *Accountability*, concerns the institutional arrangements through which decisions to retain or employ a vulnerability are reviewed, authorised, and monitored. Offensive cyberspace doctrine and rules of engagement (ROE) highlighted in JP 3-12 and the Newport Rules of Engagement Handbook stress that cyber operations must be governed by clear authorities, transparent decision-making processes, and oversight mechanisms that ensure alignment with legal and policy frameworks. The U.S. VEP operationalises this requirement through the Equities Review Board, which convenes representatives from multiple agencies to evaluate competing equities, document rationales, and ensure that retention decisions reflect national-level interests rather than the operational preferences of a single unit (United States Government, 2017). The United Kingdom's Equities Process adopts a similar structure by imposing senior oversight, periodic reassessment, and escalation pathways that compel continuous justification for withholding a vulnerability (GCHQ and National Cyber Security Centre, 2021). These governance arrangements demonstrate that ethical exploitation requires an institutional environment that allows for deliberation, records decisions, evaluates downstream consequences, and constrains operational actors through legal review and political authorisation.

Measured against these criteria, the decision to retain or disclose a vulnerability becomes a structured ethical evaluation rather than a tactical calculation shaped solely by operational convenience. States must therefore determine whether their pursuit of operational advantage justifies the risks associated with allowing vulnerabilities to persist; whether safeguards and targeting constraints sufficiently mitigate the chance of unintended propagation; whether proportionality favours disclosure in cases where systemic risk is high; and whether institutional oversight mechanisms can ensure accountability for decisions that may generate strategic effects. When applied rigorously, these criteria often counsel restraint, particularly in environments where vulnerabilities underpin essential services or where the potential for cascading effects is high. Anticipatory ethics reinforces this conclusion by requiring that each decision be evaluated not only for its immediate utility but also for the norms it sets and the future risks it creates. Ultimately, because cyber capabilities can generate strategic effects through ostensibly non-violent means, rigorous ethical governance is essential for maintaining stability, managing risk, and upholding the responsibilities of a state operating in and through cyberspace.

5.4 Policy Frameworks for Vulnerability Management

This section examines how governments formalise decision-making mechanisms for the handling of newly discovered software vulnerabilities, focusing on the institutional structures that enable states to balance the operational utility of undisclosed exploits with the broader public interest in maintaining secure digital infrastructures. Although doctrines for OCO emphasise that military and intelligence activities must comply with legal frameworks and established authorities, as reflected in JP 3-12's requirement that cyberspace operations "must be consistent with applicable domestic and international law" (JP 3-12, p. II-7), national policy mechanisms for vulnerability management extend this logic by requiring that the retention or disclosure of zero-day vulnerabilities be subject to interagency deliberation and political oversight. The following subsections present the United States' Vulnerabilities Equities Process (VEP), the United Kingdom's Equities Process, the Dutch disclosure-first model, and the Swiss Coordinated Vulnerability Disclosure (CVD) mechanism (National Cyber Security Centre (NCSC), Switzerland, 2025), illustrating how each system operationalises a structured balance between offensive requirements and societal protection.

The United States' VEP represents the most institutionalised model for managing newly discovered, non-public vulnerabilities. It is designed to "balance equities and make determinations regarding disclosure or restriction," ensuring that multiple agencies can assess whether a vulnerability should be reported for patching or retained for operational use (United States Government, 2017). The process is chaired by the National Security Council, which introduces a strategic perspective that extends beyond the priorities of any individual agency and ensures that exploit retention is not treated as an exclusively intelligence-driven decision. Submissions to the VEP must include technical details, affected products, and a recommendation for either dissemination or restriction. An Equities Review Board (ERB) then assesses operational utility, defensive risk, prevalence, potential for adversary discovery, and projected societal impact. In effect, the VEP imposes a structured mechanism for weighing offensive cyberspace advantages against defensive consequences, a logic that mirrors JP 3-12's requirement that commanders consider the "consequences, including collateral effects" of cyberspace operations (JP 3-12, p. III-6). The implication is that exploit retention is justified only when the operational value clearly outweighs the risks to national infrastructure and the broader digital ecosystem.

The United Kingdom applies a comparable mechanism, administered through the National Cyber Security Centre (NCSC). Although fewer public details are available, official statements indicate that disclosure is the default expectation unless a compelling national-security rationale requires temporary retention (GCHQ and National Cyber Security Centre, 2021). This position aligns with the principle—visible throughout the Newport Rules of Engagement Handbook—that the use of force in any domain must be governed by clear authorities, legal advice, and senior political direction (Newport ROE, pp. 12–14). The UK's model therefore reflects the same structural logic as the U.S. VEP: retention is permissible only when justified at the national level, and decisions must be periodically re-evaluated to ensure that the rationale remains valid. In practice, this reinforces the idea that vulnerabilities constitute national-level equities that affect defence, intelligence, and civilian security simultaneously, necessitating governance that captures the interdependence among those sectors.

Switzerland employs a CVD system administered by the National Cyber Security Centre (NCSC), which functions as an intermediary rather than a stockpiling authority (National Cyber Security Centre (NCSC), Switzerland, 2025). Under this policy, vulnerabilities affecting government systems must be reported directly to the NCSC, whereas vulnerabilities affecting non-government systems should be reported to the product vendor first, with the NCSC intervening only when the affected party cannot be reached or fails to respond. In addition, the NCSC acts as a CVE Numbering Authority and may coordinate public disclosure when national-level infrastructures or widely deployed software is implicated. This model reflects a governance posture that privileges disclosure, transparency, and systemic protection. It does not establish a mechanism for operational retention comparable to the U.S. VEP; instead, it institutionalises a societal protection function in which the state coordinates vulnerability management to reduce systemic risk. This aligns with the Newport ROE Handbook's emphasis on clearly defined authorities and oversight for any activity that might generate cross-domain effects (Newport ROE, pp. 23–25), illustrating that Switzerland's model approaches vulnerabilities as shared national assets requiring coordinated management rather than potential tools for offensive use.

A parallel logic is visible in the Netherlands, where CVD has been institutionalised through national guidelines that structure communication, define responsibilities, and protect good-faith researchers during the reporting process (National Cyber Security Centre (NCSC), Netherlands, 2018). Unlike equities-based mechanisms, the Dutch model does not adjudicate between offensive and defensive governmental priorities but instead focuses on ensuring that vulnerabilities are remediated cooperatively before disclosure, thereby strengthening national resilience.

These cases collectively illustrate the range of institutional designs that states apply when handling newly discovered vulnerabilities, enabling a structured comparison of how national frameworks balance offensive utility, defensive risk, and public accountability.

These four systems illustrate different institutional interpretations of the same underlying problem: vulnerability management involves weighing operational value against the risks associated with unpatched flaws. The U.S. and UK models incorporate mechanisms that enable exploit retention but impose interagency oversight, periodic review, and political direction; the Dutch and Swiss models elevate public disclosure as the normative baseline, reducing the scope for operational retention and emphasising the protection of the national digital infrastructure. The implication is that policy frameworks for vulnerability management reflect each state's broader conception of how OCO should be governed, how national resources should be organised, and how decision-making mechanisms should balance security, intelligence, and societal protection. These differences also indicate that vulnerability management has become a domain in which national policy choices shape operational latitude, defensive readiness, and international trust. Table 5.1 compares four national vulnerability-handling frameworks by authority, default bias, retention mechanisms, participation, transparency, and operational orientation.

TABLE 5.1
Comparison of National Vulnerability-Handling Frameworks

Feature	**United States (VEP)**	**United Kingdom**	**Netherlands (NL)**	**Switzerland (CVD)**[a]
Primary Authority	NSC-chaired Equities Review Board	NCSC/GCHQ senior oversight	National Coordinator for Security and Counterterrorism (NCTV)	NCSC (intermediary function)
Default Bias	Disclosure unless compelling national-security rationale for retention	Disclosure as default; retention only exceptionally justified	Explicit disclosure-first principle	Disclosure-first; no operational retention mechanism
Retention Mechanism	Yes—structured process with periodic review	Yes—limited, mandatory reassessment	Minimal—retention rare and time-limited	No retention mechanism
Interagency Participation	Intelligence, DoD, DHS, FBI, others	Intelligence and security community	Cross-government participation when relevant	Vendor-focused; state intervenes if vendor contact fails
Public Transparency	Published charter; sometimes aggregate statistics released	Limited, high-level principles only	High transparency in national CVD policy	High transparency; publishes CVE information
Operational Orientation	Balances offensive and defensive equities	Balances offensive and defensive equities	Predominantly defensive; offensive utility secondary	Defensive societal protection; no offensive latitude

Abbreviations: CVD, Coordinated Vulnerability Disclosure; DHS, Department of Homeland Security; DoD, Department of Defense; GCHQ, Government Communications Headquarters; NCSC, National Cyber Security Centre; NSC, National Security Council; VEP, Vulnerabilities Equities Process.
[a] See citation (National Cyber Security Centre (NCSC), Switzerland, 2025).

5.5 Case Studies of Policy in Action

Evaluating how states manage vulnerabilities requires examining concrete incidents in which decisions to retain, disclose, or operationalise exploits produced observable strategic, operational, or societal consequences. These cases illustrate how the abstract principles discussed earlier acquire practical meaning under conditions of uncertainty, political pressure, and time-sensitive operational requirements. They also reveal that misjudging the offensive–defensive balance can generate spillover effects that extend far beyond the intended target, thereby reinforcing why structured decision-making mechanisms—such as VEP-like processes—are necessary to document assumptions, revisit their validity, and mitigate risks associated with exploit retention.

Stuxnet: Operational Gains and Strategic Externalities

The Stuxnet operation (2007–2010) demonstrates how the deliberate exploitation of multiple zero-day vulnerabilities can offer significant operational advantages while simultaneously introducing systemic risks that are difficult to contain once a cyber capability is deployed. Historical and doctrinal analyses indicate that the operation disrupted Iran's enrichment programme and delayed the escalation of the nuclear crisis by providing decision-makers with temporal and diplomatic space (Kaplan, 2016; Bronk, 2016). Because Stuxnet relied on a suite of previously unknown vulnerabilities, it reflected a calculated choice to retain offensive capabilities rather than disclose them for patching. Yet the worm's escape from its intended environment demonstrated a core limitation of cyber operations highlighted in existing doctrine: even capabilities designed with restrictive logic may propagate in unpredictable ways once released into interconnected systems (Mandsager et al., 2022). In this sense, Stuxnet established a precedent for using zero-days to produce physical effects while simultaneously revealing the proliferation risks inherent in sophisticated malware. Subsequent technical analyses underscored that elements of Stuxnet's propagation logic were later examined and repurposed by other actors, illustrating the long-term costs associated with exploit retention (Kaplan, 2016). The episode therefore highlights the need for post-operational reassessment, including disclosure once the continued secrecy of an exploit no longer yields strategic value.

Heartbleed: Evaluating Disclosure in the Context of Systemic Risk

The disclosure of Heartbleed (2014), a critical flaw in OpenSSL, illustrates how vulnerabilities embedded in widely deployed cryptographic libraries generate risk profiles that make retention indefensible from both a policy and societal-security perspective. Heartbleed allowed attackers to extract memory contents from servers, compromising passwords, encryption keys, and other sensitive information. Because the library was integrated across critical sectors—including financial services, communications, and elements of national infrastructure—the vulnerability constituted a systemic risk. Public speculation at the time regarding whether intelligence agencies had prior knowledge compelled governments to clarify their vulnerability-handling philosophies. In parallel, academic research used a fictional scenario to illustrate how potential intelligence benefits must be weighed against the risk that the same vulnerability could jeopardise national systems (Huskaj and Wilson, 2021). This combination of public concern, academic scrutiny, and governmental clarification highlighted a key threshold criterion: when a vulnerability affects core Internet infrastructure, the defensive and societal equities decisively outweigh any temporary operational gain. The case therefore underscores the importance of transparent communication regarding vulnerability-handling mechanisms, as public trust can erode quickly when disclosure decisions appear opaque or politically contested.

WannaCry: When Stockpiling Enables Adversarial Exploitation

The WannaCry ransomware attack (2017) provides a stark illustration of the liabilities associated with retaining offensive exploits, particularly when operational security around those exploits fails. The worm's propagation relied on EternalBlue, a sophisticated SMB exploit reportedly developed and retained by a state until a breach resulted in its theft and subsequent release by the Shadow Brokers (Newman, 2018). Once leaked, the exploit was rapidly incorporated into criminal and state-linked malware campaigns, enabling groups such as North Korea's Lazarus Group to conduct a global ransomware operation that disrupted hospitals, logistics networks, and government agencies. Although Microsoft issued patches once informed, the episode demonstrated a structural limitation of exploit retention: patch availability does not equate to patch adoption, particularly across legacy or unsupported systems where vulnerabilities persist despite vendor mitigation (Newman, 2018). Within the policy community, WannaCry intensified debates regarding governmental obligations to disclose vulnerabilities once retention no longer serves a clear national-security purpose. Research further emphasised that exploit retention carries inherent blowback risks, particularly when intelligence services cannot guarantee long-term operational control over their tools (Huskaj, 2024*c*). The incident therefore validated arguments for periodic reassessment within VEP-like processes and demonstrated the global consequences of misaligned IGL calculations.

Cross-Case Assessment

Across these cases, several cross-cutting insights emerge. First, exploit retention confers short-term operational advantages only when accompanied by rigorous risk assessment, continuous monitoring, and a willingness to disclose once defensive or systemic equities dominate. Second, poorly governed stockpiles create liabilities that can materialise unexpectedly, as demonstrated by WannaCry's exploitation of an assessed state-developed tool and Stuxnet's unintended proliferation pathways. Third, vulnerabilities embedded in foundational technologies such as OpenSSL require heightened scrutiny because exploitation would undermine broad segments of the digital ecosystem, rendering retention strategically unsound. Finally, these cases indicate that national processes for vulnerability management—whether formalised through VEPs or guided by institutional norms—shape the credibility of governmental claims regarding responsible behaviour in cyberspace. States that cannot demonstrate a defensible rationale for retaining high-risk vulnerabilities, or that lack documented decision-making processes, tend to face political criticism, diplomatic questioning, and public scrutiny—particularly after incidents that expose the consequences of exploit retention. These lessons motivate the need for structured, transparent, and periodically re-evaluated mechanisms for vulnerability management, which the next section develops in greater conceptual detail.

5.6 Towards a Normative Framework for Vulnerability Management

The preceding analysis demonstrates that decisions concerning the retention, disclosure, and operationalisation of software vulnerabilities cannot be managed through technical discretion or ad-hoc operational judgement alone. Because vulnerability exploitation directly conditions intelligence access, operational readiness, and systemic exposure across interconnected infrastructures, it requires formalised governance arrangements that allocate authority, constrain discretion, and document rationale. Absent such structures, decisions default to unit-level preferences shaped by short-term operational incentives rather than national-level assessments of risk, legality, and consequence. A normative framework for vulnerability management is therefore required not to resolve ethical tension in the abstract, but to institutionalise how competing intelligence, operational, and societal equities are weighed under conditions of uncertainty. Accordingly, the framework developed below integrates ethical criteria with institutional design by moving from normative constraint to procedural governance.

Operationally, the framework functions by structuring how decision-makers evaluate, compare, and document competing intelligence, operational, and societal equities when determining whether a newly identified vulnerability should be retained, deployed, or disclosed. One way to conceptualise this assessment is through a disclosure–exploitation matrix that maps the offensive value of a vulnerability against the systemic risk associated with withholding it. Offensive value refers to the specific operational advantages a state expects to derive from retaining or employing a vulnerability, such as sustained access to adversary command-and-control systems or the ability to disable targeted military capabilities at a critical moment. Systemic risk encompasses the potential harm that may arise domestically or internationally if an unpatched flaw is independently discovered or widely exploited by criminal or state-linked actors. Vulnerabilities that combine high offensive value with low systemic exposure may, under strict oversight, be temporarily retained. Conversely, vulnerabilities characterised by high systemic risk and limited operational utility should be disclosed promptly. The most difficult judgements arise in high–high cases, where substantial offensive value coincides with significant systemic exposure. In such situations, anticipatory mitigation enables a retain–then–release posture, in which limited operational use is paired with concurrent preparation for disclosure in order to minimise long-term harm.

Operationalisation begins at the point of discovery, where each newly identified vulnerability is subjected to a structured decision procedure rather than informal expert judgement. This procedure requires explicit assessment of intelligence value, operational utility, systemic exposure, and anticipated persistence of advantage before any decision to retain, deploy, or disclose is authorised. Additional considerations include the vulnerability's relevance to ongoing or planned operations, the feasibility of protecting national and allied systems without disclosure, and the expected persistence of operational advantage if retained. Structured evaluation of these factors enables a reasoned comparison between national-security benefits and cumulative defensive costs. This reflects the broader argument that vulnerabilities constitute strategic resources that must be governed with the same discipline as intelligence assets rather than treated as expendable technical artefacts (Huskaj, 2024*c*). Consequently, decisions should rest on documented, evidence-based reasoning rather than organisational intuition or parochial interest.

The framework requires defined governance mechanisms that assign authority, impose review obligations, and constrain discretionary exploit retention over time. Any decision to retain a vulnerability must therefore be time-bound, documented, and subject to mandatory reassessment at predefined intervals or upon completion of a specified operational phase. These review points function as control gates that prevent dormant exploit stockpiles from persisting without renewed justification. Retained vulnerabilities should be subject to scheduled review cycles, such as re-evaluation at fixed intervals or at the conclusion of defined operational phases, to prevent dormant stockpiles from persisting without scrutiny. Deliberation should involve actors beyond the immediate offensive user community. While the United States Vulnerabilities Equities Process exemplifies interagency participation, additional perspectives—potentially including independent advisors with appropriate clearances or indirect consultation with private-sector experts through established severity-scoring practices—can introduce broader risk awareness into the process. All decisions to delay disclosure should be formally justified in writing, enabling later oversight through inspectors general or legislative bodies and creating an institutional record that supports organisational learning when retained exploits subsequently generate negative externalities.

At the operational level, the framework imposes planning requirements that integrate second- and third-order risk assessment into exploit development, deployment, and exit decisions. Offensive cyber operators and intelligence analysts are required to account for second- and third-order effects when employing an exploit, including the possibility of unintended propagation, adversary adaptation, or long-term reputational consequences.

Embedding such considerations into planning cycles encourages the development of preplanned exit strategies, such as notifying affected vendors after mission completion or implementing containment measures if operational security is compromised. These practices operationalise the retain–and–release principle by aligning offensive actions with predefined mitigation pathways and reducing strategic exposure while preserving time-sensitive operational effects.

An ethical vulnerability management framework must also recognise that national decisions generate transnational consequences. Modern software ecosystems are globally integrated, and a state's choice to retain a vulnerability may expose other jurisdictions to cascading risks. International coordination and norm development therefore constitute natural extensions of the framework. Allies may establish shared guidelines for when vulnerabilities should be communicated across defence partnerships, while multilateral institutions such as NATO and the European Union already treat vulnerability disclosure as a component of cooperative cyber defence. More ambitious proposals envision secure international mechanisms for exchanging information on high-risk vulnerabilities under strict protocols. Although political sensitivities limit the scope of such arrangements, even incremental norm development elevates ethical and strategic considerations and reinforces expectations of responsible state behaviour in cyberspace.

Taken together, this framework indicates that decisions concerning zero-day vulnerabilities should not emerge from opaque or discretionary processes. By systematising how offensive value and systemic risk are weighed, and by embedding oversight, documentation, and anticipatory ethics into procedural routines, states can navigate the inherent tension between exploiting vulnerabilities for national advantage and preserving the stability of the broader digital ecosystem. Vulnerability management thus constitutes a governance function rather than a purely operational activity. This conclusion provides a direct bridge to the next chapter, which examines how offensive cyberspace capabilities depend on whole-of-society arrangements that integrate governmental authority, industrial expertise, and academic knowledge into a coherent national framework.

5.7 Conclusion

This chapter has examined how states balance the operational utility of exploiting undisclosed software vulnerabilities against the systemic risks associated with leaving widely deployed systems unpatched. The analysis has shown that zero-day exploitation enables states to project power in and through cyberspace by creating access vectors that circumvent defensive architectures, yet the same practice generates long-term exposure when vulnerabilities persist across interconnected infrastructures. Case studies such as Stuxnet, Heartbleed, and WannaCry illustrate that decisions to retain or disclose vulnerabilities produce effects that operate across strategic, operational, and societal levels and that poorly governed retention can enable adversarial exploitation or generate cascading disruptions that extend far beyond the intended target environment.

The chapter has also demonstrated that ethical decision-making in this domain requires integrating principles of necessity, proportionality, distinction, and accountability into procedural mechanisms such as the United States. Vulnerabilities Equities Process and comparable national models. These mechanisms institutionalise deliberation, broaden the range of considerations incorporated into vulnerability-handling decisions, and establish review pathways that constrain operational preferences by embedding legal, policy, and societal perspectives. The proposed normative framework builds on this logic by formalising how states can evaluate offensive value, systemic risk, and anticipated secondary effects within an evidence-based and documented decision process.

The overall implication is that vulnerability management constitutes a governance function rather than a solely operational activity. Decisions to retain, disclose, or operationalise vulnerabilities influence national security, public trust, and the wider stability of the digital environment. States therefore require institutional architectures that enable structured evaluation, periodic reassessment, and coordination across agencies responsible for offensive operations, defensive posture, and societal protection. This conclusion provides the basis for the next chapter, which examines how effective offensive cyberspace capabilities depend on whole-of-society arrangements that integrate governmental, industrial, and academic resources into a coherent national framework.

Decision Exercise: Governing the Retain–Disclose Dilemma for High-Value Vulnerabilities

Scenario. A credible report describes a previously unknown vulnerability in widely deployed software used across government, essential services, and partner systems. Defence and intelligence argue for short-term retention to preserve a time-sensitive access opportunity. The national CERT and regulators argue that withholding sustains systemic exposure and creates blowback risk. A decision is required within 72 hours: disclose, retain under restrictions, or retain briefly then disclose. The decision must be defensible under oversight and compatible with partner consultation obligations.

Analytical question 1—Decision rule. State a binding rule for your choice (for example, disclose by default; retain only when time-sensitive and non-substitutable). Specify the primary purpose for the next 30 days and one uncertainty you accept inside 72 hours.

Analytical question 2—Exposure vs operational value. Specify two indicators of *high systemic risk* (prevalence/criticality; plausibility of exploitation at scale) and two indicators of *high operational value* (priority access; short-lived window). State the minimum patch/mitigation timeline assumption you use.

Analytical question 3—Option and trigger. Choose **one** posture: disclose now; retain; retain–then–disclose. Specify (i) the intended advantage (access/collection/contingency), (ii) the IGL trade-off, and (iii) one trigger that forces immediate disclosure (parallel discovery, criminal exploitation, loss of containment).

Analytical question 4—Governance minimum requirements. Specify minimum governance conditions: participants (defence, intelligence, CERT, legal, foreign affairs/regulator), documentation requirement, sunset/review rule for retention, and auditability standard. Add one rule that prevents a single operational stakeholder from dominating the decision.

6

Organising Cyber Capabilities: A Whole-of-Society Approach

This chapter examines how a cyberliterate state can organise OCO through a whole-of-society approach that integrates government agencies, private companies, and academic institutions under a unified governance architecture.

The analytical starting point is a distributional problem: the specialised competence, infrastructure, and research environments required to discover vulnerabilities, develop exploit capability, and sustain readiness are dispersed across society rather than concentrated inside government organisations. The implication is that organisational design conditions capability. A state can expand operational options only if it can mobilise these dispersed resources while preserving unity of authority, legal accountability, and operational security (Huskaj and Axelsson, 2023; Huskaj, 2024*c*).

The purpose of this chapter is to treat cross-sector integration as a capability variable and to specify which institutional arrangements convert distributed competence into decision-ready options for authorised offensive action. The central claim is conditional: whole-of-society participation increases capability potential, yet it increases loss-of-control risk because additional actors expand the interfaces where information handling, deconfliction, and mandate boundaries can diverge. Therefore, whole-of-society models are sustainable only when governance mechanisms translate political and ethical constraints into enforceable operating conditions (Huskaj, 2025*b*).

The analysis relies on publicly available material and does not infer or describe classified thresholds, targeting practices, or national decision procedures. The term *smart state* is used as an analytical proxy for cyberliterate small or medium-sized states in which competence is distributed across industry and academia and must be mobilised under democratic oversight.

The chapter addresses the following analytical question: Which configurations of cross-sector partnership—linking government agencies, private companies, and academic institutions—can increase a cyberliterate state's offensive cyber capability under democratic oversight, and through which resource-sharing and institutional-alignment mechanisms can they do so while preserving state control and legal accountability (Huskaj and Axelsson, 2023; Huskaj, 2024*c*)?

The chapter uses the Multi-Level, Multi-Dimensional (MLMD) framework as the organising structure for assessing partnership models against operational constraints. Ethical and legal constraints developed in Chapter 5 are treated as design parameters for cross-sector mobilisation rather than external considerations applied after capability is built (Huskaj and Blix, 2022; Huskaj, 2025*b*).

The remainder of the chapter proceeds as follows. Section 6.1 defines the conceptual and analytical frame and specifies the core distinctions used to examine organisation for cyber capability. Section 6.2 establishes the smart-state baseline by specifying the mobilisation problem created by high digital dependence and distributed ownership of critical functions. Section 6.3 specifies partnership configurations as organisational build options and clarifies how roles and contributions can be allocated across public authority, operators, and

DOI: 10.1201/9781003655183-6

supporting stakeholders. Section 6.4 identifies governance mechanisms that render these configurations governable under legal authority and oversight, including control points, accountability, and decision interfaces. Section 6.5 traces the policy-to-payload workflow and locates where deconfliction and coordination are required to preserve coherence across intelligence, defence, and authorised offensive activity. Section 6.6 provides an implementation roadmap and proposes measurement approaches for tracking capability development, coordination performance, and readiness over time. Section 6.7 analyses risk and escalation management as design constraints that condition political usability and operational sustainability. Section 6.8 concludes by synthesising the organisational argument and preparing the transition to the case material in Chapter 7 (Granåsen et al., 2019; Huskaj and Blix, 2022).

6.1 Conceptual and Analytical Frame

This section specifies the analytical frame used to examine whole-of-society organisation for OCO. The unit of analysis is a socio-technical capability system that links political authority, intelligence support, and specialised technical work into decision-ready options for authorised action. The organising assumption is that capability emerges from how roles, authorities, and control mechanisms are designed and integrated across organisational boundaries, because competence, infrastructure, and innovation capacity are distributed across government, industry, and academia.

Cyberspace is treated as a human-built domain composed of internetworked information systems and the people and organisations that operate them. This domain enables intelligence collection and operational interference at a high tempo, while simultaneously producing systemic risk because vulnerabilities persist and are exploited by state, proxy, and criminal threat actors. The implication is that a state's capacity to conduct OCO is conditioned by how political intent is translated into operational planning constraints and into bounded technical action under uncertainty.

For the purposes of this chapter, OCOs are defined as coordinated actions conducted by a state, or by actors operating under state authority, intended to project power in or through cyberspace against adversary systems by affecting confidentiality, integrity, or availability, including through manipulation of data and system behaviour. This definition treats OCO as a sequenced activity that depends on target selection, access conditions, payload behaviour, and post-operation assessment. The implication is that capability assessment must incorporate authorisation procedures, intelligence processes, engineering workflows, and accountability arrangements, because these elements condition feasibility, controllability, and political sustainability.

The chapter uses a MLMD frame to structure analysis of organisational choice. At the strategic level, the analysis examines how national intent, legal authority, and deterrence signalling specify objectives and constraints for capability development and employment, because deterrence credibility depends on an adversary's perception of capacity and authorised willingness. At the operational level, the analysis examines how planning functions coordinate intelligence requirements, resource allocation, deconfliction, and approval gates across institutions, because distributed expertise produces usable options only when roles, authorities, and sequencing rules are explicit. At the tactical level, the analysis examines how access operations, payload engineering, testing, and execution control condition whether technical effects remain bounded and reversible under real-world uncertainty. Across all levels, political oversight, legal mandates, ethical constraints, technical risk, and organisational culture are treated as interacting variables that shape whether cross-sector participation expands national option space while preserving state control.

Within this frame, the chapter distinguishes between *partnership configurations* and *governance mechanisms*. Partnership configurations specify structural forms through which government organisations, industry, and academia are combined into a capability architecture. Governance mechanisms specify the instruments and processes through which information, personnel, infrastructure, and authorities are integrated into a coherent workflow across those structures. This distinction matters because similar actor sets can yield different operational outcomes when authority allocation, information handling, and deconfliction routines vary across institutional designs.

Whole-of-society organisation is defined here as the mobilisation and integration of government agencies, private sector capacity, and academic training and research as enduring capability inputs for OCO under political direction. Authorisation and responsibility are anchored at the national policy level through strategy, legal authority, and ROE, while execution and capability development draw on controlled cooperation arrangements, including co-location and resource pooling, reserve and "posted" personnel models, secure testing and training environments, and formal coordination channels for deconfliction and OPSEC. In some models, non-governmental actors may conduct state-directed tasks under explicit authorisation and accountability conditions, which makes interface design and boundary management central to preserving unity of authority.

A further premise is that intelligence is the operational mechanism that connects deterrence policy to OCO planning and execution. Offensive units rarely possess complete knowledge of target systems at the outset, and therefore must generate intelligence requirements and collect cyber intelligence to characterise targets, vulnerabilities, dependencies, and access conditions. The implication is that cross-sector organisation must prioritise intelligence–operations fusion because access is perishable and disclosure can collapse both collection pathways and effect options (Huskaj and Iftimie, 2020; Huskaj and Blix, 2022). Organisational designs that separate intelligence production from operational preparation without structured integration can produce delays, misalignment between legal intent and technical feasibility, and increased loss-of-control risk during execution under time compression.

To make organisational design empirically traceable along the policy-to-payload workflow, the chapter employs a four-step planning model as an organising structure for later sections: Indicators and Warnings, Planning Timelines, Operational Considerations, and a Decision Point (Huskaj and Iftimie, 2020; Huskaj and Blix, 2022). The analytic purpose is to locate where whole-of-society participation intersects with decision gates and where governance mechanisms must constrain drift beyond authorised intent. At each step, the analysis asks three questions: which actor holds authority at that point; which actor provides inputs, including intelligence and technical artefacts; and which mechanism enforces boundaries for legality, proportionality, and operational security.

Deconfliction is treated as a core governance requirement because whole-of-society participation increases the number of actors conducting reconnaissance, testing, threat-hunting, and capability development against overlapping target environments. Deconfliction is defined as structured coordination that prevents operational overlap, inadvertent interference, and unintended escalation arising from uncoordinated activity across agencies and sectors. The implication is that organisational designs must produce shared situational awareness and enforceable coordination routines, because self-inflicted compromise can occur when parallel activities collide, expose access, or generate ambiguous signals to adversaries.

Ethical and legal constraints developed in Chapter 5 are incorporated as operational design variables that shape partnership design, authority allocation, and testing requirements. The organisational implication is that legality and proportionality must inform authorities, permissible action categories, and assurance requirements early enough to bound operational options. Reversibility, cascading-effects risk, and collateral exposure therefore function as decision criteria at approval gates because bounded effects condition the political sustainability of authorisation under democratic oversight (Huskaj and Blix, 2022). This framing also anticipates the governance dilemma associated with national vulnerability policy, where the same undisclosed flaw can support intelligence access and offensive effect while also exposing domestic systems if retained; institutional design must therefore allocate decision authority and oversight responsibility in ways that preserve legitimacy while sustaining capability potential (Huskaj, 2025*b*).

The term *smart state* is used as an analytical proxy for cyberliterate small- or medium-sized states in which competence and innovation capacity are distributed across industry, universities, and specialised communities. In this usage, smart-state capability denotes the capacity to mobilise those knowledge communities as instruments of state power under democratic oversight (Huskaj and Axelsson, 2023). The implication is that the binding constraint often lies in the design of organisational interfaces that convert dispersed competence into controlled operational capability, including security vetting, compartmentalisation regimes, contractual controls, auditability of artefacts, and enforceable accountability for decisions.

Taken together, this conceptual and analytical frame establishes three chapter-level claims. First, whole-of-society OCO should be analysed as governance of a socio-technical capability system spanning policy authority, intelligence processes, and engineering workflows. Second, partnership configurations specify structural options for mobilisation, and governance mechanisms determine how those options produce decision-ready capability under oversight. Third, the policy-to-payload workflow provides a structured sequence for locating authority, responsibility, assurance, and deconfliction across levels of analysis. The subsequent sections therefore specify baseline mobilisation conditions in cyberliterate states, compare partnership configurations as organisational blueprints, and identify governance mechanisms that preserve state control while managing escalation exposure.

6.2 A Smart-State Baseline

A whole-of-society approach to OCO is best understood as a response to how cyber power is produced and distributed in advanced digital societies. Many cyberliterate small states combine a high degree of digitisation with governance traditions that mobilise expertise, innovation, and specialised networks as instruments of national power. The implication is that offensive capability development cannot be treated as an internal, military-technical programme alone, because the knowledge, infrastructure, and human resources needed to generate controlled effects are structurally dispersed across state, industry, and academia (Sundelius, 1995; European Commission, 2023; The Agency for Growth Policy Analysis, 2015; Huskaj and Axelsson, 2023).

A later section uses a single national case to illustrate how these baseline conditions shape partnership design and governance choices, without describing operational arrangements.

The "smart state" baseline is therefore defined less by scale than by mobilisation capacity. From a whole-of-society approach perspective, executive-level authority is commonly treated in policy discussion as the locus of political authorisation for OCO and the authority for providing strategic direction, while the chapter does not describe decision procedures. This matters because whole-of-society participation increases operational surface area: more actors can contribute capability, but more actors also create additional pathways for loss of control, leakage, and misalignment. Centralised political authority reduces this risk by anchoring offensive activity in explicit authorisation, translated into rules and instructions that shape how agencies and partners may contribute to offensive missions (Huskaj, 2024*c*).

A distinctive feature of the smart-state baseline is that the model explicitly allows for industry participation under state direction in defined circumstances. The dissertation material notes that the private sector can conduct OCO where the executive authorises narrowly scoped action under explicit commissioning and supervision from government-related infrastructure, and frames this as a mechanism through which the smart state remains in charge while still leveraging competence that is concentrated outside government. The implication is that the baseline assumption is not merely "cooperation," but conditional delegation under state command authority, where the state defines purpose, boundaries, and accountability while external actors supply scarce expertise and capability components (Huskaj, 2024*c*; Huskaj, 2025*b*).

The distribution of institutional responsibilities helps explain why a whole-of-society approach is analytically plausible. Open sources in many cyberliterate states describe a division of labour in which intelligence support, civilian resilience and incident response, and military cyber capability are organised in distinct institutions with different mandates and accountability regimes. The implication is that offensive capability sits inside a wider system of interdependent functions, and governance design must prevent interference and responsibility ambiguity across these mandates (Huskaj, 2024*c*; Huskaj and Axelsson, 2023).

The baseline is also shaped by a human-capital constraint that favours integration rather than institutional self-sufficiency. The dissertation explicitly contrasts the time required to train conventional operators with the time required to train offensive cyber operators, noting that offensive cyber skills may take years to build and that multiple distinct skill sets are required. This matters because long training pipelines create a structural incentive to pool and share scarce expertise across organisations rather than duplicating capability development inside isolated institutional silos. The implication is that whole-of-society organisation is not only a political choice; it is a capacity-management response to a scarcity condition in which the limiting factor is skilled labour rather than policy intent (Huskaj, 2024*c*).

A further enabling condition is the existence of national training and experimentation infrastructures that already assume multi-actor participation. Publicly described arrangements indicate that state-affiliated research and training environments provide education support and applied experimentation capacity, while universities educate and train human resources subsequently recruited by agencies and industry. The implication is that the smart-state baseline already contains a production pipeline—education, recruitment, and training environments—that can be organised into an intentional national system if governance, vetting, and information-handling rules are made explicit (Huskaj, 2024*c*; Granåsen et al., 2019).

The organisational logic of the baseline is further clarified by the argument for co-location. Pooling and sharing scarce specialist competence benefits from co-location of key cyber functions within an intelligence-supporting environment, and links this argument to two mechanisms: overlap between offensive cyberspace work and SIGINT work, and the need for short decision paths and rapid deconfliction. The implication is that whole-of-society organisation is best understood as controlled integration: sensitive functions are kept within a shared, governable operational setting to reduce coordination delay and to limit misalignment between intelligence collection and offensive action (Huskaj, 2024*c*).

This co-location argument also provides a baseline explanation for why governance and risk tolerance must be designed around different operational logics. The dissertation distinguishes offensive operations from intelligence collection on a risk dimension: the commander executing offensive effects may accept operational risk, whereas intelligence collection aims to remain unnoticed and therefore tends to reject risk that could expose access.

The implication is that whole-of-society organisation must internalise this tension as a standing coordination problem, because a partnership architecture that accelerates offensive action without protecting intelligence equities can reduce long-term access and thereby degrade future options. Co-location functions here as a structural mitigation because it reduces the distance between communities with different risk tolerances and enables rapid deconfliction under time pressure (Huskaj, 2024*c*).

A final baseline condition concerns how the smart state's governance principles can enable or constrain cross-sector mobilisation. The dissertation material frames executive-level authority as setting vision, law, and rules for the cyber capability, while also warning that the principle of responsibility can generate fragmentation effects when resources and mandates are distributed across agencies that must coordinate against cross-cutting threats. The implication is that whole-of-society organisation must be treated as an institutional design problem, not as a coordination slogan: the state can mobilise national resources only if it builds mechanisms that counteract predictable fragmentation produced by distributed responsibility and legally bounded agency mandates (Huskaj, 2024*c*; Government, 2024*b*).

Taken together, a smart-state baseline can be summarised as a configuration in which (i) political authority is centralised in a cabinet-level function for authorisation and boundary-setting, (ii) operational and intelligence capabilities are specialised across agencies with distinct mandates, (iii) competence production and innovation capacity are distributed across society, and (iv) the scarcity of skilled personnel creates an incentive to pool, share, and co-locate sensitive functions to sustain tempo and control. The implication is that such states are analytically suitable for a whole-of-society model because they already contain the institutional components and coordination logics that the model presupposes; the remaining question is how partnership configurations and governance mechanisms can mobilise these components without weakening legal control, operational security, or the ethical constraints specified in Chapter 5 (Huskaj, 2024*c*; Huskaj and Axelsson, 2023).

6.3 Partnership Configurations (What to Build)

Many cyberliterate countries find that offensive cyberspace capability is constrained less by strategic intent than by the distribution of the resources required to translate intent into operational options. The skills and infrastructures that sustain access, toolchains, testing, and operational tempo are dispersed across intelligence organisations, defence organisations, critical-infrastructure operators, specialised cybersecurity firms, and research environments. The purpose of this section is therefore to specify partnership configurations that convert nationally distributed competence into a governed capability, while preserving unity of command, legal responsibility, and operational security. The underlying claim is conditional: a state can expand the scope and tempo of authorised offensive activity only if cross-sector participation is structured as a component of state capability rather than as parallel activity that merely coexists with it (Huskaj, 2024*c*; Huskaj and Axelsson, 2023).

The configurations below are presented as organisational blueprints. Each blueprint is defined by (i) where authority sits, (ii) how civilians and non-military organisations are incorporated, and (iii) which parts of the policy-to-payload workflow they are designed to touch. The configurations are complementary rather than mutually exclusive because the capability gaps they address are different in kind: some concern operational planning and deconfliction, others concern sustained capability development, and others concern talent pipelines and testing environments. The design constraint across all configurations is the intelligence–operations tension: access and collection are perishable resources, and whole-of-society participation increases the number of interfaces where uncoordinated activity can compromise access, reveal intent, or create effects misaligned with authorised risk tolerance (Huskaj and Blix, 2022; Huskaj, 2024*a*).

Configuration 1: A government-led integrated offensive unit with controlled civilian incorporation

The first configuration is a state-led offensive unit that incorporates civilian competence under government authority through structured roles such as secondments, reserve-style arrangements, and cleared advisory functions. The operational rationale is that vulnerability research, exploit development, and target-environment understanding evolve faster than public staffing cycles, meaning that an exclusively governmental staffing model tends to lag the technology it must exploit. Civilian incorporation reduces this lag if it is designed as an internal capability function rather than as external support delivered at arm's length (Huskaj, 2024*c*; Huskaj and Axelsson, 2023).

This configuration also addresses cyberliterate countries' of limited specialist manpower. The capability implication is not merely a larger headcount but a deeper skill mix within the same command structure, which matters because offensive missions require tightly coupled roles across intelligence preparation, exploit engineering, testing, and execution control. The organisational requirement is therefore a personnel architecture that separates *authority* from *technical contribution*: civilians can design, test, and advise, but execution authority remains with the responsible agency and is exercised through defined command channels and approval gates (Huskaj and Blix, 2022).

A practical anchoring mechanism is co-location. Prior work argues that co-locating cyber capability within an intelligence-supporting environment can enable pooling and sharing of scarce specialist personnel and support rapid deconfliction between offensive activity and intelligence collection, which is treated as a condition for mission success (Huskaj and Axelsson, 2023). Within this configuration, co-location does not imply that all functions are physically centralised. It implies that coordination authority and the deconfliction function are positioned where intelligence support and offensive planning can be integrated with short decision paths and clear ownership of access.

Configuration 2: A joint cross-sector operational hub for planning, targeting support, and deconfliction

The second configuration is a joint operational hub that co-locates, or tightly networks, planners and specialised contributors from relevant public authorities, select private operators, and research environments to support planning, targeting support, and deconfliction. The purpose is to raise the quality and speed of operational design by integrating (i) government intelligence holdings and authorities, (ii) private-sector knowledge of technologies and dependencies, and (iii) research-driven methods for modelling and validation. This matters because targeting in modern ICT environments is often dependency-driven: cloud platforms, telecom infrastructures, industrial control systems (ICS), and software supply chains create propagation and spillover pathways that a single organisation rarely understands fully on its own (Huskaj, 2024*c*; Huskaj and Blix, 2022).

This configuration must be bounded by explicit sequencing rules. The validated four-step model positions deconfliction as a design constraint early enough to shape resourcing and tool selection, rather than as a late administrative check at the decision gate (Huskaj and Blix, 2022). A joint hub is therefore most defensible when it is defined as a planning and assurance function that informs the execute/no-go decision, not as an execution collective.

The causal claim is straightforward: the more actors that contribute, the more coordination is required to keep access and intent coherent, and the less viable it becomes to rely on informal coordination to prevent collisions.

The hub also functions as a trust mechanism. Research on intelligence sharing emphasises that structured sharing depends on personal ties, compatible policies, streamlined processes, and leadership support, and that alliances often separate multilateral exchange from more sensitive bilateral compartments to reduce manipulation and leakage risks (Huskaj, 2024*a*). A domestic analogue implies that some information is shared broadly inside the hub to support planning, while the most sensitive methods and sources remain compartmented under bilateral or agency-internal controls. The configuration therefore requires an explicit information-handling model rather than a generic expectation of "sharing."

Configuration 3: State-authorised private-sector action under commissioning, supervision, and liability design

The third configuration is state-authorised private-sector action under a commissioning framework that specifies scope, constraints, oversight, and termination conditions. The configuration is included as an analytical possibility discussed in the literature; it is not presented as a recommended default, and its permissibility is jurisdiction-dependent. This configuration exists because some operational problems are scale problems: for instance, dismantling non-state infrastructures or conducting narrowly bounded disruption against criminal command-and-control may exceed public capacity in time-sensitive settings, especially when the private sector holds unique visibility into adversary tooling, hosting patterns, or service abuse. The policy risk is that delegating coercive action can erode accountability and escalate conflicts if authorisation and monitoring are underspecified (Huskaj, 2025*b*).

A common constraint is constitutional and institutional: private entities do not hold coercive authority by default, and offensive action conducted by non-state actors can create ambiguity about responsibility attribution, legal accountability, and escalation ownership. The configuration is therefore defensible only if private execution is treated as an *extension of state action* through commissioning instruments that specify (i) who authorises, (ii) who supervises, (iii) what evidence must exist at approval time, and (iv) what penalties apply if the mandate is exceeded. Prior work develops this logic by discussing modernised commissioning approaches and liability arrangements intended to keep private participation bounded by state direction (Huskaj, 2025*b*).

Operationally, the key design choice is the mission type. Commissioned private action is most coherent where objectives and effects can be specified narrowly and verified quickly, and where reversibility and bounded payload logic are feasible constraints. This aligns with the ethical and escalation considerations developed earlier in the book: if civilian contributors are used, the mandate can prioritise controlled effects and clear abort conditions because the political cost of unintended consequences is higher when responsibility appears diffused across sectors (Huskaj and Blix, 2022). The configuration can therefore be treated as selective and exceptional, not as a default method for high-end state-on-state operations.

Configuration 4: A structured research and capability pipeline linking universities and operational stakeholders

The fourth configuration is a long-horizon research and capability pipeline that links universities, state-affiliated research environments, and operational stakeholders through programmes that combine open research, cleared research, and application-focused prototypes. The purpose is to ensure that operational capability is sustained as a learning system that produces methods for targeting, modelling, validation, and post-operation assessment, rather than being reduced to episodic tool acquisition. The strategic claim is that offensive capability depreciates when it is decoupled from research environments that can test assumptions, formalise lessons, and build repeatable models for planning and assurance (Huskaj, 2024*c*; Huskaj and Axelsson, 2023).

This pipeline is also a governance instrument. When research relationships are institutionalised, the state can set problem frames and ethical boundaries early, before capability work becomes operationally urgent and therefore harder to steer. The practical form of the pipeline includes doctoral and postdoctoral programmes aligned to national priorities, joint appointments, and managed mobility between government and academia. The intent is to create continuity of competence without normalising uncontrolled information flows. This corresponds to the intelligence-sharing insight that skill compatibility and controlled process design are prerequisites for sustained cooperation, especially when sensitive methods are involved (Huskaj, 2024*a*).

A further implication is talent formation. Earlier research on offensive operations highlighted that the field suffers from fragmentation between highly technical work and highly qualitative work and called for research that explains operational processes and governance without collapsing into implementation detail. A structured pipeline is one way to prevent that fragmentation from becoming an institutional weakness, because it produces cadres who can translate between policy constraints, operational design, and technical feasibility under secrecy constraints (Huskaj, 2024*c*).

Configuration 5: Joint training and testing infrastructure as a national cyber range network

The fifth configuration is a shared training and testing infrastructure centred on a national cyber range network used for rehearsal, validation, and cross-sector coordination training. Offensive operations rely on verification: untested exploits can crash hosts, expose access, and produce effects that violate authorised bounds, so testing is a control function rather than a technical luxury (Huskaj and Blix, 2022). A national range network supports this control function by enabling mixed teams to validate payload logic, evaluate reversibility, and assess cascading-effects risk under conditions that can be instrumented and reviewed.

Empirical work on cyber defence exercises shows that inter-organisational teams can be formed at scale, with governmental institutions and private companies contributing personnel in a time-bounded operational setting, and that such settings reveal coordination structures and information practices that are otherwise difficult to observe in live environments (Granåsen et al., 2019). While a defensive exercise is not an offensive mission, the organisational lesson is transferable: complex cyberspace operations are socio-technical, and training therefore has to develop command-and-control, not only technical skills. A range network is a mechanism through which many cyberliterate countries can institutionalise those rhythms while maintaining compartmentation and auditability.

The configuration is also a deconfliction mechanism. When multiple sectors share a controlled training environment, they can learn the interfaces that later reduce friction in planning and preparation, and they can test information-handling rules before those rules are stressed by time pressure. This aligns with the validated framework's emphasis on treating deconfliction and risk as elements that shape planning timelines rather than as concerns postponed to the final authorisation gate (Huskaj and Blix, 2022).

Synthesis: assembling configurations into a governed portfolio

Taken together, the configurations specify a portfolio logic. The government-led integrated unit is the core executor. The joint operational hub is the planning and deconfliction amplifier that raises design quality when dependencies and tempo strain a single organisation. The commissioning framework is a selective scaling mechanism for bounded mission types where private visibility and tempo provide marginal capacity without dissolving accountability. The research pipeline sustains methods, models, and talent formation over multi-year horizons. The range network provides verification capacity and trains cross-sector coordination under controlled conditions. The portfolio implication is that whole-of-society organisation is not a single institution; it is a governed set of interfaces that each exist to reduce a specific failure mode: skill scarcity, dependency blindness, planning delay, loss of control, and unverified effects (Huskaj, 2024*c*; Huskaj and Axelsson, 2023; Huskaj and Blix, 2022).

This portfolio must also be shaped by the alliance environment in which many cyberliterate countries operate. As interoperability requirements deepen, partnership design has to ensure that whole-of-society participation does not create ambiguity in multinational coordination, intelligence release rules, or operational deconfliction with allies. The intelligence-sharing literature shows that "release" defaults, shared classification protocols and process streamlining determine whether cooperation scales without policy contradiction, and that expanding the number of participants increases both coordination difficulty and perceived exclusion risks if compartments are not explained and governed (Huskaj, 2024*a*). The implication is that domestic configurations can be designed with explicit releasability and liaison patterns, so that whole-of-society participation strengthens national options without generating friction in coalition settings where rules, terminology, and authorities differ.

The next step in the chapter is to move from *what to build* to *how it works*. The mechanisms section therefore treats these configurations as inputs and specifies the governance instruments, information-sharing rules, and deconfliction practices that prevent the configurations from becoming parallel structures that compete for access, talent, and authority rather than supporting a single national capability.

6.4 Mechanisms and Governance (How They Work)

Whole-of-society partnership configurations only produce operational utility when they are connected to mechanisms that translate dispersed resources into authorised options for action. The governance problem is therefore not the existence of competence in government, industry, and academia, but the conversion of that competence into a controlled sequence of decisions, information flows, and technical preparations that preserve national intent. The purpose of this section is to specify the mechanisms that make this conversion possible and to define how those mechanisms preserve unity of authorisation even when execution draws on distributed expertise.

The governance control system: authority, fusion, deconfliction, and assurance

A whole-of-society posture presupposes that political intent is translated into binding mission categories, target constraints, and escalation boundaries that planners can treat as fixed parameters. This steering function matters because offensive actions are state acts whose legitimacy depends on traceable authority and attributable responsibility. A design that disperses technical work without centralising authorisation risks producing activity that is operationally plausible but politically unauthorised. The structural requirement is therefore a single strategic gate that specifies who may initiate planning, what classes of effects are permissible, and what legal and policy constraints must be satisfied before an execute decision can be issued (Joint Chiefs of Staff, 2018).

This strategic gate is not sufficient on its own because offensive options depend on intelligence about access conditions, target profiles, and time-sensitive opportunities. Intelligence–operations fusion is therefore a governance mechanism, not an auxiliary function. The state must establish routinised interfaces for two-way exchange in which government actors provide classified intent, targeting priorities, and legal constraints, while private operators contribute architecture and dependency knowledge, and academic partners contribute methods, testing capacity, and analytical techniques. This exchange becomes operationally meaningful only when it is structured through liaison roles, access tiers, and defined procedures for sanitisation and compartmentation, because episodic briefings do not sustain feasibility assessment under changing access conditions (Huskaj, 2024*a*).

Deconfliction and assurance then convert fused information into controlled options. Deconfliction protects access, sequencing, and intelligence equities when multiple actors touch overlapping infrastructures, because uncoordinated activity can burn scarce access positions or expose intent (Joint Chiefs of Staff, 2018). A whole-of-society posture therefore requires a deconfliction authority that can detect collisions and impose sequencing rules without forcing uniform visibility across all partners, which preserves operational coherence while protecting compartmentation. Assurance complements this function by converting uncertainty into authorisation-relevant evidence. Testing and evaluation must be treated as evidence requirements rather than technical preferences, because the approval chain must be able to assess boundedness, reversibility, and cascading-effects exposure before execution (Huskaj and Blix, 2022). The implication is that authority, fusion, deconfliction, and assurance operate as a single control system: each mechanism constrains the next stage so that dispersed competence produces decision-ready options rather than dispersed discretion.

Contracting, commissioning, and state-authorised private action

Cross-sector cooperation requires legal and contractual instruments that allocate responsibility, specify liability, and define the consequences of deviation from the mandate. These instruments matter because offensive activity creates ambiguity when conducted by actors with commercial incentives or academic norms of openness. Governance therefore has to formalise who is authorised to act, under what conditions action is permitted, what oversight is required, and what protections apply when authorised actions create unintended technical spillover.

A controlled form of state-authorised private action can be treated as a contingency mechanism rather than a default model. Its purpose is to enable time-sensitive disruption against bounded target sets—particularly non-state infrastructures—without normalising unsanctioned hack-back practices that collide with intelligence collection and diplomatic constraints. The commissioning logic is only coherent when authorisation is centralised and oversight is integrated into each stage of the activity, including legal review, operational review, and diplomatic risk review (Huskaj, 2025*b*). In other words, private execution can be distributed, but authority to initiate, approve, and terminate operations must remain within the state.

Security, compartmentation, and insider-risk controls

Expanding participation can increase operational tempo, yet it also increases the risk of compromise through insider threat, inadvertent disclosure, or adversary penetration of partner environments. Governance must therefore treat security controls as preconditions for participation, not as optional enhancements. The control problem is institutional: partners differ in information-handling culture, and those differences become operational risks when offensive capability knowledge is involved.

A workable approach is tiered compartmentation aligned with role necessity. External partners can receive the minimum information required to perform a bounded task, and access can be time-limited, auditable, and monitored. Vetting and continuous evaluation become governance mechanisms because they determine whether the state can rely on distributed contributors without creating persistent exposure. The implication is that offensive capability development and counterintelligence are coupled functions in whole-of-society models, because the same structures that enable participation also create exploitable seams.

Institutional learning and controlled feedback

Whole-of-society models require a mechanism for converting operational experience into updated procedures without leaking sensitive details. Learning is necessary because toolchains, target environments, and adversary behaviour change, and because coordination failures recur when they are not formalised into new rules. Structured planning artefacts and post-operation assessment concepts help bound what is evaluated and what is retained for future planning, which enables learning without requiring broad dissemination of sensitive operational detail (Huskaj and Blix, 2022).

The governance mechanisms specified above are operationalised through the validated four-step planning model used earlier in this book, which is employed in the next section solely as a workflow frame for locating deconfliction points and cross-sector interfaces (Huskaj and Iftimie, 2020; Huskaj and Blix, 2022).

The workflow is the operational expression of the governance mechanisms above, because it locates authority, evidence, and deconfliction in a sequence that can be audited.

6.5 Policy-to-Payload Workflow and Deconfliction

This section specifies how whole-of-society organising principles are translated into a mission workflow that preserves unity of authority while allowing distributed competence to contribute to planning, preparation, and assurance. The purpose is to locate (i) where cross-sector participation is defensible and capability-relevant, and (ii) where deconfliction must be resolved as an authorisation-relevant gate, because multi-actor participation increases the probability that parallel activities collide across intelligence collection, access operations, payload engineering, and defensive network operations (Joint Chiefs of Staff, 2018; Huskaj and Blix, 2022). The implication is that deconfliction cannot be treated as a late-stage administrative check; it must be embedded early enough to shape target selection, sequencing, and evidentiary thresholds for authorisation.

Deconfliction is treated here as a control function that protects perishable access and constrains escalation exposure. The mechanism is that the same infrastructure can simultaneously host intelligence collection, defensive remediation, and offensive preparation,

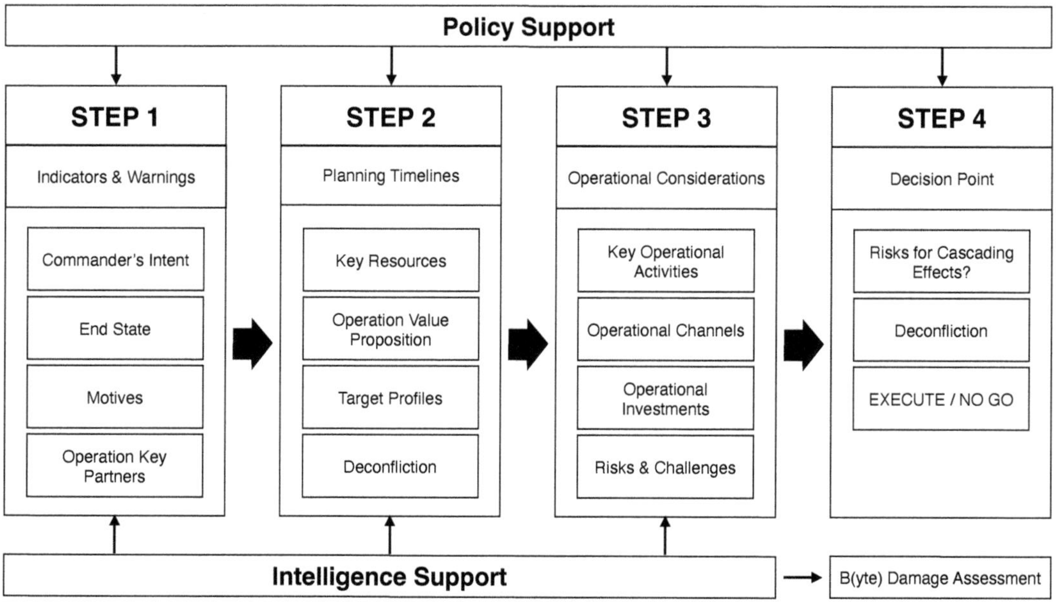

FIGURE 6.1
A validated four-step model for translating policy intent into technical effect.

meaning that uncoordinated activity can invalidate access conditions, expose tooling, or trigger political externalities through unintended collateral or cascading effects (Joint Chiefs of Staff, 2018). The implication is that the policy-to-payload workflow is required not only to generate tempo, but to preserve boundedness, accountability, and predictability when society-wide resources are mobilised.

The section uses the validated four-step model as an analytic template for locating authority, whole-of-society interfaces, and deconfliction gates across the sequence from intent to decision (Huskaj and Iftimie, 2020; Huskaj and Blix, 2022). The model is employed here as an organising device rather than a claim of universality. Its value is that it renders the policy-to-technical translation legible as a sequence of checkpoints that can be governed under democratic oversight.

A validated four-step model for translating policy intent into technical effect

The validated model in Figure 6.1 structures OCO into four steps—Indicators & Warnings, Planning Timelines, Operational Considerations, and Decision Point—under continuous policy and intelligence support (Huskaj and Iftimie, 2020; Huskaj and Blix, 2022). In the context of whole-of-society organisation, the relevant question is not the internal logic of each step as such, but where cross-sector participation can increase decision quality without dispersing authority, and where deconfliction must be treated as a binding constraint before planning hardens into sunk cost.

Step 1: Indicators & Warnings (partner selection and classification boundary-setting).

Step 1 fixes intent, end state, and key partners, which becomes operationally constraining because it defines what must be achieved and which relationships must be protected through coordination (Huskaj and Blix, 2022). For whole-of-society models, the critical decision at this stage is participation design: which non-government actors may contribute to preparation and assurance, and under what clearance and compartmentation conditions. The implication is that early partner selection reduces later pressure to improvise information-sharing arrangements under time constraints.

Step 2: Planning Timelines (deconfliction as a binding planning constraint).

Step 2 translates intent into a target-development and resourcing problem and treats deconfliction as a named planning element, because access and tool exposure are shared constraints across intelligence and operations (Huskaj and Blix, 2022). Whole-of-society participation is most defensible here when it is bounded to target profiling, dependency mapping, and verification design, because these inputs increase fidelity regarding configurations and operational dependencies that are decisive for controlled targeting (Joint Chiefs of Staff, 2018). The deconfliction gate at Step 2 is therefore the point where off-limits environments and sequencing restrictions are fixed, so that later preparation does not proceed on incompatible assumptions.

Step 3: Operational Considerations (assurance production under joint constraints).

Step 3 converts the plan into a controllable capability through operational preparation, risk assessment, and assurance practices (Huskaj and Blix, 2022). In whole-of-society designs, this is where interface risk becomes concrete: shared ranges, shared toolchains, and shared telemetry can create collisions in operational security, while parallel defensive activity can expose offensive preparation patterns. The implication is that Step 3 requires explicit scheduling rules and information-handling constraints for joint testbeds, because these constraints preserve need-to-know boundaries while still enabling the production of authorisation-relevant evidence on boundedness, reversibility, and cascading-effects exposure (Joint Chiefs of Staff, 2018; Huskaj and Blix, 2022).

Step 4: Decision Point (authorisation anchored in accumulated evidence).

Step 4 is the authorisation gate where leaders evaluate readiness, deconfliction status, and cascading-effects exposure before issuing an execute or no-go decision (Huskaj and Blix, 2022). The control claim is that deconfliction can be resolved at Step 2 and evidenced through Step 3 preparation, so that the Decision Point is not a venue for late-stage reconciliation but an evidence-based judgement about whether the intended effect remains controllable under realistic uncertainty (Huskaj and Blix, 2022). The implication is that whole-of-society participation contributes most when it increases the quality of decision-relevant evidence upstream, not when it expands discretion at the point of authorisation.

Finally, the four-step sequence clarifies scope. It supports pre-execution planning and preparation and produces decision-ready representations, but it does not substitute for real-time execution control, which depends on continuous monitoring and operational judgement during the mission (Huskaj and Blix, 2022).

6.6 Implementation Roadmap and Measurement

This section provides an implementation roadmap for a whole-of-society approach to organising OCOs, while keeping the analysis at the level of institutional design rather than administrative programme management. The purpose is to specify how the partnership configurations and governance mechanisms identified earlier can be sequenced into a credible national capability, because whole-of-society integration generates operational value only when authority, deconfliction, and assurance practices are institutionalised rather than improvised (Huskaj and Axelsson, 2023; Huskaj, 2025*b*). The roadmap is therefore a phased logic of institutionalisation: each phase establishes preconditions that reduce loss-of-control risk, protect intelligence equities, and preserve legal and ethical constraints as operational requirements rather than after-action considerations (Huskaj and Blix, 2022; Huskaj, 2025*b*).

The phases are an analytical sequencing device, not a proposed national programme. The roadmap also aligns with the chapter's MLMD framing. Strategic-level work concentrates on political authorisation, mandate clarity, and deterrence signalling, because credible OCO depends on an adversary perceiving both capacity and authorised willingness (Government, 2024*a*). Operational-level work concentrates on governance arrangements, planning processes, and deconfliction routines, because distributed expertise becomes operational options only when roles, authorities, and sequencing rules are explicit (Huskaj and Iftimie, 2020; Huskaj and Blix, 2022). Tactical-level work concentrates on assurance, verification, and bounded payload logic, because controllability under uncertainty determines whether planned effects remain discriminating and reversible in practice (Huskaj and Blix, 2022; Granåsen et al., 2019). Across phases, measurement is treated as an instrument of governance: indicators are selected to test whether the system is becoming more controllable, more disciplined, and more predictable under stress.

Phase 1—Foundational Alignment (Year 1)

Phase 1 establishes the legal-political and organisational preconditions for whole-of-society participation without yet assuming that participation must extend to operational execution. The sequencing matters because many cyberliterate countries organise security and crisis-management responsibilities across multiple agencies with legally bounded mandates, which creates predictable fragmentation when cyber activity cuts across institutional boundaries. This fragmentation risk becomes sharper when external competence is introduced into sensitive workflows, because additional actors increase the number of interfaces where authority, information handling, and timing can diverge (Huskaj and Axelsson, 2023). The immediate aim is therefore to reduce ambiguity regarding who may authorise what, who may know what, and who carries responsibility for effects.

At the strategic level, Phase 1 can formalise a shared governmental interpretation of OCO authorisation and control. In many cyberliterate states, OCO are treated as a government-authorised military capability supported by intelligence, and Phase 1 operationalises that premise into an explicit authorisation grammar: defined triggers for option development, defined cautions for escalation assessment, and a defined routing of decisions into executive-level authority (Huskaj and Axelsson, 2023). The point is not to publish thresholds, but to ensure that the internal system can translate political intent into bounded operational parameters and a documented decision trail.

At the operational level, Phase 1 can establish a standing deconfliction and coordination routine across the institutions that sit at the centre of a cyberliterate state's cyber security system: the armed forces, signals intelligence (SIGINT) and security services, and the civilian authorities responsible for incident response and national resilience. The reason to start here is that whole-of-society integration fails first through interference: duplicated tasking, inadvertent exposure of access paths, and timing conflicts between intelligence collection and action (Huskaj, 2025*b*). A minimal viable design is therefore a shared operational picture for sensitive cyber activities, paired with a defined mechanism for adjudicating trade-offs when intelligence equities and operational imperatives diverge.

At the tactical level, Phase 1 can treat assurance rules as entry conditions for any later integration. The validated planning model emphasises that reversibility, cascading-effects assessment, and verification in test environments shape the decision to authorise execution (Huskaj and Iftimie, 2020; Huskaj and Blix, 2022). Phase 1 therefore institutionalises two constraints: (i) capabilities must be testable in controlled environments before they can be proposed as executable options, and (ii) operational participation by external actors must be bounded by information-handling rules, compartmentalisation, and counterintelligence hygiene designed for offensive contexts (Huskaj, 2025*b*).

Measurement in Phase 1 can assess governance readiness rather than operational output. The appropriate indicators test whether the system can make disciplined decisions under uncertainty: whether roles and mandates are documented, whether deconfliction routines are used rather than bypassed, whether clearance and vetting processes exist for any external participation, and whether the authorisation path produces auditable traces of proportionality and necessity reasoning consistent with the ethical constraints developed in Chapter 5 (Huskaj, 2025*b*; USAF LeMay Center, 2023). The implication is that Phase 1 is successful if it creates a stable perimeter for later capability growth.

Phase 2—Capability Development and Structured Integration (Years 2–3)

Phase 2 develops capability through controlled integration, where the central design choice is to expand participation in ways that increase competence while keeping authority centralised. This matters because whole-of-society designs can create capacity without creating control, and in offensive contexts capacity without control produces escalation exposure, legal uncertainty, and intelligence loss (Huskaj, 2025*b*). Phase 2 therefore treats integration as a function of defined roles and bounded interfaces, not as a generalised expansion of collaboration.

At the operational level, Phase 2 can institutionalise joint planning and preparation functions that link intelligence, target development, and operational design. Military cyber doctrine treats timely intelligence, operational preparation of the environment (OPE), and deconfliction as prerequisites for OCO, and many cyberliterate states rely on close integration between defence and intelligence organisations to provide planning support, access positioning, and technical foundations (Joint Chiefs of Staff, 2018). Phase 2 therefore concentrates on standing planning cells and liaison structures that permit rapid option development without relying on ad hoc coordination.

At the tactical level, Phase 2 can concentrate on testable capability development and repeatable rehearsal. The Cyberia validation and the broader cyber-range literature emphasise that rehearsal environments make operational behaviour observable and support verification of bounded effects (Huskaj and Blix, 2022; Granåsen et al., 2019). This phase therefore expands range-based practices as governance instruments: tool testing, payload-behaviour verification, and red-team challenge processes that force teams to account for failure modes, discovery likelihood, and unintended propagation. The point is not to pursue technical detail in the monograph, but to make assurance a standing institutional practice rather than a situational judgement.

Structured whole-of-society integration in Phase 2 can prioritise contribution types that remain compatible with constitutional constraints and democratic legitimacy. In practice, this means emphasising roles that strengthen planning, testing, analytic baselining, and training pipelines, while treating private-sector execution as an exceptional arrangement that requires explicit legal commissioning and supervision logic (Huskaj, 2025*b*). The reason is that delegating coercive action to private actors can create ambiguity about responsibility and legal accountability and can expose civilians to adversary retaliation, which constitutes a legal and ethical constraint rather than a design preference (Huskaj, 2025*b*). Where external competence is integrated, it can be incorporated through mechanisms that preserve unity of command, such as secondments, reserve constructs, or tightly scoped contracts that specify authority, liability, and information-handling obligations.

Measurement in Phase 2 can shift from governance readiness to capability maturity while still treating outcome claims cautiously. Indicators can test whether integration improves the quality and speed of option generation without degrading control. Appropriate measures include the time-to-produce an operational option from an agreed intelligence requirement; the proportion of candidate capabilities that pass verification gates in test environments; evidence that deconfliction decisions are made early in planning rather than at the authorisation gate; and the extent to which legal-ethical constraints are translated into operational parameters that engineers and planners can apply consistently (Huskaj and Iftimie, 2020; Huskaj and Blix, 2022; Huskaj, 2025*b*). The implication is that Phase 2 is successful if it increases disciplined capacity while preserving the strategic premise that authority remains centralised.

Phase 3—Full Integration and Operational Expansion (Years 4–5)

Phase 3 expands from development and rehearsal into sustained operational readiness, where the key question becomes whether the system can operate at tempo without sacrificing deconfliction, discipline, and assurance. The causal risk is that greater tempo increases the probability of interference: internal collisions between intelligence and operations and external collisions with allied activities and shared dependencies (Huskaj, 2025*b*). Phase 3 therefore treats operational expansion as an interoperability and control problem as much as a capacity problem.

At the strategic level, Phase 3 can integrate EU and NATO constraints into a whole-of-society design. Many cyberliterate countries operate inside EU legislative and crisis-management frameworks and within NATO's collective-defence context, which means offensive capability must be organised so it can contribute to allied objectives without creating releasability failures, coordination delays, or attribution ambiguity (Government, 2024*a*). The practical implication is that authorisation and deconfliction routines must be capable of handling multinational dependencies: when intelligence is jointly produced, when targets are allied-relevant, and when operations risk spillover into shared infrastructure. This does not require identical structures across states, but it does require a national model that can interface predictably with allied planning rhythms and coordination requirements.

At the operational level, Phase 3 can formalise a national system for prioritising and adjudicating intelligence–operations trade-offs. The literature emphasises that intelligence access is perishable and that action can burn collection, yet delayed action can permit adversary harm to continue (Huskaj, 2025*b*). Phase 3 therefore requires an explicit decision routine that resolves precedence under defined conditions, because otherwise those trade-offs will be negotiated informally, which increases the probability of institutional conflict and operational leakage. The whole-of-society contribution in this phase is primarily to improve option breadth and verification capacity, not to fragment operational authority.

At the tactical level, Phase 3 can treat operational assurance as an operational tempo enabler. The validated model's logic is that decision gates depend on accumulated evidence: intelligence quality, preparation, and verification of bounded effects (Huskaj and Blix, 2022). Under higher tempo, this implies standardised verification artefacts, repeatable test protocols, and documentation practices that allow decision-makers to compare options and risks without depending on personality-driven persuasion. The implication is that Phase 3 maturity is visible when the organisation can say "no-go" for technical-assurance reasons without collapsing the strategic intent to act.

Measurement in Phase 3 can remain modest in claims about deterrence while still testing operational responsiveness and control. Indicators can include mobilisation time for joint planning teams, the stability of deconfliction outcomes (measured as avoided internal collisions or late-stage rework), and the reliability of assurance gates (measured as detected failures before execution rather than after) (Huskaj and Blix, 2022; Granåsen et al., 2019). Strategic-level evaluation can use proxies rather than declarative deterrence claims: assessments of adversary adaptation, shifts in observed operational patterns, and allied demand for national participation as an indicator of perceived competence and predictability (Government, 2024*a*). The implication is that Phase 3 succeeds when a state can generate and sustain controlled operational options at tempo, while remaining interoperable with allied frameworks.

Phase 4—Sustainment, Adaptation, and Continuous Improvement (Year 5+)

Phase 4 concerns long-term sustainment under continuous technological change and adversary adaptation. The reason sustainment is analytically distinct is that offensive capability depreciates: access decays, vulnerabilities are patched, platforms change, and operational techniques become detectable once reused (Huskaj and Blix, 2022). A whole-of-society model is therefore valuable in Phase 4 primarily because it provides a national renewal mechanism, where research environments, industrial competence, and state operational requirements can be aligned into a repeatable pipeline rather than treated as episodic collaboration.

At the strategic level, Phase 4 can stabilise democratic legitimacy through bounded oversight that matches the sensitivity of offensive activity. Oversight is not an external add-on; it is a credibility condition, because political authorisation and public trust constrain whether offensive options are politically usable under crisis pressure (Government, 2024*a*; Huskaj and Axelsson, 2023). The practical design requirement is therefore an oversight model that can review compliance, proportionality reasoning, and mandate adherence without forcing disclosure that would compromise sources, methods, or allied equities. In whole-of-society designs, this requirement becomes sharper because private incentives and public legitimacy can diverge unless governance is explicit (Huskaj, 2025*b*).

At the operational level, Phase 4 can treat organisational learning as a controlled process. Lessons learned in offensive contexts cannot be disseminated as ordinary best practice, because dissemination can reveal capability and targeting preferences. The appropriate mechanism is therefore structured after-action review with controlled distribution, coupled to doctrine and training updates that preserve secrecy while still preventing institutional amnesia. Cyber ranges and repeat exercises provide a governance-compatible means to rehearse updated techniques and evaluate decision routines under stress without requiring operational disclosure (Granåsen et al., 2019; Huskaj and Blix, 2022).

At the tactical level, Phase 4 emphasises continuous assurance and counterintelligence integration. Increasing the number of participants and interfaces increases the attack surface for insider threats and external compromise, and offensive toolchains are themselves high-value targets (Huskaj, 2025*b*). The implication is that sustainment depends on disciplined compartmentalisation, continuous vetting where legally permissible, and defensive monitoring across partner environments that are part of the offensive preparation pipeline. This phase also consolidates the ethical constraints from Chapter 5 into engineering routines: reversibility assumptions must be tested, civilian exposure must be treated as a design constraint, and uncertainty must be documented rather than rhetorically minimised (USAF LeMay Center, 2023; Huskaj and Blix, 2022).

Measurement in Phase 4 can prioritise resilience of the capability pipeline rather than the volume of operations. Indicators can include: the renewal rate of validated capabilities (without exposing their nature), the stability of recruitment and retention in key roles, the frequency with which assurance gates detect failure modes before execution, and the reliability of deconfliction routines when partners, platforms, and allied dependencies change (Huskaj, 2025*b*; Huskaj and Blix, 2022). Where strategic signalling is used, measurement can assess whether signalling remains consistent with authorised capability and legal constraints, because signalling that outpaces institutional control creates credibility risk rather than deterrence value (Government, 2024*a*). The implication is that Phase 4 succeeds when a cyberliterate state can sustain a controlled, legally bounded, and interoperable offensive capability as a standing national function, rather than as an episodic project.

In sum, the roadmap treats implementation as the progressive institutionalisation of control. Phase 1 establishes mandate clarity, deconfliction routines, and assurance entry conditions. Phase 2 develops verified capabilities and bounded integration mechanisms. Phase 3 expands operational readiness while embedding allied interoperability constraints. Phase 4 sustains capability renewal, democratic legitimacy, and continuous assurance under change. This sequencing supports the chapter's core claim: whole-of-society participation strengthens offensive capacity only when governance mechanisms preserve unity of command, protect intelligence equities, and translate legal and ethical constraints into operational practice (Huskaj and Axelsson, 2023; Huskaj, 2025*b*; Huskaj and Blix, 2022). Chapter 7 then uses empirical cases to illustrate how these control conditions shape outcomes under time pressure, dependency complexity, and uncertainty (Granåsen et al., 2019; Huskaj and Blix, 2022).

The risk categories that follow can be read as failure modes of the roadmap when these control conditions are weak, because each phase assumes that mandates, deconfliction routines, and assurance gates remain enforceable under time pressure and cross-sector participation.

6.7 Risks and Escalation Management

This section examines the structural risks and escalation dynamics that arise when OCO are organised through whole-of-society arrangements. The organising claim is that distributing capability development and support across government, private industry, and academia increases access to scarce expertise, yet it also increases the number of decision-points, interfaces, and information pathways where control can be lost. This matters because OCO depend on fragile access conditions and time-sensitive intelligence, meaning that governance weaknesses do not remain administrative; they shape operational feasibility and political exposure. The implication is that whole-of-society OCO requires escalation management as an institutional design problem rather than as a purely technical safeguard.

The analysis extends Chapter 5's ethical constraints into an organisational setting. Chapter 5 treated legality, proportionality, reversibility, and anticipatory governance as decision criteria that bound vulnerability exploitation and payload design. In a whole-of-society model, these criteria must be translated into repeatable organisational controls—authorisation gates, deconfliction routines, assurance practices, and oversight—because civilian participation expands both the opportunity surface for innovation and the risk surface for unintended consequences. The implication is that ethical and legal constraints only become operational constraints when they are embedded in governance routines and enforced through accountable authorities.

Risk Category 1: Loss of control through distributed participation

A first risk category concerns loss of governmental control when actors outside the standard chain of command contribute to planning, capability development, or execution support. The mechanism is organisational distance: as additional institutions receive partial tasking, partial information, or partial access to tooling, the lead agency's ability to maintain unity of intent weakens unless authority and responsibility are explicitly centralised. This risk is amplified in cyberspace because small deviations in timing, access management, or tooling changes can expose operations, degrade intelligence positioning, or create outcomes beyond the authorised end state. The implication is that distributed execution cannot be allowed to imply distributed authority.

Loss of control also manifests as mandate drift, where operational objectives expand as technical opportunities emerge. This is a predictable failure mode because vulnerability discovery and access operations tend to reveal adjacent targets, additional privileges, and alternative effect pathways. In the absence of strict authorisation rules, the operational community can rationalise incremental expansion as "opportunistic efficiency," even when it changes the political meaning of the action. The implication is that whole-of-society participation requires explicit "scope locks" that bind operational action to pre-authorised targets, pre-authorised effect types, and pre-authorised collateral tolerance, with re-authorisation required for scope change (Huskaj, 2025*b*).

Governance design mitigates this risk by specifying a single accountable authorising authority and by separating technical contribution from execute authority. Technical partners may develop payload components, test exploit chains, or provide system-specific expertise, yet the right to activate operational effects must remain within the responsible state authority. This separation matters because it preserves a single political decision-point where intent, legal basis, and escalation exposure can be evaluated. The implication is that whole-of-society models remain viable only if the organisational architecture enforces a strict difference between "contributing capability" and "triggering effect."

Risk Category 2: Deconfliction failure and intelligence–operations interference

A second risk category concerns deconfliction failure across intelligence collection, operational preparation, and offensive action. The mechanism is shared dependence on access and secrecy. Intelligence services may maintain persistent access to adversary systems for collection purposes, while offensive units may require time-bound disruptive action that increases discovery risk. When additional civilian partners contribute—through threat hunting, vulnerability research, or range-based validation—the probability of self-inflicted interference increases because more actors can inadvertently change target conditions, burn access, or reveal operational patterns through routine defensive activity. The implication is that deconfliction is not a late-stage coordination check; it is a core governance function that decides which national interest takes precedence under time pressure.

The validated four-step model already positions deconfliction as a planning constraint rather than as a final administrative barrier. The empirical result from the Cyberia validation is that additional deconfliction at the decision gate was unnecessary when deconfliction had been handled earlier in planning, indicating that sequencing rules must be applied before capability work and access operations harden into sunk costs (Huskaj and Blix, 2022; Huskaj and Iftimie, 2020). The implication is that whole-of-society arrangements can treat deconfliction as a design variable that shapes the mission timeline, the division of labour, and the allowable technical pathways.

Doctrine strengthens this point by emphasising that the pace of cyberspace operations requires coordination and deconfliction in advance and that deconfliction depends on detailed analysis of both capabilities and the target environment to avoid unintended consequences (Joint Chiefs of Staff, 2018). This requirement becomes sharper in many cyber-literate states because intelligence, military, and civilian actors often hold different equities in the same infrastructure, including foreign-intelligence priorities, domestic resilience concerns, and commercial dependencies. The implication is that deconfliction must be institutionalised as a continuous process that maintains a current register of equities, target restrictions, and access conditions across the relevant community.

One generic mitigation discussed in doctrine and prior practice is a centralised deconfliction function that maintains visibility of sensitive equities and adjudicates sequencing when multiple actors operate against overlapping environments. Precedent exists in earlier computer network operations practice, where intelligence community organisations maintained a shared register to deconflict exploitation and attack activities. The organisational principle is that any actor—governmental or cleared non-governmental—who intends to touch an operationally relevant target must trigger a deconfliction check, because "access is critical" and is perishable under interference (Joint Chiefs of Staff, 2018; Huskaj and Blix, 2022). The implication is that whole-of-society OCO requires a common situational picture of "who is where" in cyberspace that is treated as operational infrastructure, not as optional coordination.

Risk Category 3: Technical uncertainty, capability assurance, and cascading effects

A third risk category concerns technical uncertainty and the possibility of unintended secondary or tertiary effects. The mechanism is the combination of complex dependencies and incomplete knowledge. Cyberspace targets are embedded in layered systems, supply chains, and shared services, which means that payload behaviour can propagate through relationships that are not visible in the planning stage. Doctrine defines cascading effects as effects that can move laterally to peer systems or upward to higher-level systems, including through links "not evident to the planner" (Joint Chiefs of Staff, 2018). The implication is that whole-of-society participation increases the number of components and dependencies that must be understood, because partner-provided infrastructure, partner-provided tooling, and partner-provided knowledge may each introduce additional coupling.

Capability assurance is therefore not a technical luxury but an escalation control. The validated framework emphasises that decision-makers require accumulated assurance about capability behaviour, including reversibility and cascading-risk exposure, and that an inability to answer these questions can block execution through a no-go outcome (Huskaj and Blix, 2022). The mechanism is straightforward: if planners cannot specify how an effect is bounded, they cannot credibly claim proportionality, reversibility, or political controllability. The implication is that whole-of-society OCO can invest in repeatable evaluation practices—range testing, dependency mapping, and controlled rehearsals—because distributed innovation without verification produces escalation risk.

Reversibility is a central design variable because it shapes the decision-maker's ability to terminate effects once political conditions change. In doctrinal terms, reversibility concerns the degree of control over the duration of effects and distinguishes between operator-controlled and non-operator-controlled outcomes (Joint Chiefs of Staff, 2018). The Cyberia validation illustrates why this distinction matters: the assessed absence of cascading effects and the availability of reversibility were treated as decisive inputs at the decision gate, enabling authorisation in a scenario where the political and legal officer roles were explicitly represented (Huskaj and Blix, 2022). The implication is that "bounded payload logic" becomes an escalation-management mechanism only when it is demonstrated under conditions that approximate the target environment.

Whole-of-society models can support assurance if they use civilian competence to expand testing capacity and analytic depth, yet the governance condition remains: testing must be conducted under secure rules, with configuration control and accountability for toolchain changes. The reason is that shared development environments and shared ranges can become sources of error propagation if baseline configurations drift or if validation results are not reproducible. The implication is that governance must treat the test environment as part of the operational system, including access control, auditability, and a disciplined process for promoting code or payload components from "lab" to "operational candidate."

Risk Category 4: Civilian participation, legal exposure, and ethical vulnerability

A fourth risk category concerns legal and ethical vulnerability created when civilians participate in offensive operations or in direct operational support. The mechanism is ambiguous status and ambiguous liability. Whole-of-society approaches deliberately integrate non-state expertise, yet this integration can create questions about responsibility attribution, lawful authority, and the legal status of individuals who contribute to coercive action. This risk increases when operations approach thresholds where international humanitarian law concepts become politically salient, because adversaries may interpret civilian participation as escalatory, illegitimate, or as justification for retaliation against non-military entities. The implication is that legal clarity is not merely compliance; it is part of escalation management because it shapes how adversaries and domestic audiences interpret the legitimacy of action.

A governance response is to centralise legal basis and to use contractual and organisational forms that incorporate civilian contributors into clearly bounded roles. One approach is to restrict private and academic participation primarily to capability development, verification, training, and analytic support, while limiting execution to state personnel operating under explicit mandates. Where direct operational support is required, temporary reserve-like incorporation mechanisms can clarify authority, duty status, and information-handling rules. The implication is that whole-of-society OCO can use civilian participation to expand competence without normalising ambiguous coercive authority outside the state.

This risk category links directly to Chapter 5's emphasis on proportionality and civilian harm minimisation. In a whole-of-society model, proportionality becomes harder to evaluate because the operational system includes more infrastructure and more actors, increasing the probability that a "small" technical action has larger social consequences. The implication is that ethical review and legal review can not be parallel advisory functions; they can be embedded as mandatory inputs at defined stages of the policy-to-payload workflow, including at least one formal decision gate before capability activation (Huskaj and Blix, 2022; Huskaj and Iftimie, 2020).

Risk Category 5: Alliance interoperability, multinational equities, and signalling hazards

A fifth risk category concerns alliance interoperability and the escalation hazards created by multinational dependencies. In many cyberliterate countries, deeper alliance integration increases the probability that national OCO will be planned, coordinated, or sequenced alongside allied cyber activity and wider joint operations. Doctrine notes that joint forces will often operate as part of multinational coalitions and that overlaps between global and theatre missions in cyberspace require close coordination with allied and interagency partners (Joint Chiefs of Staff, 2018). The implication is that whole-of-society models must be designed to interoperate with allied deconfliction practices, classification regimes, and operational timelines.

The mechanism of escalation here is misinterpretation through signalling and sequencing. An action intended as limited denial can be interpreted by an adversary as preparation for broader attack if it coincides with allied posture changes, kinetic deployments, or information operations. Conversely, allied partners may judge a whole-of-society model as insufficiently controlled if roles, decision rights, and accountability are not legible under shared standards. The implication is that escalation management requires not only technical bounding but also deliberate sequencing across national and allied planning cycles.

A mitigation is to separate national whole-of-society collaboration from multinational execution interfaces. In practice, this means that many cyberliterate countries can use whole-of-society structures to build tools, train teams, and generate planning options, yet present operational choices to allies through a narrow and controlled interface where decision rights, target constraints, and assurance evidence are explicit. The implication is that interoperability is improved when partners see stable organisational primitives: a clear authorising authority, a defined deconfliction mechanism, and a transparent assurance logic for bounding effects.

Risk Category 6: Insider threats, information leakage, and capability compromise

A sixth risk category concerns insider threats and compromise risks created by expanded participation. The mechanism is simple arithmetic: as more individuals and organisations gain access to sensitive information, the probability of inadvertent leakage, intentional disclosure, or adversary recruitment increases. The Cyberia validation explicitly modelled an insider threat role in the scenario design, underscoring that offensive planning must assume adversary intelligence pressure and compromise attempts (Huskaj and Blix, 2022). The implication is that whole-of-society OCO must pair integration with counterintelligence and security engineering, rather than treating these as separate organisational silos.

Capability compromise is especially costly in OCO because the disclosure of exploits, payload logic, and operational infrastructure can eliminate future access opportunities and create blowback risk if adversaries repurpose the tools. Chapter 5's discussion of exploit retention and later misuse provides a concrete mechanism: once a high-value exploit escapes, patch availability does not translate into patch adoption, and the exploit can be used against civilian infrastructure at scale. The implication is that whole-of-society participation requires strict compartmentalisation, need-to-know enforcement, and continuous monitoring of partner environments, because the integration that accelerates innovation also widens the exposure surface.

A mitigation is to treat sensitive capabilities as "high-value capabilities with rapid depreciation" governed by lifecycle rules. These rules include: (i) compartmented access and controlled distribution; (ii) audit logs and configuration management for toolchains; (iii) mandatory reassessment of continued retention as system equities change; and (iv) post-operation review that updates both technical mitigations and governance assumptions. The implication is that security governance must be designed to survive routine personnel rotation and institutional churn, because whole-of-society models are sustained through long-term relationships rather than one-off projects.

Escalation management as a multi-level control system

Escalation management can be treated as a multi-level control system spanning the strategic, operational, and tactical levels of the MLMD framework. At the strategic level, escalation management requires explicit political intent, defined thresholds for acceptable exposure, and a legal basis that frames action as authorised and bounded. At the operational level, escalation management requires deconfliction routines, sequencing rules, and assurance evidence that is legible to decision-makers. At the tactical level, escalation management requires payload design choices—reversibility, propagation limits, and operational security—backed by validation in controlled environments and disciplined execution control (Huskaj and Blix, 2022; Joint Chiefs of Staff, 2018). The implication is that escalation management fails when any one level treats its responsibility as "someone else's problem."

The four-step policy-to-payload planning sequence provides a concrete place to embed escalation controls. Indicators and Warnings define what the operation is allowed to optimise for, because they establish end state and risk tolerance. Planning Timelines embed deconfliction early, preventing sunk-cost dynamics from pressuring decision-makers to approve marginal operations. Operational Considerations impose assurance requirements on capability behaviour, including cascading-effects analysis and reversibility assessment. Decision Point functions as an authorisation gate that can be passed only when accumulated evidence supports bounded effects and when deconfliction and legal review have been completed (Huskaj and Blix, 2022; Huskaj and Iftimie, 2020). The implication is that escalation management becomes credible when it is proceduralised into decision gates that are difficult to bypass.

Doctrine reinforces that deconfliction and coordination in cyberspace requires close analysis of capabilities and the target environment and must occur in advance of execution to prevent unintended consequences (Joint Chiefs of Staff, 2018). For whole-of-society OCO, this doctrinal requirement implies that escalation management must be institutionalised as an always-on coordination function, not as a crisis-only activity. In practical terms, this supports the case for a standing coordination body or centre that maintains target equities, tracks planned activities, and enforces notification rules across participating entities. The implication is that escalation management is inseparable from governance; it is governance applied under uncertainty.

Synthesis and transition

Synthesising across categories, the risks of whole-of-society OCO do not arise because cross-sector participation is inherently destabilising. The risks arise because distributed capability development increases the number of interfaces where authority, information, and timing can diverge. This divergence becomes politically salient in cyberspace because unintended consequences can propagate through interconnected systems, and because adversaries interpret actions through uncertain attribution and strategic signalling. The implication is that many cyberliterate countries face a central organisational challenge: to design whole-of-society structures that increase competence without increasing ambiguity about who decides, who is responsible, and how effects are bounded.

Chapter 7 builds on this logic by examining case material that exposes these risk pathways under empirical constraints. The purpose of the transition is to move from organisational design principles to observed behaviour in scenarios and incidents, including how test environments shape assurance, how deconfliction is handled under time pressure, and how cascading-effects risk is interpreted when decision-makers face uncertainty about target dependencies and propagation boundaries (Huskaj and Blix, 2022; Granåsen et al., 2019).

6.8 Conclusions

This chapter examined how a cyberliterate state can organise OCO through a whole-of-society approach that mobilises competence distributed across government, industry, and academia while preserving unity of command, legal accountability, and operational security. The starting point was a distributional problem: the resources required for vulnerability discovery, capability development, verification, and sustained readiness are not concentrated inside the state. The implication is that organisational design is a capability determinant, because capability depends on how dispersed resources are aligned and controlled across institutional boundaries (Huskaj and Axelsson, 2023; Huskaj, 2024*c*).

The chapter separated *partnership configurations* from *governance mechanisms*. Configurations specify what a cyberliterate state builds—an integrated state-led capability with controlled civilian incorporation, planning and deconfliction hubs, selective commissioning for bounded mission types, research and talent pipelines, and shared training and testing infrastructures. Mechanisms specify how these arrangements remain governable in practice—mandate clarity, intelligence–operations fusion, bounded role design, commissioning and liability instruments, deconfliction authority, assurance practices, and security controls. The causal claim is that configurations mobilise actors, but mechanisms determine whether mobilisation produces controlled capability or fragments authority and increases exposure (Huskaj, 2024*a*; Huskaj, 2025*b*).

Across the MLMD levels, the chapter treated whole-of-society organisation as governance of a socio-technical system rather than aggregation of tools. At the strategic level, centralised political authorisation and explicit mission boundaries were treated as preconditions for credible use, because deterrence signalling depends on an adversary perceiving authorised willingness in addition to technical capacity. At the operational level, planning and deconfliction were treated as access-protection functions, because distributed expertise becomes operational options only when decision rights, sequencing rules, and information-handling constraints are explicit. At the tactical level, assurance was treated as an evidence requirement, because controllability under uncertainty is the condition under which effects remain bounded and politically governable (Huskaj and Blix, 2022; Joint Chiefs of Staff, 2018).

The policy-to-payload workflow clarified where whole-of-society participation adds value and where it must remain bounded. By using a validated four-step planning model as a scaffold, the chapter located cross-sector contribution upstream of the decision gate—target profiling, dependency analysis, verification design, and rehearsal—while keeping execute authority and time-sensitive activation decisions inside the responsible state chain of command (Huskaj and Iftimie, 2020; Huskaj and Blix, 2022). The implication is that whole-of-society integration supports capability when it increases the quality of decision-relevant evidence rather than dispersing coercive authority.

Finally, the chapter treated escalation management as an institutional design problem. Distributed participation expands innovation capacity, yet it also expands the number of interfaces where authority, timing, and information handling can diverge, and divergence is politically salient because cyberspace effects can propagate through dependencies that are not evident to planners (Joint Chiefs of Staff, 2018). The implication is that legality, proportionality reasoning, boundedness, and reversibility must be embedded in authorisation gates, deconfliction routines, and assurance practices, because these mechanisms operationalise the ethical constraints developed in Chapter 5 as enforceable control conditions (USAF LeMay Center, 2023; Huskaj and Blix, 2022; Huskaj, 2025*b*).

Taken together, the conclusion is conditional: many cyberliterate countries can expand offensive capability and strengthen deterrence credibility only if they mobilise dispersed competence through controlled interfaces that preserve unity of authorisation, protect intelligence equities, and require test-derived evidence of bounded effects before execution (Huskaj and Axelsson, 2023; Huskaj, 2024*c*).

Decision Exercise: Organising Offensive Cyber Capability Through Whole-of-Society Integration

Scenario. A cyberliterate state faces a sustained campaign combining intrusion, data theft, and preparatory activity affecting services owned and operated largely outside government. The state has limited in-house offensive cyber capacity and relies on private operators and universities for key expertise, test environments, and visibility into dependencies. Political leaders request an option set within 10 days that can generate decision-ready offensive options while preserving unity of authorisation, rule-of-law oversight, operational security, and partner interoperability obligations. Agencies disagree on how far cross-sector participation can extend, and the intelligence community warns that uncoordinated defensive and investigative activity could compromise access positions.

Analytical question 1—Capability objective and participation boundary. State the capability objective for the next 90 days (option generation speed, assurance quality, access preservation, coordinated signalling, or a bounded combination). Define a participation boundary: which functions may involve non-government actors (training, testing, analytic support, tool validation, targeting dependency analysis), and which functions remain exclusively governmental (authorisation, execute decisions, sensitive source handling).

Analytical question 2—Partnership configuration choice. Select one organising configuration for the period:

- integrated government unit with cleared secondees,
- joint planning and deconfliction hub,
- research and talent pipeline with controlled access tiers,
- contracted support for bounded technical tasks under government supervision.

Specify one capability gain you expect and one loss-of-control risk created by your choice.

Analytical question 3—Governance controls under time pressure. Specify minimum governance controls required to operate the model:

- approval threshold for initiating option development and for execution,
- legal review and documentation requirement,
- information-handling model (need-to-know tiers; releasability rule),
- audit and logging standard for artefacts, tooling changes, and access to test environments.

Add one rule that prevents mandate drift when technical opportunity expands scope.

Analytical question 4—Deconfliction and IGL rule. Define a deconfliction mechanism that prevents interference between intelligence collection, defensive remediation, and offensive preparation. State one explicit IGL trigger that forces replanning or a pause, and explain how the trigger preserves political control.

Short task—MLMD mapping (one page). Create a 3-row mapping (Strategic / Operational / Tactical) listing:

1. the decision at each level,
2. the key dependency (authority and legitimacy; coordination and assurance; feasibility and boundedness),
3. one misalignment failure mode where cross-sector activity diverges from authorised intent.

Part III

Cyber Power in Practice

7

Case Studies and Practical Applications

This chapter uses empirical case material to demonstrate how OCO unfold as practical activity constrained by time compression, partial intelligence, and technical volatility. The purpose is to show how the book's causal claims account for observed operational trajectories, including how technical action can propagate beyond intended boundaries and how institutions attempt to preserve control under uncertainty. The chapter applies the Multi-Level Multi-Dimensional (MLMD) framework as an analytic coding frame that links political intent to operational design and tactical execution. OCO outcomes are shaped by vertical dependencies across levels and interaction effects across political, ethical, organisational, intelligence, and technical dimensions (Huskaj, 2024*c*).

The guiding question is: how do real-world and exercise-based cases illustrate the structural conditions under which OCO are planned and executed, and what do those conditions imply for maintaining alignment across the strategic–political, operational–ethical/intelligence, and tactical–technical layers specified in MLMD? The chapter treats the question causally. In cyberspace, small technical choices can generate disproportionate system effects because interdependence and automation can propagate outcomes faster than institutions can interpret and govern them. The implication is that empirical analysis must account for both upward propagation (tactical behaviour producing strategic consequences) and downward constraint (strategic intent delimiting permissible technical action).

Two cases are selected because each case isolates key mechanisms under different control conditions. WannaCry represents an uncontrolled, high-tempo incident in which automated propagation and uncertainty about intent and attribution compressed defensive decision cycles and produced cascading disruption across critical sectors (Huskaj and Iftimie, 2020). The cyber range scenario represents a controlled environment in which an offensive action is planned, authorised, rehearsed, and executed under explicit political constraints and structured intelligence support, thereby exposing the organisational and judgemental work required to translate intent into technical pathways (Huskaj and Blix, 2022). Together, the cases clarify a single control problem: WannaCry shows how technical dynamics can outrun institutional control, while the cyber range case shows which institutional practices are required when the purpose is to preserve control.

The chapter operationalises MLMD by tracing each case through a common three-level structure and by specifying the causal couplings between levels. At the strategic level, the analysis focuses on political purpose, risk tolerance, and thresholds, because these parameters determine what kinds of cyber effects can be authorised and how escalation risk is managed. At the operational level, the analysis focuses on intelligence integration, ethical judgement, and governance mechanisms, because these mechanisms translate political direction into a feasible concept of operation under uncertainty. At the tactical level, the analysis focuses on access vectors, exploit and payload behaviour, and environmental dependencies, because these factors determine what is technically possible and how effects propagate once execution begins. The structure is used consistently across both cases so that cross-case comparison becomes a comparison of mechanisms rather than a juxtaposition of narrative sequences.

DOI: 10.1201/9781003655183-7

The chapter proceeds as follows. Section 7.1 recaps the interpretive lenses used in the chapter—MLMD as the analytic architecture, the ambidextrous planning model as the planning lens, and anticipatory ethics as the evaluation lens for vulnerability retention, disclosure, and foreseeable spillover (Huskaj and Iftimie, 2020; Huskaj and Wilson, 2021; Huskaj, 2024*c*). Section 7.2 analyses WannaCry with emphasis on automation, incomplete situational awareness, and fragmented coordination under time pressure (Huskaj and Iftimie, 2020). Section 7.3 analyses the cyber range operation as scenario-based exercise material, focusing on intelligence preparation, planning timelines, deconfliction, and operator judgement under explicit political constraints (Huskaj and Blix, 2022). Section 7.4 conducts the cross-case synthesis. Section 7.5 analyses interaction with adjacent domains as specified in joint doctrine (Joint Chiefs of Staff, 2018; USAF LeMay Center, 2023). Section 7.6 derives practical lessons for capability development and governance. Section 7.7 concludes by linking the empirical implications to Chapter 8 (Huskaj, 2024*c*).

7.1 Frameworks in Context

This section specifies how the chapter reads the two cases. MLMD is used to structure inference across levels and dimensions so that claims about intent, control, and consequence remain traceable to observable dependencies. The ambidextrous planning model is used to interpret how authorisation, sequencing, and intelligence generation shape feasibility under uncertainty. Anticipatory ethics is used to evaluate decisions where operational advantage reallocates systemic risk through vulnerability retention, disclosure, and foreseeable spillover. Together, these lenses define the criteria applied in the case analyses and the cross-case synthesis.

MLMD as the coding scheme for the chapter

This chapter uses the MLMD framework as a coding scheme rather than as a re-statement of first principles. The two cases are read as sequences of interacting dependencies across the strategic, operational, and tactical levels and across political, ethical–intelligence, organisational, and technical dimensions, because observed cyber activity becomes analytically tractable only when the pathways of propagation are specified. This coding choice matters because the same technical event can either propagate upward into political crisis through organisational and ethical–intelligence mechanisms (as in uncontrolled incidents) or be driven downward from political intent through planning and control mechanisms (as in structured operations). The chapter therefore treats MLMD as the mapping device that keeps causal claims bounded: it anchors each inference about intent, control, and consequence in an explicit level–dimension linkage rather than in the surface appearance of the malware or the exploit chain (Huskaj, 2024*c*).

Ambidextrous planning model as the planning lens

The ambidextrous planning model functions as the planning lens for interpreting how cyber units translate intent into executable action under uncertainty. It is operationalised through four components—Indicators and Warnings, Planning Timelines, Operational Considerations, and the Decision Point—which together structure what must be known, when it must be known, and how residual uncertainty is accepted or mitigated before authorisation. The model matters in this chapter because it specifies the mechanism by which alignment and adaptation are reconciled: indicators and warnings define what triggers attention; timelines bound preparation and constrain reversibility; operational considerations force explicit treatment of dependencies such as access, tooling behaviour, deconfliction, and attribution risk; and the decision point concentrates authority by turning these assessments into a go/no-go judgement (Huskaj and Iftimie, 2020; Huskaj and Blix, 2022).

Anticipatory ethics as the evaluation lens

Anticipatory ethics functions as the evaluation lens for decisions where operational advantage is purchased through systemic exposure, particularly in the handling of undisclosed vulnerabilities. The core problem is an IGL dilemma: retention preserves access, operational optionality, and strategic leverage, while disclosure reduces systemic risk by enabling remediation across affected infrastructures, and the trade-off cannot be reduced to a technical optimisation because it reallocates risk across civilian, governmental, and allied systems (Huskaj and Wilson, 2021). Anticipatory ethics therefore requires forecasting foreseeable secondary and tertiary effects—including uncontrolled propagation, cascade pathways across interdependent services, and political blowback from collateral disruption—before capability deployment or continued withholding. In this chapter, that evaluative stance bounds the interpretation of both cases by treating "control" as a governance property: an operation is judged not only by intended effects but by whether the institutional arrangements for review, oversight, and consequence assessment are sufficient to justify exposing others to long-lived vulnerability risk (Huskaj and Wilson, 2021).

7.2 Case Study I: WannaCry

This section analyses WannaCry as an uncontrolled, high-tempo incident in which automated propagation compressed organisational decision cycles and produced cascading disruption across sectors. The analysis treats propagation dynamics, continuity constraints, and intelligence discontinuities as the operational mechanisms through which technical behaviour acquired strategic meaning. The purpose is to show how a capability that is bounded at the level of a technical exploit can become unbounded in consequence once embedded in interdependent infrastructure. The section closes by mapping the episode to MLMD to make explicit which level–dimension couplings account for the observed loss of control.

Operational trajectory and propagation dynamics

WannaCry (May 2017) is analytically useful because it shows how a capability that is tactically bounded in design can become operationally unbounded in consequence once it is embedded in globally interconnected infrastructure. The malware combined a ransomware payload with worm-like propagation and relied on EternalBlue, an exploit against Microsoft's SMB implementation that was reportedly developed and retained as an intelligence capability before being stolen and released by the Shadow Brokers (Newman, 2018). The mechanism that matters for operational analysis is not the encryption routine in isolation, but the coupling of remote exploitation with automated scanning and lateral movement. This coupling reduced the attacker's requirement for continuous operator control and accelerated spread through machine-speed propagation, which reduced the role of human-paced tasking in governing tempo. The implication is that the operation's realised effect was shaped as much by network topology, patch posture, and service exposure as by the attacker's initial intent.

The case also illustrates how loss of control is not a residual risk but a structural feature of self-propagating tools. Once execution begins, the propagation mechanism selects targets through reachability, not through political discrimination, which means that effect pathways follow interdependence rather than strategy. The worm therefore moved across organisational boundaries and sectors because SMB was widely deployed and because segmentation and patching practices were uneven across legacy environments (Newman, 2018). In practice, this produced a pattern in which a technically straightforward mechanism generated systemic disruption, since local outages propagated into service-level disruption where institutions depended on shared digital services, outsourced IT, or tightly coupled operational technology (OT) and administrative networks. The implication is that offensive capability design choices at the tactical–technical level can pre-commit an operation to cascading effects that neither the attacker nor the defender can fully bound once automation takes over.

A further feature of the trajectory is that the exploit's provenance matters for strategic interpretation. WannaCry is not simply a ransomware incident; it is also an instance where the leakage of a stockpiled capability altered the global threat environment by lowering the marginal cost of high-impact intrusion for a wide range of actors (Huskaj, 2024*c*). The mechanism is diffusion: once an exploit becomes public, it migrates into toolchains, proof-of-concept repositories, and derivative malware families. The implication is that vulnerability retention decisions made under intelligence incentives can generate a delayed externality, where subsequent campaigns exploit the same vulnerability against third parties that were never part of the original intelligence purpose.

Decision-making and organisational response under time pressure

WannaCry demonstrates how automation compresses organisational decision cycles because defenders face a propagation tempo that outpaces ordinary governance and change-management processes. When infections scale rapidly, response shifts from planned risk management to crisis containment, since the time available to interpret telemetry, decide on mitigations, and implement changes collapses from days to hours or minutes. The mechanism is interaction between malware tempo and institutional friction: patch deployment, system isolation, and restoration all require coordination across teams, approvals, and service dependencies, yet those procedures were built for routine operations rather than for worm-speed incidents (Huskaj and Iftimie, 2020). The implication is that the defender's early posture becomes improvised, decentralised, and uneven across organisations, even when technical guidance exists.

The organisational response also revealed continuity constraints that shaped what "containment" meant in practice. Many affected organisations could not simply shut down networks or reboot core services without generating unacceptable secondary harm, particularly where digital systems were integrated into time-sensitive service delivery. This is an operational constraint rather than a purely technical one: defenders must trade off rapid isolation against continuity of essential functions, which in turn shapes where segmentation is feasible, how restoration is sequenced, and what residual risk is tolerated during triage. The mechanism is that continuity obligations create asymmetric response capacity: institutions with rehearsed procedures, tested backups, and pre-authorised emergency playbooks can move faster and with clearer priorities, while institutions with brittle legacy estates face slower decision-making and higher restoration cost (Huskaj and Iftimie, 2020). The implication is that preparedness is not a generic virtue but a determinant of how quickly an organisation can convert technical advice into operational action under time pressure.

WannaCry further indicates that crisis response is conditioned by prior governance of vulnerability and patch management. Microsoft's patch availability did not produce uniform protection because adoption depends on inventory visibility, maintenance windows, procurement cycles, and the presence of unsupported systems (Newman, 2018). The mechanism is organisational: patching competes with uptime incentives and resource constraints, and it is often deprioritised until disruption forces action. The implication is that the operational impact of a widely exploited vulnerability is shaped by institutional routines long before the incident, meaning that the same technical threat produces different outcomes across organisations because their governance and resilience posture differ.

Intelligence discontinuities: warning, attribution, and interpretation

The WannaCry episode highlights an intelligence discontinuity between warning and action. Even when indicators exist—such as disclosure of a critical vulnerability and vendor patch release—institutions frequently fail to translate warning into mitigation at scale (Newman, 2018). The mechanism is that warning intelligence is only actionable if it is disseminated to the right operators, prioritised against competing risks, and implemented through change processes that reach legacy and peripheral systems. The implication is that defensive outcomes depend on an intelligence-to-operations pipeline, not on the existence of technical knowledge, and that gaps in this pipeline convert known vulnerabilities into realised disruption.

A second discontinuity concerns attribution and interpretation during the early phase of the incident. Technical responders can often characterise malware behaviour quickly, but strategic interpretation of actor intent and political meaning lags because it depends on higher-confidence attribution, contextual intelligence, and assessments of whether observed effects reflect deliberate targeting or opportunistic propagation (Huskaj, 2024*c*). The mechanism is evidentiary asymmetry: telemetry can show exploitation and lateral movement, but it rarely reveals command intent, tasking structure, or policy purpose with comparable clarity. The implication is that political decision-makers face a temporal dilemma. They must decide on thresholds, signalling, and potential response options while the intelligence picture is still incomplete, which increases the probability of either under-reaction (because intent is uncertain) or over-reaction (because worst-case assumptions dominate).

These discontinuities matter because they shape escalation management and response thresholds. If early uncertainty prevents timely political attribution, deterrence by punishment becomes difficult to activate in a controlled manner, since proportionality and target selection require confidence about the actor and the operational purpose (Huskaj and Wilson, 2021). At the same time, the case indicates why deterrence by denial remains structurally salient: the most reliable way to reduce the operational utility of widely reusable exploits is to reduce exposure through patching, segmentation, and recovery capacity (Newman, 2018). The implication is that intelligence does not merely describe the incident; it conditions which strategic options are feasible under time pressure, and it determines whether response is anchored in political intent or dominated by technical crisis management.

MLMD mapping: what the case validates

WannaCry validates MLMD's core proposition that tactical–technical actions generate strategic consequences through operational mechanisms that are organisational, ethical, and intelligence-mediated rather than purely technical (Huskaj, 2024*c*). At the strategic–political level, the case foregrounds how vulnerability retention and stockpiling decisions create systemic exposure when control over an exploit is lost, thereby transforming an intelligence asset into a global risk externality (Huskaj and Wilson, 2021). At the operational level, the case shows that crisis outcomes depend on preparedness, governance of patch adoption, and the ability of intelligence functions to convert warning and attribution into timely decision-support under uncertainty (Huskaj and Iftimie, 2020). At the tactical–technical level, the coupling of remote exploitation with automated propagation reduced operator control and amplified cascading effects through interdependence (Newman, 2018). The implication is that a persuasive analysis of cyber operations must trace how political decisions about capability and disclosure condition operational resilience and intelligence interpretation, which in turn shape the scale, duration, and strategic meaning of technical effects.

7.3 Case Study II: A Cyber Range Exercise Scenario

This section uses a scenario-based cyber range exercise (hereafter Northwind) to observe how an offensive action is organised when political constraints are explicit and operational secrecy is not the limiting variable. The case is analysed as a sequence in which intent is translated into design requirements, intelligence is generated to reduce uncertainty, and authorisation is conditioned on boundedness, deconfliction, and reversibility. The focus is organisational and judgemental work and does not address technical tradecraft. The section concludes by mapping the scenario to MLMD to show how strategic constraints shape tactical feasibility through operational processes.

Exercise boundary and strategic context

This section draws on a cyber range exercise scenario. The events analysed here, designated Exercise Northwind, are scenario-based simulations and do not describe historical OCO (Huskaj and Blix, 2022). The analytical purpose of using an exercise setting is to isolate planning, intelligence integration, and operator judgement under controlled conditions where the scenario can be instrumented, replayed, and discussed without operational secrecy becoming the limiting variable. The case provides empirical material for evaluating how an offensive operation is organised when political intent, rules of engagement (ROE), and technical feasibility must be aligned before execution (Huskaj and Blix, 2022).

The simulated security environment is explicitly a below-threshold situation. A fictitious country (Cyberia) experiences repeated unwanted reconnaissance flights by a neighbouring state, producing a deteriorating security condition that remains short of armed conflict yet requires a calibrated response (Huskaj and Blix, 2022). The strategic objective assigned to Cyberia's cyber unit is therefore deterrence-oriented and behaviour-focused: to stop the neighbour's aerospace violations by imposing operational friction on enabling dependencies rather than by escalating through kinetic action. This choice matters because it constrains what "success" can mean; the desired outcome is a change in adversary behaviour under conditions where signalling, attribution ambiguity, and proportionality concerns are integral to the political problem rather than external to it (Huskaj and Blix, 2022).

ROE function in the scenario as the mechanism that translates strategic permissibility into operational constraints. The ROE authorise Cyberia to conduct offensive cyber action that may produce collateral effects, provided the action remains plausibly deniable and aligned with the political requirement to avoid escalation (Huskaj and Blix, 2022). This form of authorisation does not simplify operational design; it shifts the burden onto planning, intelligence, and legal review because deniability, proportionality, and reversibility become design requirements rather than post-hoc justifications. Doctrinally, this reflects the general point that ROE are intended to operationalise legal and policy boundaries into actionable guidance for commanders and operators, thereby shaping what courses of action are permissible in practice (Mandsager et al., 2022).

Although the scenario is fictitious, its organisational implications intersect with the wider context in which cyber-capable states coordinate with partners and operate under information-sharing constraints. Range-based rehearsal and deconfliction procedures increasingly need to be compatible with allied coordination, interoperability expectations, and information-sharing constraints, because capability development is shaped by the institutional environment in which it will be governed and employed (Henriksén et al., 2025). The implication for the cyber range case is that the exercise does not serve as a proxy for NATO, yet the organisational problems surfaced by Exercise Northwind—authority, deconfliction, and information integration—belong to the same class of challenges that become more demanding when operations must be coordinated across partners and institutional boundaries.

Planning and intelligence integration

Planning in Exercise Northwind is organised through the ambidextrous planning model, which structures OCO around indicators and warnings, planning timelines, operational considerations, and a decision point (Huskaj and Blix, 2022). The operational significance of this structure is that it treats uncertainty as a planning condition. The initial operation order does not provide sufficient information to populate target profiles and operational assumptions, so the unit treats intelligence collection as an enabling operation that must be executed before the operation can be responsibly authorised (Huskaj and Blix, 2022). This is a practical demonstration of a recurring feature of OCO: access, effects, and risk cannot be specified credibly unless the intelligence required to characterise the target environment is generated as part of the planning process.

To reduce intelligence gaps, the unit conducts a dedicated reconnaissance sub-operation as Cyber ISR, iteratively collecting and validating information about services, vulnerabilities, and access opportunities until "enough intelligence" exists to link prospective cyber actions to the political end state (Huskaj and Blix, 2022). The key point is procedural rather than technical: the unit repeats intelligence collection as needed because the target environment is treated as partially observed and dynamically uncertain. This approach converts intelligence requirements into concrete RFIs embedded in the planning artefacts (the canvas), which in turn constrains what planners can credibly propose at the decision point (Huskaj and Blix, 2022).

The scenario's target logic is dependency-oriented. Rather than aiming at the aircraft directly, the unit maps enabling institutions and informational dependencies that influence aviation decision-making, including meteorological services and adjacent administrative functions (Huskaj and Blix, 2022). This target selection reflects the strategic requirement to halt reconnaissance flights without escalating to overt force: the desired mechanism is to degrade confidence in, or availability of, an informational input that aviation operations rely upon, thereby producing a behavioural effect through institutional decision processes rather than through physical destruction (Huskaj and Blix, 2022). The implication is that operational planning is inseparable from an institutional understanding of how information moves through the adversary's socio-technical system.

Uncertainty management also appears as an organisational problem of coordination. Scenario injects and planning timelines incorporate deconfliction requirements, including the need to avoid interference with other friendly activity in adjacent network segments (Huskaj and Blix, 2022). This constraint matters because it restricts the feasible target set and shapes access choices even before execution begins. It also illustrates why OCO planning cannot be treated as a purely adversary-centric optimisation exercise: planners must preserve friendly freedom of action, protect intelligence equities, and avoid operational collisions, which in turn requires explicit coordination mechanisms and authority to adjudicate trade-offs across activities (Huskaj and Blix, 2022).

Execution dynamics and operational friction

Execution in Exercise Northwind is designed to preserve political constraints while producing a controlled effect. The scenario employs deniable operational pathways and relies on widely available tooling and access infrastructure so that observed activity does not trivially resolve attribution to Cyberia (Huskaj and Blix, 2022). This is not a technical preference; it is a political design requirement derived from the ROE and the deterrence objective. The implication is that tactical implementation is constrained by strategic intent, because the operation must remain compatible with plausible deniability while still producing an effect that is salient enough to alter adversary behaviour.

The case also surfaces a central friction in offensive cyber practice: tool behaviour and target system response introduce operational uncertainty at the point of execution. The capability used in the scenario can produce instability on the target, including system crashes that complicate assessment of what the compromised host does and whether the intended operational pathway remains available (Huskaj and Blix, 2022). This matters because instability is not merely a technical inconvenience; it creates political and operational risk. If the tool's behaviour causes overt disruption beyond what planners anticipated, it can undermine proportionality judgements, increase escalation risk, and reduce the credibility of claims that the operation is reversible and bounded (Huskaj and Blix, 2022).

Real-time judgement therefore becomes the operational mechanism that preserves alignment between intent and action during execution. Operators must integrate feedback from the environment, adapt exploitation pathways, and reassess risk when system behaviour diverges from expectations (Huskaj and Blix, 2022). The case is especially instructive because the framework being validated supports planning and order-giving, yet it is less suited to supporting operator actions during ongoing operations when real-time data, human discretion, and rapid reassessment are required (Huskaj and Blix, 2022). The implication is that planning frameworks need to be complemented by command-and-control practices that can incorporate live data and update risk assessments during execution; otherwise, the organisation's ability to keep tactical action within strategic bounds depends disproportionately on individual operator competence.

Finally, the decision to proceed is framed through assessed reversibility and boundedness. The scenario concludes that cascading effects are unlikely and that effects can be recalled or limited, which provides decision-makers with the confidence required to issue the go-order under uncertainty (Huskaj and Blix, 2022). Whether this judgement is always warranted outside an exercise environment is not the claim; the analytical point is that reversibility and low cascading risk are treated as gating criteria at the decision point, demonstrating how ethical and political constraints are converted into operational tests that shape authorisation (Huskaj and Blix, 2022).

MLMD mapping: what the case validates

Exercise Northwind validates MLMD's core proposition by showing that strategic intent constrains tactical feasibility through operational mechanisms that institutionalise intelligence integration, risk evaluation, and deconfliction. At the strategic–political level, the operation is defined by a below-threshold deterrence objective, an escalation-avoidance requirement, and ROE constraints that prioritise plausible deniability and bounded effects (Huskaj and Blix, 2022; Mandsager et al., 2022). At the operational level, the ethical and intelligence dimensions function as the translation layer: planners treat incomplete information as a structural condition, conduct Cyber ISR iteratively, update planning artefacts as intelligence accumulates, and manage deconfliction as an organising constraint that is built into planning timelines (Huskaj and Blix, 2022). At the tactical–technical level, execution is shaped by capability behaviour and environmental response, including tool instability and the need for real-time judgement and reassessment to keep action aligned with the authorised risk envelope (Huskaj and Blix, 2022). The case therefore demonstrates that "policy-to-payload" coherence depends on institutionalised operational processes that reconcile strategic constraints with technical opportunity under uncertainty.

7.4 Cross-Case Synthesis

This section compares WannaCry and the cyber range simulation to extract mechanisms that persist across uncontrolled incidents and deliberate-control operations. The comparison is organised around time compression, partial information, cascading effects, and control limits, with attention to how each constraint is generated and where it becomes decisive in the chain from tactical behaviour to political consequence. The purpose is to separate shared structural conditions from case-specific context and to specify which governance implications follow from each control condition.

Shared constraints across structured and unstructured settings

A comparative reading of WannaCry and the cyber range simulation indicates that OCO are shaped by recurring structural conditions that persist across divergent operational contexts. WannaCry unfolded as a high-velocity incident driven by automated propagation. Exercise Northwind unfolded as a planned activity within a bounded exercise environment in which decision-makers could structure reconnaissance, sequencing, and authorisation. The shared analytical result is that time compression, partial information, cascading effects, and control limits recur across both settings because technical dependencies can shift rapidly while institutional decision and response processes proceed through approval, coordination, and implementation cycles, creating a persistent timing mismatch between technical tempo and institutional tempo (Huskaj and Iftimie, 2020; Huskaj and Blix, 2022; Huskaj, 2024*c*).

Technical effects can propagate, and access conditions can change, within seconds to minutes. Political authorisation, intelligence assessment, legal review, and cross-unit coordination typically require longer cycles. This timing gap exposes offensive cyber activity—whether emergent in consequence (WannaCry) or deliberate in design (Northwind)—to loss of alignment between the authorised purpose and the realised operational trajectory. In practical terms, decision-makers may authorise a bounded purpose (for example, a limited disruption intended to shape behaviour while preserving deniability), while realised outcomes expand in scope, duration, or collateral spillover (for example, wider service disruption, unintended propagation pathways, or effects that generate escalation pressure beyond the original risk assumptions).

Time compression appears as a shared constraint, but it is generated through different mechanisms. In WannaCry, time compression is produced by tool behaviour: self-propagation accelerates the operational tempo and forces defenders into improvised containment decisions under severe uncertainty, because spread and harm are driven by automated scanning and exploitation, which reduces the role of continuous operator judgement in pacing the incident (Huskaj and Iftimie, 2020). In Northwind, time compression is produced by opportunity and synchronisation, where access conditions, deconfliction constraints, and signalling requirements can narrow the window for a meaningful execute decision: planners still face narrow windows in which access conditions, deconfliction constraints, and strategic signalling requirements can be aligned before an execute decision is meaningful, which is why the planning model treats decision-making as a gated sequence that culminates in a decision point (Huskaj and Blix, 2022). The implication is that governance cannot assume "available time" as a function of whether an operation is planned; cyberspace compresses decision cycles either through automated technical tempo (WannaCry) or through fragile alignment conditions that can change faster than institutional procedures (Northwind).

Partial information is the second shared constraint and functions as the main driver of operational risk in both cases. WannaCry illustrates how early-stage interpretation is dominated by fragmented technical indicators and uncertain attribution, which forces decision-makers to act before intent and scope can be reliably inferred from observed effects. Exercise Northwind shows that partial information is not eliminated by planning or by operating in a controlled environment: the validation study describes that the operation order did not provide sufficient information to fill the planning canvas and that the unit had to conduct Cyber ISR to close intelligence gaps before viable execution pathways could be identified (Huskaj and Blix, 2022). This matters because the operational problem is not "lack of data" in the abstract; it is that the intelligence needed for proportionality assessment, collateral estimation, and escalation control is frequently incomplete at the time when authorisation choices must be made. The implication is that intelligence integration is not a preparatory add-on but the mechanism by which operations become governable under time pressure, because it is the only way to reduce uncertainty about access conditions and downstream effects to a level compatible with political constraints.

Cascading effects constitute the third shared constraint and provide the clearest linkage between tactical events and strategic consequence. Doctrinally, cascading effects arise because effects can travel laterally across peer systems or upward into higher-level systems due to the interconnected nature of the operating environment (Joint Chiefs of Staff, 2018). WannaCry operationalised this risk in the strongest possible form: the worm-capable exploitation path created an explicit risk of cascading effects, because propagation was not limited to a narrowly profiled target set but instead followed network reachability and patch disparity (Huskaj and Iftimie, 2020). In Northwind, cascading risk was treated as an explicit authorisation variable rather than as an incidental by-product: the decision point was justified in part by an assessment of negligible cascading effects and the possibility of reversibility, paired with prior deconfliction in the planning timelines step (Huskaj and Blix, 2022). The implication is that cascading effects must be treated as a governance object rather than as an after-action observation, because the core control problem in cyberspace is that tool behaviour can create secondary and tertiary consequences that propagate beyond the operational hypothesis.

Control limits constitute the fourth shared constraint and emerge from the combination of environmental dependencies and imperfect capability behaviour. In WannaCry, control limits follow from autonomy: once a worm is released, tactical execution is largely delegated to software logic and network topology, and the resulting operational trajectory can hinge on technical contingencies that are not anchored in attacker intent (for example, termination conditions and infrastructure artefacts). In Northwind, control limits appear as instability and uncertainty at the point of exploitation: the validation notes that EternalBlue-based tooling could blue screen targets and create uncertain effects that complicated assessment of target function, even in an exercise environment with structured planning (Huskaj and Blix, 2022). The implication is that "control" in cyberspace cannot be reduced to intent and authorisation; it depends on how capabilities behave under real conditions, which requires evidence practices (testing, profiling, reversibility design) that translate technical uncertainty into decision-relevant risk statements.

Taken together, these shared constraints clarify why the MLMD framing remains analytically useful in a case-study chapter: each constraint is generated at the tactical–technical level but becomes decisive only when it interacts with operational intelligence processes and strategic political thresholds. Across both cases, planning and rehearsal function as organisational mechanisms that enable time compression, partial information, cascading risk, and control limits to be handled as explicit trade-offs during authorisation and execution (Huskaj and Blix, 2022; Huskaj, 2024*c*).

Divergent control conditions and governance implications

The key divergence between WannaCry and Northwind concerns the locus of control. WannaCry illustrates an automation-dominant condition where operational tempo and spread are driven primarily by capability design and environmental exposure. Exercise Northwind illustrates a deliberate-control condition where planners seek to preserve operator discretion, sequencing, and boundedness through intelligence-driven preparation and explicit decision gates. The governance implication is that oversight mechanisms cannot be uniform across operation types, because the feasible degree of ex ante control differs sharply depending on whether the capability is designed to propagate and generalise or to remain target-bounded and reversible (Huskaj and Iftimie, 2020; Huskaj and Blix, 2022).

Automation changes who bears risk, because it externalises uncertainty onto actors outside the authorising chain. In an automation-heavy incident, a tool can traverse heterogeneous infrastructures and impose costs on third parties that were not part of the operational hypothesis, which becomes a strategic and ethical problem regardless of whether the initiating actor sought that outcome. The WannaCry canvas explicitly treats worm capability as a driver of cascading risk, which captures the core mechanism: propagation characteristics shift operational risk from the initiating unit to the broader ecosystem of exposed systems, including critical services that may have no meaningful agency over their inherited technical debt (Huskaj and Iftimie, 2020). By contrast, the Northwind validation treats risk as something that can be bounded through reversibility and deconfliction, which shifts the burden back onto the authorising institution: decision-makers are responsible for demonstrating that the operation can be contained and recalled, and that it does not collide with other friendly activities that depend on shared access conditions (Huskaj and Blix, 2022). The implication is that governance must distinguish between operations where risk is structurally exportable (automation, broad targeting, worm behaviour) and operations where risk is structurally internal to the authorising state (bounded targeting, reversible payloads, deconflicted access).

Divergent control conditions also change what can be anticipated. In deliberate-control settings, anticipation is possible because intelligence collection and testing practices can be organised to reduce environmental uncertainty. The ambidextrous model's emphasis on indicators and warnings, planning timelines, operational considerations, and a decision point reflects this logic: it structures anticipation as a cumulative evidence process rather than as a single predictive act (Huskaj and Blix, 2022). In automation-dominant settings, anticipation is bounded because the operation's trajectory depends on network reachability, patch distribution, and emergent defender behaviour, which are not fully knowable at the point of release. The implication is that anticipatory governance in cyberspace is less about "forecasting everything" and more about designing capabilities and approval processes around explicit uncertainty: identifying which uncertainties can be reduced through intelligence and rehearsal, and which uncertainties must be treated as non-negotiable constraints on permissible tool classes and targeting approaches.

These differences drive a further governance question: where oversight must sit in the chain of authority. When a capability's behaviour can rapidly create cross-system propagation, oversight must operate upstream of execution because the time available for real-time intervention is structurally limited. This pushes governance towards strategic and operational constraints on capability design, deployment doctrines, and vulnerability handling, rather than relying on tactical discretion after release. When an operation is designed for boundedness and reversibility, oversight can be distributed more credibly: strategic authorities define thresholds and acceptable risk; operational authorities enforce evidence gates (deconfliction status, cascading-risk assessment, legal review); and tactical operators retain discretion to adapt to technical friction without changing the operation's authorised end state (Joint Chiefs of Staff, 2018; Huskaj and Blix, 2022). The implication is that oversight is not a single institutional location; it is a set of linked control points that must be placed where time, uncertainty, and tool behaviour make intervention feasible.

Finally, the divergent cases clarify why governance must treat deconfliction as a primary design constraint rather than as late-stage coordination. The dissertation discussion traces deconfliction to the fact that access is critical and that offensive and intelligence activities can collide when they share target surfaces or infrastructure, historically requiring joint mechanisms to avoid interference (Joint Chiefs of Staff, 2018). The Northwind validation aligns with this principle by noting that additional deconfliction was not required at the decision point because it had already been managed earlier in planning timelines (Huskaj and Blix, 2022). WannaCry, by contrast, illustrates what deconfliction cannot solve after the fact: once a worm-capable exploit is released into exposed infrastructure, there is no meaningful interagency register or targeting discipline that can retroactively re-bound effects. The implication is that deconfliction is governance for deliberate control, not a remedy for automation-driven spread, and that policy must therefore constrain the adoption and release of self-propagating tool characteristics where the operational requirement is bounded coercion rather than uncontrolled disruption.

7.5 Cyber Effects in Adjacent Domains

OCO generate outcomes that are rarely confined to a single technical environment because cyberspace functions as connective tissue for activities in air, land, maritime, space, and the information environment (Joint Chiefs of Staff, 2018; USAF LeMay Center, 2023). The implication is that an operation that begins as a technical intrusion must be planned and governed as a cross-domain activity whenever its mechanism of action targets dependencies that shape decision-making, mobility, sensing, or command and control in adjacent domains. In MLMD terms, this section addresses horizontal propagation: how tactical–technical actions produce operational and strategic consequences through non-cyber pathways, and how that propagation constrains planning, ROE, and escalation management.

Cyber can enable cross-domain effects by degrading, manipulating, or delaying information flows that adjacent-domain organisations require to act. This enabling function is visible in the cyber range scenario, where the mechanism for influencing air activity is not the disruption of aircraft or air-defence systems, but the manipulation of a meteorological dependency that aviation decision-makers treat as authoritative (Huskaj and Blix, 2022). The implication is that target selection in OCO cannot be reduced to "systems the adversary owns"; it must focus on the organisational nodes and data dependencies that translate information into action in another domain. This shifts the planning problem from a narrow compromise-and-payload sequence to a dependency-mapping exercise in which planners must specify how a cyber-induced change in one system will predictably alter behaviour elsewhere.

Cyber can also substitute for kinetic action when political constraints, attribution risk, or escalation sensitivity make physical effects undesirable. The strategic attraction of substitution lies in reach and reversibility: planners may seek to impose costs or alter behaviour without crossing thresholds associated with visible military force, while preserving the ability to terminate effects if political conditions change (Huskaj and Wilson, 2021). The Northwind scenario illustrates this substitution logic: the desired behavioural change (halting airspace violations) is pursued through a cyber pathway that is designed to remain below escalation thresholds and to preserve deniability within the scenario's ROE constraints (Huskaj and Blix, 2022). The implication is that substitution demands a tighter coupling between political intent and technical design than many cyber operations receive in practice, because the political value of "non-kinetic" coercion depends on disciplined control over scope, duration, and collateral pathways.

A third cross-domain pattern is unintended spillover, where a cyber capability produces disruption in societal functions that were not part of a deliberate operational design. WannaCry illustrates this mechanism: a technical exploit and automated propagation produced disruption across healthcare, transport, and industrial operations because vulnerable systems were embedded in essential services and could be reached through ordinary network connectivity (Huskaj and Iftimie, 2020). The implication is that cross-domain effects can emerge even when neither the attacker nor the defender treats the incident as "multi-domain" at the outset. For planning and governance, this means that the multi-domain problem is not optional: any operation that leverages widely deployed vulnerabilities or self-propagating mechanisms creates a non-trivial probability of effects that manifest as service disruption, political pressure, and crisis dynamics outside cyberspace.

These cross-domain pathways impose specific requirements on planning. First, planners must translate a cyber action into an adjacent-domain mechanism that is explicit enough to be tested, rehearsed, and bounded. In the cyber range, this is operationalised through an intelligence-driven planning process that treats Cyber ISR as a prerequisite for validating assumptions about the target environment and for assessing whether the intended effect can be generated without uncontrolled side effects (Huskaj and Blix, 2022). Second, planners must treat deconfliction as a cross-domain requirement, not only as a cyber–cyber collision problem. When an operation aims to influence air activity through meteorological services, deconfliction includes coordination with those responsible for aviation safety, crisis communication, and defensive continuity measures, because those actors may counteract or amplify the intended effect through standard procedures. The implication is that OCO planning must incorporate institutional channels that connect cyber teams to the relevant adjacent-domain authorities, even when those authorities are external to the military organisation.

ROE and operational authorities become more constraining when cyber effects are expected to manifest outside the digital substrate. Joint doctrine distinguishes cyberspace exploitation (CE) from cyberspace attack (CA), and that distinction matters most when a technical act can plausibly create non-cyber consequences, because authorisation thresholds, collateral constraints, and reporting requirements tend to differ by mission type (Joint Chiefs of Staff, 2018). In practice, cross-domain targeting increases the importance of specifying permitted actions (e.g., manipulation versus denial), bounded target scope (systems, subnets, functions), and termination conditions (reversibility and recall). The cyber range's emphasis on reversibility, tool behaviour uncertainty, and blue-screen risk illustrates why ROE cannot be written only in terms of intended outcomes; it must be written in terms of technical behaviours and failure modes that shape collateral pathways (Huskaj and Blix, 2022). The implication is that ROE for cross-domain cyberspace operations may encode not only "what may be targeted" but also "how effects may be generated," because the method often determines whether adjacent-domain harm is foreseeable.

Escalation management is complicated by the interpretive ambiguity of cross-domain effects. A disruption in an aviation-related dependency can be interpreted as a safety incident, a coercive signal, preparation of the environment, or the opening move of a wider campaign, depending on timing and context. This ambiguity matters because adversaries may respond to perceived intent rather than to the operator's internal authorisation logic. The WannaCry case shows the converse problem: large-scale disruption can occur without a clear strategic message, which increases uncertainty for decision-makers and complicates proportionality assessments and response options under time pressure (Huskaj and Iftimie, 2020). The implication is that escalation control in OCO cannot rely on intent alone; it requires mechanisms that reduce misinterpretation risk, including disciplined target selection, restraint in self-propagating tools, and governance procedures that anticipate how adjacent-domain authorities and publics will interpret disruption.

Taken together, the two cases show why adjacent-domain effects must be treated as a planning and governance variable rather than as a post hoc observation. Exercise Northwind demonstrates deliberate cross-domain design: political intent is translated into an operational concept that targets an information dependency shaping air decision-making (Huskaj and Blix, 2022). WannaCry demonstrates uncontrolled cross-domain consequence: technical propagation created disruption in societal functions that rapidly became a political and crisis-management problem (Huskaj and Iftimie, 2020). The implication for Chapter 8 is that emerging automation, tighter cyber–physical coupling, and faster decision cycles are likely to increase both the opportunity for substitution effects and the risk of spillover, thereby raising the importance of institutionalised planning, ROE specificity, and escalation-aware governance for OCO (Joint Chiefs of Staff, 2018; USAF LeMay Center, 2023).

Interaction with the information environment: disinformation, disclosure, and legitimacy risk

OCO frequently interact with the information environment because technical events are interpreted through public narratives, political contestation, and adversary influence activity. This interaction matters for control and credibility because strategic effect depends on how action is understood by multiple audiences under attribution uncertainty, including domestic institutions, coalition partners, and the adversary. In practice, the information environment becomes a coupling mechanism: tactical cyber events can trigger political interpretation that constrains subsequent operational choices, while strategic messaging requirements can constrain technical design by imposing boundedness and evidentiary discipline. Joint doctrine's emphasis on cross-domain interaction implies that cyber planning should treat narrative consequences as foreseeable pathways when the operation touches public services, electoral processes, or critical infrastructure (Joint Chiefs of Staff, 2018; USAF LeMay Center, 2023; Joint Chiefs of Staff, 2022).

Here, *disinformation* refers to intentional deception through fabricated claims or through a mismatch between content and context that produces a misleading message even when isolated statements are factually correct. This definition matters for OCO because cyber incidents and disclosures supply raw material that adversaries can reframe, repackage, and amplify into legitimacy challenges for democratic institutions. The governance implication is that countermeasures operate under a legitimacy constraint: measures that degrade freedom of information and expression can be weaponised rhetorically as evidence of hypocrisy, thereby creating a second-order credibility risk that persists beyond the technical incident (Wasinger, 2023).

Cyber-enabled disclosure is one recurrent pathway. Data theft, selective release, and forged or context-stripped material can be used to shape political perceptions without requiring sustained disruption of systems. The operational relevance is that a cyber intrusion can become a credibility problem even when the technical effect remains limited, because the political consequence arises from claims about intent, legality, and target class rather than from measurable service degradation. This dynamic increases governance demand: authorisation and review must address how evidentiary uncertainty and public communication interact with proportionality assessments, coalition coordination, and escalation boundaries (Reitz, 2024; Huskaj, 2024*a*).

Disinformation can also follow from major cyber incidents even when the initiating actor did not design a messaging campaign. High-tempo disruption creates an interpretive vacuum in which adversaries, opportunistic actors, and domestic political entrepreneurs can introduce causal claims about responsibility, competence, and intent. Under time compression, institutions face a dual burden: restoring functionality while preserving public trust and resisting premature attribution claims that could lock leaders into escalatory commitments. AI toolchains further tighten this constraint because they reduce the labour required to generate persuasive impersonation, synthetic media, and tailored narratives, increasing the volume and speed of influence outputs during election-adjacent windows. This is an MLMD linkage in practice. Tactical disruption shapes strategic constraints through organisational capacity to communicate, verify, and coordinate across government and critical operators (Huskaj, 2024*b*; SOCRadar Cyber Intelligence Inc., 2025; Klepper and Tucker, 2024).

A recent case illustrates how these mechanisms can emerge outside formal military or intelligence structures. The "Equalise/Beyond" network, exposed in 2024, aggregated confidential state and private data into searchable dossiers on political and business elites while claiming tacit state approval. The operation combined insider access, open-source aggregation, and coercive disclosure to influence decision-makers and clients. The case demonstrates how intelligence-like capabilities operated without lawful oversight can blur the boundary between state authority and private coercion, creating disinformation and legitimacy risks that mirror those faced in OCO when evidentiary control and authorisation diverge (Roussi and Roberts, 2025).

Table 7.1 applies the MLMD framework illustratively to the Equalise/Beyond case to show how intelligence-like data exploitation and coercive disclosure generate legitimacy risk when authorisation, governance, and evidentiary control diverge.

Read against the two core cases, the Equalise/Beyond case clarifies how the MLMD coupling mechanisms identified in this chapter also operate when intelligence-like data exploitation and disclosure occur outside formally authorised OCO, thereby sharpening the interpretation of information-environment dynamics in WannaCry and the cyber range scenario.

The chapter's two core cases also illuminate information-environment coupling under different control conditions. In WannaCry, rapid propagation and uneven situational awareness created a divergence between operational containment tempo and public interpretation tempo. That divergence increased the premium on disciplined public communication, cross-agency information sharing, and attribution statements calibrated to evidentiary confidence, because inconsistent narratives can erode institutional trust and complicate partner coordination. In the cyber range scenario, deniability and boundedness function as design requirements with downstream narrative consequences: planners seek technical pathways that limit the probability that exposure generates political effects exceeding authorised purpose, while maintaining auditability of the authorisation chain and a release posture compatible with partner consultation and evidentiary limits. The governance implication is that credible

TABLE 7.1
Illustrative MLMD Matrix: Disinformation, Disclosure, and Loss of Control in the Equalise/Beyond Case

Level	Dimension		
	Political	**Ethical**	**Technological**
Strategic	Blurred boundary between state authority and private actors through claims of tacit approval, undermining political accountability and public trust	Absence of legitimate mandate reallocates coercive power over elites without proportionality or due process	Concentration of sensitive data creates structural leverage that substitutes technical capability for formal authority
Operational	Intelligence-like collection and analysis conducted outside authorised governance and oversight structures, with no formal deconfliction or tasking control	Systematic violation of IGL discipline through uncontrolled aggregation, retention, and monetisation of sensitive information	Platformisation of collection and analysis enables scalable exploitation and rapid conversion of data into influence and coercion
Tactical	Individual data accesses and disclosures executed without binding mission scope, release criteria, or accountability for downstream effects	Selective disclosure and dossier construction amplify harm by repackaging information to maximise reputational and political pressure	Automated aggregation, search, and retrieval functions lower the cost and increase the tempo of disclosure and disinformation activity

OCO requires a communications and evidence posture integrated with operational planning, including release criteria, consultation triggers, and documentation practices that preserve accountability (Joint Chiefs of Staff, 2022; Reitz, 2024; Huskaj, 2025*a*; Oleson, 2016).

7.6 Practical Lessons for Capability Development and Governance

This section consolidates the case-derived implications into four non-overlapping requirements for how a state may build, maintain, and control OCO. The intent is not to restate the cases, but to specify organisational and governance conditions that reduce decision latency, preserve political control, and limit foreseeable second- and third-order consequences under time pressure and partial intelligence. The observations in this section concern organisational control, legal–policy constraint, and risk governance; they do not provide procedural guidance for planning or executing offensive operations.

Institutionalise rehearsals and playbooks

Offensive cyber capability is not only a stock of tools; it is a repeatable organisational performance that must remain controllable under uncertainty. Rehearsals in cyber ranges are typically institutionalised as a standing preparation function, because range conditions can expose operational friction that is difficult to identify in abstract planning documents. In particular, rehearsals allow teams to test exploit behaviour, reversibility, and instability risks against representative target configurations, which matters because untested capability behaviour can crash hosts, compromise access, and trigger uncontrolled effects that exceed authorised scope.

Playbooks can operationalise this rehearsal function by translating doctrinal intent and planning models into sequenced, role-bound procedures that can be executed within compressed timelines. The purpose of a playbook is to reduce discretionary drift under stress by specifying (i) minimum intelligence requirements before transitions between phases, (ii) mandatory deconfliction checks, and (iii) decision criteria for abort, pause, or rollback when tool behaviour diverges from assumptions. Rehearsals may therefore culminate in explicit abort criteria tied to observable technical indicators (e.g., loss of reversibility, unexpected propagation pathways, or host instability) that mandate termination or rollback rather than discretionary continuation. This codification matters because cyber operations often depend on perishable accesses and narrow windows of opportunity; without routinised procedures, units trade speed for improvisation, which increases variance in outcomes. Rehearsals and playbooks therefore function as a mechanism for converting specialised expertise into institutional reliability, while preserving operator judgement for genuinely novel contingencies.

Embed intelligence cycles throughout planning and execution

OCO depends on intelligence not as a preliminary input, but as a continuous mechanism for reducing uncertainty, validating assumptions, and constraining action as conditions change. The practical implication is that intelligence cycles must be embedded throughout planning and execution rather than sequenced as "collection first, action later." This embedding is required because target environments evolve, access conditions degrade, and adversaries adapt; plans that are not continuously updated become misaligned with technical reality, which increases the probability of unintended effects and operational failure.

Embedding intelligence cycles requires institutionalising intelligence–operations fusion at the operational level. This includes structured cyber ISR to enumerate services, map dependencies, and elicit behaviour; corroboration mechanisms that reconcile HUMINT claims with technical evidence; and feedback loops that update risk assessments as exploitation proceeds. To prevent conjecture from becoming an execution premise, units often enforce verification gates at phase transitions, where key claims about configuration, segmentation, and dependencies must be corroborated through technical observation or cross-source consistency before proceeding. Intelligence support must also incorporate "own-force" considerations, because deconfliction is partly an intelligence problem: parallel collection or exploitation in adjacent network segments can collide, expose accesses, or degrade priority operations. The operational requirement is therefore to treat intelligence as a live control function that governs phase transitions, not as a static product delivered to planners. When intelligence is treated as continuous, decision-makers can impose tighter bounds on scope, duration, and intensity of technical action while retaining the ability to adapt tactics as evidence accumulates.

Clarify authority, ROE, and governance for OCO

Because cyber operations can generate strategic consequences through fast technical propagation and ambiguous attribution, governance must prioritise clear authority and legally grounded constraint rather than discretionary agility. The basic requirement is an explicit authorisation chain that translates political intent into operational orders and tactical permissions, and that specifies who may (i) approve target categories, (ii) accept collateral and escalation risk, and (iii) issue time-sensitive go/no-go decisions. This clarity matters because OCO is often executed under compressed timelines; absent delegated decision competence and pre-defined thresholds, states either delay action until windows close or accept informal workarounds that weaken oversight.

ROE should function as the binding instrument that connects legal authority to operational guidance under uncertainty. ROE must specify permissible effects, target constraints, and termination conditions, while accounting for the lack of stable international thresholds for what constitutes use of force or armed attack in cyberspace. The practical governance implication is that a state must define internal thresholds and response options even when international consensus remains incomplete, because commanders and operators require executable constraints when confronted with partial intelligence and ambiguous intent. Governance must also address inter-organisational coordination, including deconfliction between intelligence equities and attack objectives, and—where relevant—compatibility with allied coordination and information-sharing constraints. In institutional terms, OCO governance is credible when it produces fast decisions that remain traceable to political authority and legally defined limits.

Integrate anticipatory ethics and multi-domain planning

The cases indicate that ethical evaluation is not an external "compliance layer," but a planning requirement driven by the predictable tendency of cyber effects to cascade across interconnected infrastructures. Anticipatory ethics should therefore be embedded as an operational practice that evaluates foreseeable secondary and tertiary consequences before deployment, including propagation risk, spillover into civilian services, and long-term exposure created by vulnerability retention and capability leakage. This requirement matters because the benefits of exploitation are often immediate and localised, while the systemic risk distribution is delayed and broad; without an anticipatory mechanism, institutions systematically privilege short-term operational advantage over long-term stability.

Multi-domain planning must be integrated alongside anticipatory ethics because cyber effects rarely terminate within a purely technical boundary. Even when an operation is designed as a cyberspace action, its strategic value often derives from how it shapes decision-making in adjacent domains and the information environment. The practical implication is that planners should treat cross-domain interaction as a design constraint: cyber actions that manipulate, deny, or degrade information can alter air, land, maritime, or societal processes indirectly, and may be interpreted by an adversary as preparation for escalation. Integrating multi-domain planning therefore requires explicit coordination mechanisms that synchronise cyber timing, messaging, and deconfliction with other instruments of national power, while maintaining political control over escalation pathways. In combination, anticipatory ethics and multi-domain planning provide a structured way to align technical feasibility with proportionality, escalation control, and strategic intent.

7.7 Conclusion

This chapter asked how real-world and exercise-based cases illuminate the structural problem that OCO are planned and executed under narrow decision windows, partial intelligence, and technically volatile effects, and what these conditions imply for maintaining alignment across the strategic–political, operational–ethical/intelligence, and tactical–technical layers specified in MLMD. The cases show that these constraints are not contingent anomalies but recurring properties of the domain: interdependence and automation compress time for interpretation, intelligence is structurally incomplete at the moment authorisation decisions must be made, and technical behaviour can propagate outcomes faster than institutions can reassess intent, scope, and tolerable risk. The operational implication is that alignment is produced through institutionalised control points—rehearsal, intelligence refresh, deconfliction, and termination design—rather than through declaratory policy intent alone.

WannaCry demonstrates how tactical–technical design choices can generate strategic consequences through operational mechanisms that were not designed to absorb worm-speed propagation. The coupling of remote exploitation with automated spread shifted control from human pacing to software logic and network topology, meaning that disruption followed reachability and patch disparity rather than political discrimination. This dynamic clarifies why political decision-making under cyber crisis conditions is dominated by uncertainty about intent and attribution, and why defensive governance routines (patching, segmentation, continuity planning) shape strategic outcome before the incident occurs. It also illustrates a delayed externality of exploit retention: when a stockpiled capability is leaked and diffuses into criminal and state-linked campaigns, the strategic environment changes even if the original intelligence purpose has ended.

The cyber range simulation demonstrates the inverse problem: when the intent is to keep control, institutions must invest in the organisational work that turns political constraint into executable practice. The ambidextrous planning structure operationalises this translation by treating intelligence generation as an enabling sub-operation, elevating deconfliction into an explicit planning element, and using the decision point as a governance gate conditioned on reversibility and negligible cascading risk. The scenario also shows that technical volatility persists even under controlled settings, which makes real-time judgement and feedback integration a standing requirement rather than an exceptional skill.

Taken together, the cases provide a direct MLMD validation: WannaCry shows upward propagation in which tactical automation and interdependence generate strategic disruption through organisational and intelligence discontinuities. Northwind shows downward alignment in which strategic intent is translated into bounded technical action through embedded intelligence cycles, deconfliction, and decision gates. The implication for capability development is that governance and control cannot be appended after technical capability is built; they must be co-developed as institutional functions that preserve political traceability and constrain foreseeable spillover, including vulnerability-handling decisions assessed through anticipatory ethics.

These conclusions bridge to Chapter 8 by defining the problem that future capability trajectories intensify rather than resolve: as automation increases, cyber–physical coupling tightens, and decision cycles shorten, the gap between machine-speed effects and institution-speed interpretation widens. The forward-looking question is therefore how states design governance architectures, rehearsal regimes, and intelligence–operations fusion arrangements that preserve boundedness, reversibility, and escalation control when operational tempo and technical volatility reduce the margin for correction during execution.

Decision Exercise: MLMD Control Under Time Compression, Partial Intelligence, and Narrative Risk

Scenario. Over ten days, a worm-capable ransomware incident spreads across health, transport, and local-government networks. Intelligence indicates a state-linked actor is exploiting the incident to access a defence-adjacent research environment and to prepare disclosure material for an election-adjacent influence push. Attribution is uncertain, partner reporting is uneven, and political leadership requests a 72-hour recommendation that preserves oversight, protects intelligence equities, reduces cascading disruption, and limits legitimacy erosion.

Analytical question 1—Strategic purpose and control objective. State the strategic purpose for the next 14 days (one sentence). Specify:

- one control objective that must hold under attribution uncertainty,
- one observable indicator that would show the control objective is being met.

Analytical question 2—Go/no-go gates for coordinated action. Define the minimum gating conditions required to move from crisis containment into a coordinated posture that can include offensive options:

- **Strategic.** authority clarity, thresholds, escalation boundary, and accountability for public claims,
- **Operational.** intelligence integration, deconfliction across agencies and partners, and a validated picture of critical dependencies,
- **Tactical.** evidence of boundedness (termination criteria and plausible failure modes).

State one reason to recommend **no-go** even when a technically feasible option exists.

Analytical question 3—IGL rule and documentation. Specify one rule that governs whether to preserve access for intelligence or shift towards delivery of effects. Include:

- one trigger that permits action despite incomplete attribution (required confidence and evidentiary posture),
- one trigger that forces restraint due to high-value access, diffusion risk, or plausible cascade pathways,
- one documentation requirement that preserves traceability of political control.

Analytical question 4—Information environment and legitimacy constraint. State how disinformation and cyber-enabled disclosure change your recommendation. Specify:

- one release-posture principle for the first 72 hours,
- one rule for partner consultation and releasability,
- one legitimacy risk where a countermeasure can increase political exposure through claims of censorship, manipulation, or selective disclosure.

Analytical question 5—Adjacent-field case: dossier platform and coercion risk. A private network of insiders and technical specialists aggregates state and open-source data into searchable dossiers on political and business elites and markets access to selected clients, while claiming tacit state approval. Specify:

- the primary MLMD control failure at **each** level (Strategic / Operational / Tactical),
- one governance intervention that reduces recurrence while preserving lawful intelligence activity and due process,
- one communications choice that reduces legitimacy loss during investigation and prosecution while avoiding premature claims.

Deliverable—MLMD synthesis (3 lines). Write three lines (Strategic / Operational / Tactical), each stating: (i) the decision, (ii) the key dependency, (iii) one misalignment failure mode.

8

Future Directions in OCO

Offensive Cyberspace Operations (OCO) have become a central instrument of state power as security competition increasingly unfolds through networked infrastructures and data-dependent decision systems. Joint doctrine defines OCO as actions intended "to project power by the application of force in and through cyberspace" (Joint Chiefs of Staff, 2018). This definition matters for the chapter because it places cyber effects within the same category of state action as other coercive instruments, while recognising that cyber operations remain conditioned by intelligence, access, and technical volatility.

This chapter is prospective and analytic. It does not provide procedural guidance, targeting methods, techniques, or operational tradecraft for OCO. It uses public material to examine how technological change interacts with controllability, legality, and escalation risk under time compression. References to country cases, where included, are illustrative and do not infer non-public institutional arrangements.

The purpose of this chapter is to examine how emerging technologies—particularly artificial intelligence and quantum computing—together with evolving norms and legal interpretations, are likely to shape the opportunities and constraints of OCO over the coming decade. The motivation is twofold. First, AI-enabled toolchains can compress the interval between disclosure, analysis, proof-of-concept development, and deployment, which tightens decision windows for both attackers and defenders. Second, quantum computing may undermine widely deployed public-key cryptography, which would change the confidentiality and authentication assumptions that underpin intelligence collection, operational preparation, and strategic signalling. The central causal claim is that innovation expands what OCO can technically achieve, yet strategic utility remains conditioned by political control, legal authority, and ethical constraint.

This chapter extends the Multi-Level, Multi-Dimensional (MLMD) framework into a changing environment by linking technological change to strategic incentives and operational feasibility. Technological acceleration reshapes tactical–technical feasibility and the reliability of cyber effects. Normative development and alliance practice reshape strategic–political incentives and thresholds. Organisational design, intelligence governance, and ethical review mediate whether new technical options can be translated into authorised and bounded action. The implication is that future OCO cannot be assessed as a technical question alone; it must be assessed as an alignment problem across levels and dimensions under tighter time constraints and deeper uncertainty.

Compression of decision cycles propagates into the intelligence–operations relationship. Faster reconnaissance, vulnerability discovery, targeting, and adaptation change command-and-control assumptions because machine-speed decision points can arise faster than human oversight can intervene. The operational payoff is speed and scale. The strategic risk is reduced interpretability and reduced control, which increases the probability that limited actions are misread or spill beyond intended boundaries. Quantum computing introduces a parallel pressure: even before large-scale quantum capability exists, "harvest-now, decrypt-later" strategies can shift incentives during cryptographic migration windows and weaken trust in communications and authentication (Mosca, 2018).

DOI: 10.1201/9781003655183-8

For many innovation-driven, highly digitalised states, this environment creates a persistent dilemma. High digital dependency increases exposure to coercion and intelligence collection, while innovation capacity expands the range of feasible offensive options and the ability to shape norms that reduce systemic risk. The strategic question is how to retain politically authorised and legally bounded cyber options without increasing instability that would disproportionately affect digitally dependent societies.

This chapter is organised in six sections. Section 8.1 analyses technological horizons in OCO and specifies implications for command authority, intelligence, and effect reliability. Section 8.2 examines norms, treaties, and policy futures and explains how these factors shape permissible action. Section 8.3 analyses the strategic position of smart states in a contested domain. Section 8.4 uses scenarios for future OCO to specify causal pathways and decision points under time compression and partial intelligence. Section 8.5 derives policy and research implications. Section 8.6 concludes by linking technological acceleration and normative constraint to the book's wider argument about credible integration.

8.1 Technological Horizons in OCO

This section examines how technological change reshapes OCO by altering three operational variables: tempo, scale, and predictability. Tempo refers to how quickly an actor can move from information to action inside a defended environment. Scale refers to how many targets, systems, or decision points an actor can handle within the same time horizon. Predictability refers to how reliably an actor can anticipate what an offensive tool will do once deployed, including second-order effects and adversary responses. The central claim is that artificial intelligence and quantum computing increase offensive opportunity by accelerating exploitation and weakening confidentiality assumptions, yet they also increase systemic risk because faster action narrows decision windows and reduces the time available for political and legal control.

Artificial intelligence (AI) and automation expand offensive capability by accelerating parts of the exploitation lifecycle, including reconnaissance, vulnerability identification, and adaptation against defensive controls (Huskaj, 2026). The mechanism is that models can process large volumes of telemetry and generate candidate actions faster than human analysts, which increases the number of feasible operations within a fixed planning window. This does not remove skill requirements, but it changes where skill is applied: operators increasingly allocate effort to model steering, tool integration, data control, and operational security rather than manual execution. The implication is diffusion, because automation lowers the organisational burden required to coordinate fast campaigns across multiple targets.

Recent reporting suggests that large language models (LLMs) matter in this context primarily because they compress the time required to translate advisories, patches, and proof-of-concept code into operationally usable understanding (Lemos, 2025*b*). This matters because the exploitation window is often defined by the interval between disclosure and broad patch deployment. If LLM-assisted workflows reduce analysis and adaptation time, the bottleneck shifts from development time towards verification time. The operational implication is that defenders face tighter decision windows even when the underlying vulnerabilities are not new.

This compression is most consequential when exploitation occurs early in the disclosure cycle. Empirical reporting indicates that a non-trivial share of known exploited vulnerabilities are reported as exploited on or before public disclosure, which implies that operational use can precede broad defender awareness (Garrity, 2025). If analysis and weaponisation accelerate further, the probability increases that exploitation occurs before compensating controls and patch cycles can be implemented at scale. The strategic consequence is not simply "more attacks." The strategic consequence is that defenders are forced into higher-frequency authorisation and prioritisation decisions under greater uncertainty.

The same acceleration pressure exists on the defensive side. Agentic and LLM-augmented workflows can speed up vulnerability triage and propose remediations quickly, yet the relevant sources still emphasise human review and external verification to avoid incorrect fixes or the introduction of new defects (Lemos, 2025*a*). The mechanism is that automation increases throughput, but it does not remove the need to validate changes against real operational dependencies. The implication is that AI shifts labour towards higher-tempo validation and authorisation, rather than removing expert judgement. In other words, tempo increases, but so does the penalty for error.

Higher tempo also changes governance and escalation dynamics. Many machine-learning systems are difficult to interpret, and their behaviour can change under distribution shift or adversarial manipulation. The operational consequence is reduced visibility into why a system selected a specific action at a specific time. The strategic consequence is increased misinterpretation risk when action occurs at machine speed and cannot be paused for political review. This is the mechanism behind "machine-speed instability": rapid action and counteraction can produce escalation pathways driven by narrow optimisation under uncertainty rather than deliberate escalation choices (Huskaj, 2026). For states that seek bounded effects, the requirement is therefore design and doctrine that constrain target classes, define escalation-sensitive systems, and specify termination conditions in advance.

Quantum computing affects OCO primarily through cryptanalysis. Shor's algorithm implies that sufficiently capable quantum machines could break widely deployed public-key schemes (Shor, 1994). Demonstrations of "quantum advantage" remain limited, yet they indicate that states must plan for a transition period in which cryptographic assumptions become contested rather than settled (Arute, Arya, Babbush, Bacon, Bardin, Barends, Biswas, Boixo, Brandao, Buell, Burkett, Chen, Chen, Chiaro, Collins, Courtney, Dunsworth, Farhi, Foxen, Fowler et al., 2019). The strategic mechanism is anticipatory exploitation: traffic collected today may become intelligible later, which encourages "harvest-now, decrypt-later" strategies and changes incentives before full-scale capability exists (Mosca, 2018). The counterintelligence implication is that long-lived secrets, authentication credentials, and retrospective diplomatic communications become vulnerable to future decryption.

This dynamic can generate strategic surprise and asymmetric advantage. If the victim cannot detect compromise, or cannot distinguish routine intelligence collection from preparation for coercive action, information asymmetry becomes destabilising during the migration window. The risk increases if quantum capability is concentrated among a small number of actors, because capability concentration magnifies uncertainty about who can read what and when (Herman, 2018; Krelina, 2021). The implication is that confidentiality becomes a competitive variable rather than a background assumption.

The operational timeline matters because cryptographic migration is slow. Standardisation activity on post-quantum cryptography reduces uncertainty about algorithm selection, yet deployment across national infrastructures remains multi-year and uneven (National Institute of Standards and Technology, 2024). The strategic implication is a window of elevated systemic risk: heterogeneous cryptography creates weak links that can be exploited, while legacy systems remain attractive for stockpiling. For smart states, the practical point is that post-quantum transition is not only a defensive programme. It is also a determinant of intelligence exposure and offensive feasibility, because the value of intercepted data and the risk of compromise depend on migration pace. The strategic consequences therefore depend on institutional integration and operational processes, because cryptanalytic advantage translates into coercive leverage only when collection, analysis, and operational planning can absorb and exploit the information advantage (Lindsay, 2020*a*).

These technological trajectories also reshape intelligence as an operational function. AI increases collection throughput and analytic automation, yet it also increases the probability of deception and integrity attacks against analytic pipelines. Quantum risk increases the value of key management and raises the stakes of communications security for sources, collection platforms, and dissemination channels. The combined effect is that intelligence becomes faster but more contested. This matters for OCO because target selection, vulnerability exploitation, and effect assessment depend on timely and trustworthy intelligence. If intelligence becomes faster but less reliable, the probability increases that operators execute against mischaracterised targets or misread adversary intent, which undermines escalation control.

Finally, the convergence of automation, data abundance, and advanced computation blurs the boundary between espionage and attack at the level of operational sequencing. Persistent access can support intelligence collection and, if authorised, shift rapidly into effect delivery. The point is not that the categories disappear, but that decision points move closer to execution time. This increases the importance of pre-authorised constraints, auditable tool behaviour, and clear termination conditions, because control mechanisms must operate at the same tempo as the systems they govern.

In sum, technological horizons point towards higher tempo, greater autonomy, and deeper informational asymmetries. The strategic challenge is not to "adopt AI" or "prepare for quantum" as abstract goals. The strategic challenge is to preserve political control and legal authority under compressed decision cycles, while managing intelligence integrity risks that directly affect targeting, proportionality assessments, and post-execution evaluation. The next section examines how norms and legal interpretations shape the space within which these technological options remain strategically usable.

8.2 Norms, Treaties, and Policy Futures

The normative and legal environment for OCO evolves more slowly than technology, yet it remains decisive for strategic utility because legitimacy, alliance coordination, and escalation thresholds are produced through interpretation rather than through code. The central problem is divergence. Many states accept that international law applies to cyberspace, yet they disagree on what core principles require in operational practice, which means that the same cyber operation can be assessed as tolerable competition by one actor and as an unlawful violation by another (Mandsager et al., 2022). The implication for planners is higher miscalculation risk in crisis conditions, because intent and legality are assessed through competing legal positions rather than a shared threshold.

Sovereignty is a persistent point of divergence. Some states treat many intrusions as below the threshold of a sovereignty violation unless tangible effects occur, while others treat unauthorised penetration itself as a breach. The operational consequence is uncertainty about expected responses. An actor may plan activity as "below threshold" competition, yet if the target state applies a stricter sovereignty interpretation, the same activity can be framed as escalatory and demand retaliation. This uncertainty interacts with attribution politics because legal claims are often made alongside contested claims about responsibility, which complicates signalling, escalation management, and crisis communication.

Debates about "use of force" and "armed attack" generate similar uncertainty. Cyber actions that cause death, injury, or severe physical damage map more directly onto existing categories, while actions that corrupt data, disrupt services, or undermine trust can be strategically significant without producing kinetic-like harm. The result is an incentive for grey-zone behaviour. Actors can pursue disruptive operations while assuming that ambiguity lowers the probability of forceful response. The strategic risk is that accumulated disruption can still trigger escalation if it is interpreted as coercion against essential functions, even when the relevant legal category remains contested.

Alliance and regional practice shape norms by shaping consequences. NATO and EU frameworks can increase the credibility of coordinated response options and raise the political costs of repeated malicious activity even when formal thresholds remain ambiguous. For smart states embedded in such frameworks, this produces constraints and leverage at the same time. Constraints arise because offensive action must remain compatible with alliance expectations, deconfliction practices, and shared risk tolerance. Leverage arises because collective attribution, intelligence sharing, and coordinated signalling can impose costs that a small state cannot impose alone.

Treaty ambitions face structural obstacles because cyber capabilities are difficult to verify and offensive toolchains are easily concealed. Narrower instruments therefore tend to dominate, including confidence-building measures, incident communication channels, joint attribution support, and targeted commitments about specific behaviours. These instruments matter because they reduce misperception and create procedural brakes in crisis conditions even when comprehensive prohibition regimes remain politically infeasible. The implication is that norm development is likely to continue through practice and process rather than through universal treaty settlement.

AI governance is increasingly part of this normative environment. The G7 Hiroshima AI Process produced voluntary guiding principles and a code of conduct for organisations developing advanced AI systems, reflecting a policy preference for risk-based constraints rather than blanket bans (G7, 2023). In parallel, the EU AI Act entered into force on 1 August 2024 and introduces a regulatory approach that will shape how European states and companies develop and deploy certain classes of AI systems over time (European Parliament and Council of the European Union, 2024). The relevance for OCO is indirect but operational. Concepts such as risk classification, documentation, and oversight mechanisms influence what "meaningful human control" can mean when automation is integrated into security tooling. The implication is that debates about autonomous cyber capability will be conditioned by emerging regulatory templates for accountability and control rather than starting from first principles.

Quantum disruption can also become a norm-shaping driver because systemic cryptographic failure creates shared risks even among competitors. If the confidentiality of global communications is destabilised, economic and diplomatic interdependence becomes harder to sustain, which creates incentives for coordinated transition to post-quantum cryptography and for partial restraint during migration windows. These incentives compete, however, against the offensive advantages created by asymmetric capability. The likely outcome is uneven progress, where some domains become normatively protected because mutual vulnerability is widely recognised, while other domains remain competitive precisely because verification and attribution are limited.

The management of zero-day vulnerabilities remains a central ethical and normative dilemma because it links offensive advantage to collective risk. Retention preserves access and coercive options, while disclosure reduces systemic exposure for all users of affected systems (Huskaj and Wilson, 2020*b*). For smart states that prioritise rule-of-law legitimacy, the policy requirement is procedural clarity. Vulnerability decisions must be governed by accountable processes that can justify trade-offs between intelligence gain, operational opportunity, and systemic harm, because legitimacy depends on whether these trade-offs can be defended as bounded and proportionate in hindsight as well as at the point of decision.

In sum, norms and policy futures shape OCO by shaping attribution politics, response expectations, and the legitimacy of automation. Where interpretive divergence persists, risk rises because actors cannot rely on shared thresholds. Where practice converges through alliances, confidence-building measures, and governance templates, operational space becomes more predictable. The next section examines how these dynamics intersect with the strategic constraints and advantages of smart states.

8.3 Smart States in a Contested Domain

Innovation-driven smart states occupy a distinctive strategic position because the same characteristics that generate economic advantage also generate strategic exposure. High connectivity, deep digital dependency, and reliance on complex supply chains expand the attack surface available to adversaries, while innovation capacity expands the state's ability to develop selective capability and to shape norms that reduce systemic risk. The implication is a dual constraint: smart states cannot avoid exposure, but they can choose how to translate innovation into bounded capability and how to embed that capability within lawful governance.

Smart states derive influence less from scale than from agility, human capital, and institutional adaptability. Many cyber-literate countries exhibit this profile through research capacity, competitive technology sectors, and established collaboration across government, industry, and academia. These features can support selective specialisation. Rather than seeking parity with larger powers across the full spectrum of cyber capability, a smart state can concentrate on mission-relevant niches where it can sustain competence, integrate intelligence support, and maintain political control under time compression.

Exposure, however, remains structural. Networked services, cloud concentration, and interdependent industrial systems create pathways for coercion and persistent intelligence collection. Open sources and research across many cyber-literate countries indicates that adversaries exploit openness and reliance on digital services to pursue strategic objectives (Bengtsson and Huskaj, 2021). The implication is that deterrence cannot be built on defence alone. A smart state needs some capacity to impose costs and shape adversary expectations, yet that capacity has limited strategic value if it cannot be translated into lawful and politically controlled practice.

Institutional alignment is therefore a core requirement. Offensive capability is not credible if intelligence support is slow, authorities are unclear, or decision processes cannot operate inside compressed windows. The limiting factor is often organisational rather than technical. Intelligence organisations and military commanders operate under different mandates and cultures, and misalignment can delay targeting and narrow options at the point of execution. For smart states, credible OCO depends on governance arrangements that enable intelligence–operations fusion while preserving oversight and accountability.

Escalation risk management is a second structural requirement. Smart states are vulnerable to retaliation that can disrupt essential services, which increases the political cost of miscalculation and narrows the margin for error. This creates incentives for precision, bounded effects, and deconfliction, often reinforced through alliance coordination. Alliances act as force multipliers by enhancing attribution capacity, increasing intelligence reach, and enabling coordinated responses that raise the expected cost of aggression. The mechanism is altered adversary calculation under uncertainty about coalition response options, rather than reliance on protection as an abstract guarantee.

Whole-of-society resilience strengthens offensive posture indirectly. If public institutions, private operators, and citizens can absorb and recover from cyber disruption, the coercive value of adversary operations declines. Reduced coercive leverage increases freedom of action because it lowers the expected political cost of retaliation. Case-based organisational analysis treats the mobilisation of innovation capacity and public–private coordination as part of offensive credibility rather than as a separate defensive agenda (Huskaj and Axelsson, 2023).

In sum, smart states face a persistent trade-off. They must develop selective offensive options to shape adversary behaviour, while ensuring that institutional design, legal authority, and resilience reduce the probability that offensive activity generates instability that disproportionately harms the smart state itself. The next section uses scenarios to clarify how different combinations of technology and governance reshape this trade-off.

8.4 Scenarios for Future OCO

This section uses scenarios to make the chapter's causal claims tangible. The purpose is not to predict the future, but to isolate decision points and show how choices about automation, cryptographic transition, and norm development can alter the space of feasible and politically controllable OCO. The value of scenarios is that they force the analyst to state assumptions explicitly and to link those assumptions to operational and strategic implications.

The first scenario concerns high-autonomy cyber agents operating at machine speed. In this scenario, offensive and defensive systems execute actions based on broad human-defined objectives but without continuous human intervention. The risk is misinterpretation under ambiguity. Optimisation processes can treat uncertain signals as hostile intent and trigger actions that exceed political thresholds. When deployed agents act faster than oversight can intervene, reversal becomes difficult and escalation becomes more likely because action and counteraction can unfold before legal review and political direction can be applied (Huskaj, 2026). The implication for smart states is that governance must be built into the system design: target classes, termination conditions, and auditability must be specified in advance if political control is to be preserved under time compression.

The second scenario concerns quantum-enabled cryptanalytic advantage by a major power. In this scenario, confidentiality, authentication, and coordination rely on cryptographic assumptions that no longer hold. Retrospective decryption enables an intelligence advantage that is difficult for the victim to detect, and it can undermine trust in diplomatic and military communications even in the absence of visible disruption (Arute et al., 2019). The operational implication for smart states is urgency in post-quantum transition. Uneven migration produces weak links, while delayed migration increases the value of adversary stockpiling and future exploitation (Mosca, 2018). The strategic implication is that a cryptanalytic advantage can translate into coercive leverage because it alters what an actor can know about intent, plans, and mobilisation before a crisis becomes visible.

The third scenario concerns partial restraint through treaties and confidence-building measures. In this scenario, states fail to reach comprehensive prohibition regimes, but they develop narrower commitments that reduce the most destabilising practices. The mechanism resembles arms-control practice under verification limits. Once states internalise that mutual restraint yields stability gains, targeted commitments become politically feasible even when capabilities remain opaque. Constraints on targeting essential civilian systems and procedural measures for incident communication can reduce misperception and narrow escalation pathways (Mandsager et al., 2022). The implication for smart states is that bounded norms can reduce exposure to higher-end adversaries while preserving space for proportionate action within alliance expectations.

The fourth scenario concerns innovation-based deterrence by smart states through selective specialisation. In this scenario, small technologically advanced states develop niche capabilities that can impose operational costs disproportionate to size by affecting adversary dependencies in bounded ways. This approach depends on sustained innovation, intelligence integration, and resilience that reduces the coercive value of retaliation. One national case analysis illustrates how niche capability, combined with alliance leverage, can shape adversary risk calculations by increasing uncertainty about system reliability under pressure (Huskaj and Axelsson, 2023). The implication is that selective capability can matter strategically, but only when it is integrated into decision authority, intelligence support, and political control.

Taken together, these scenarios indicate that the decisive variable is not whether states acquire new tools, but whether they can align capability with control. Automation increases instability risk when governance lags. Quantum risk creates an asymmetric intelligence advantage when cryptographic migration is slow. Confidence-building measures can bound behaviour when mutual vulnerability is recognised. Smart-state specialisation can strengthen deterrence when institutions can translate innovation into authorised and bounded options. The next section presents policy and research implications that follow from these decision points.

8.5 Policy and Research Implications

The preceding analysis indicates that future OCO will be shaped by the interaction of technological acceleration, evolving norms, and institutional adaptation. The purpose of this section is to specify practical implications for policy and for research. The common constraint is time compression. As decision windows narrow, the cost of unclear authority, weak intelligence provenance, and unbounded automation increases, because errors become harder to detect and harder to reverse once action is taken.

Firstly, governments require anticipatory policy processes that specify when and why offensive cyberspace options may be used, and how they will be bounded. The scenario analysis indicates that instability can emerge from tool properties and structural asymmetry rather than from deliberate escalation intent. The implication is that states need doctrines and decision authorities that can operate inside narrow windows while still enabling legal review and political accountability. Cyber effects must also be treated as part of wider statecraft because cyber incidents can demand diplomatic, economic, informational, or kinetic responses depending on scale and intent (USAF LeMay Center, 2023). This requires rules of engagement (ROE) and delegated authorities that preserve political control while accounting for second-order effects and technical uncertainty in execution (Kehler et al., 2017).

Secondly, operational integration depends on intelligence transformation. Faster collection and analytic automation can shorten the cycle from detection to action, but integrity attacks and deception against analytic pipelines can corrupt targeting and assessment. The implication is that intelligence governance must prioritise provenance, auditability, and counter-deception measures, because operational tempo without analytic reliability increases the probability of miscalculation. This is a direct constraint on offensive credibility: threats and actions are only credible when informed by timely and trustworthy intelligence.

Thirdly, legal and ethical constraint should be treated as a determinant of legitimacy rather than as a secondary compliance layer. Vulnerability exploitation yields offensive options, but systematic retention can increase systemic insecurity and undermine normative commitments (Huskaj and Wilson, 2020*b*). The implication is that states with strong rule-of-law traditions must embed legal and ethical review into planning so that proportionality and discrimination judgements are made against realistic models of second-order effects, including spillover and escalation sensitivity. This also supports alliance interoperability, because partners require predictable standards for deconfliction and responsibility attribution.

Fourthly, post-quantum transition should be treated as a strategic security programme with offensive and defensive implications. Standardisation milestones reduce uncertainty about algorithm choice, but they do not reduce the migration burden, which remains multi-year and uneven (National Institute of Standards and Technology, 2024). The implication is a window of elevated systemic risk during transition, because heterogeneous cryptography produces weak links and legacy systems remain attractive for stockpiling. Policy should therefore prioritise long-lived secrets, critical authentication systems, and national coordination with major operators to reduce weak-link exposure during migration.

Fifthly, research priorities follow from the capability–governance gap. Empirical work on cyber deterrence remains necessary to clarify when offensive options alter adversary decision-making and when they do not. AI-related research should focus on controllability, auditability, and constraint design rather than feasibility alone, because the strategic problem is political control under time compression. Quantum-related research should focus on migration timelines, weak-link dynamics, and how asymmetric cryptanalytic advantage interacts with intelligence competition. Norm research remains central because verification limits force reliance on practice, signalling, and procedural measures.

For small, innovation-driven, digitally dependent states, the implication is that offensive cyberspace options have strategic value only when selective specialisation is combined with institutional integration and societal resilience. Innovation capacity can generate disproportionate leverage, but only when aligned with clear decision authority, intelligence support, and governance mechanisms that preserve legitimacy and manage escalation risk. Alliance frameworks can amplify these conditions through attribution support, intelligence sharing, and coordinated signalling (Huskaj and Axelsson, 2023). The strategic objective is politically controllable capability that can shape adversary expectations without increasing systemic instability.

8.6 Conclusion

This chapter has examined how emerging technologies and evolving norms may shape the future of OCO, with particular attention to the strategic constraints and opportunities facing innovation-driven smart states. The analysis indicates that artificial intelligence and automation increase tempo and scale, yet they also weaken interpretability and compress oversight. The implication is that machine-speed decision points can arise faster than legal review and political direction can intervene, which increases the risk that limited actions are misread or spill beyond intended boundaries (Huskaj, 2026).

The analysis also indicates that quantum computing creates a different pressure by threatening the confidentiality and authentication assumptions that underpin intelligence protection and societal trust in communications. The strategic mechanism is anticipatory exploitation. Traffic collected today may become intelligible later, which encourages "harvest-now, decrypt-later" strategies and shifts incentives even before full-scale capability exists (Mosca, 2018). The implication is that post-quantum migration is not only a defensive requirement; it also conditions intelligence exposure and offensive feasibility during a multi-year transition (National Institute of Standards and Technology, 2024).

Norms and policy frameworks evolve more slowly than capabilities, yet they shape strategic utility because legitimacy, response expectations, and alliance coordination are produced through interpretation. Broad agreement that international law applies to cyberspace coexists with persistent divergence on sovereignty and thresholds, which increases the probability of miscalculation under contested legal positions (Mandsager et al., 2022). Emerging governance templates for advanced AI and regulatory approaches within Europe further shape how accountability and oversight are operationalised over time (G7, 2023; European Parliament and Council of the European Union, 2024). The implication is that debates about autonomy and control in cyber capability will be conditioned by these templates rather than beginning from a blank slate.

For cyberliterate states and similar smart states, the central implication is that offensive capability strengthens deterrence only when it is integrated into lawful authority, reliable intelligence, and politically controllable practice. High digital dependency increases exposure to coercion and intelligence collection, yet innovation capacity supports selective specialisation and alliance-enabled leverage (Bengtsson and Huskaj, 2021; Huskaj and Axelsson, 2023). The strategic requirement is alignment across levels and dimensions: new technical options must be translated into authorised and bounded operational plans supported by trustworthy intelligence and resilient societal functions. This synthesis prepares the ground for the concluding chapter, which consolidates cross-chapter lessons about how strategic intent, organisational design, intelligence integration, and tactical execution jointly shape the credibility and consequences of OCO.

Decision Exercise: Preserving Political Control of OCO Under AI Acceleration and Cryptographic Transition

Scenario. Over the next 12 months, a cyberliterate state faces three linked pressures. First, AI-enabled toolchains compress the interval between vulnerability disclosure and operational exploitation, tightening decision windows for both response and authorisation. Second, post-quantum cryptography migration begins unevenly across critical sectors, creating heterogeneous security postures and incentives for retrospective decryption. Third, legal interpretations and alliance expectations remain divergent, increasing misinterpretation risk when cyber activity occurs under partial attribution. Political leaders request a decision package that preserves lawful authority and oversight under time compression, sustains intelligence integrity, and keeps response options credible in coalition settings.

Analytical question 1—Primary objective and time horizon. State the primary objective for the next 18 months (authorisation speed with oversight; assurance quality for bounded effects; intelligence integrity; post-quantum transition risk reduction; coalition interoperability). Provide one observable success condition and one measurable proxy that can be assessed without operational disclosure.

Analytical question 2—Automation policy under compressed decision cycles. Define a national policy position for AI-enabled cyber tooling in offensive planning and preparation. Specify:

- which decisions must remain human-authorised at political level,
- the minimum auditability requirement for model-influenced recommendations (inputs, outputs, versioning),
- one restriction on target classes or system categories due to escalation sensitivity.

State one failure mode where automation increases misinterpretation or reduces boundedness.

Analytical question 3—Quantum transition posture and intelligence risk. Select a posture for the cryptographic migration window that integrates national security and societal exposure. Specify:

- which assets are prioritised (long-lived secrets; authentication; critical coordination channels),
- one mechanism for coordinating migration with major operators inside 90 days,
- one policy rule for handling newly discovered weaknesses during migration (disclosure, time-bounded retention, partner notification sequencing).

State one strategic risk created by uneven migration across sectors.

Analytical question 4—Norms, signalling, and alliance constraints. Draft a two-sentence posture statement for coalition partners that clarifies (i) commitment to legal authority and bounded effects and (ii) the purpose of maintaining OCO options under democratic oversight. Identify one coordination constraint created by partner releasability rules and one mitigation that preserves credibility without amplifying uncertainty.

Short task—MLMD mapping (one page). Create a 3-row mapping (Strategic / Operational / Tactical) listing:

1. the decision at each level,
2. the key dependency (authority and legitimacy; intelligence integration and deconfliction; technical feasibility and assurance),
3. one misalignment failure mode under time compression.

9

Synthesis and Implications for Credible Offensive Cyberspace Operations

This concluding chapter synthesises the book's analytical foundations, empirical insights, and doctrinal implications to specify the conditions under which OCO (OCO) contribute credibly to national security. It restates the book's central causal claim: offensive capability generates strategic value only when it is integrated across strategic, operational, and tactical decision-making and embedded in institutional, legal, and societal arrangements that enable coherent authorisation, planning, and execution. When integration is weak, technical instruments can produce effects that diverge from political intent or exceed operational feasibility.

The chapter proceeds through a structured synthesis. Section 9.1 reassembles the overarching argument by linking the Multi-Level, Multi-Dimensional (MLMD) framework, intelligence integration, and offensive doctrine into a unified model of state practice. Section 9.2 derives cross-cutting insights that recur across the theoretical and empirical analyses. Section 9.3 develops institutional implications for cyberliterate states seeking to develop offensive capabilities. Section 9.4 expands the focus to the whole-of-society approach required for credible OCO. Sections 9.5 and 9.6 identify future security policy and future research directions shaped by technological acceleration and adversary innovation. Section 9.7 closes with final reflections.

This book advances three claims about OCO. First, strategic intent, operational design, and tactical execution remain coupled in cyberspace because access dependencies, intelligence requirements, and technical volatility create constraints that propagate across levels of analysis. Second, intelligence integration and vulnerability governance are institutional design problems that condition whether offensive capability can be authorised, controlled, and sustained over time. Third, comparative case material indicates that credible offensive cyber power depends on governance and societal arrangements that preserve decision competence under time pressure.

Chapter 1 began from a practical puzzle: states invest in offensive cyberspace capabilities, yet often struggle to translate that capability into credible deterrence and controlled state action. The analysis has shown that this difficulty arises because political objectives, legal authority, intelligence dependencies, and organisational boundaries jointly shape what can be planned, authorised, and executed within narrow decision windows.

9.1 Reassembling the Argument

This section proceeds from the book's central causal claim: offensive capability generates strategic value only when it is integrated across strategic, operational, and tactical decision-making and embedded in institutional, legal, and societal arrangements that enable coherent

DOI: 10.1201/9781003655183-9

authorisation, planning, and execution. This claim treats offensive capability as a necessary input but an insufficient condition for deterrence and strategic leverage.

Within this book, the institutional, legal, and societal arrangements referenced in the central claim are analysed through political authority, ethical constraint, organisational design, and technical feasibility.

This section reconstructs the conceptual architecture developed in earlier chapters by linking the MLMD framework, intelligence integration, and offensive cyber doctrine into a unified model of state practice.

The MLMD framework serves as the book's structural anchor because it clarifies how decisions taken at one level constrain and enable choices at other levels. Offensive cyber actions are executed in technical systems, yet their consequences unfold in political and organisational environments. For that reason, tactical effects cannot be assessed independently of strategic purpose. MLMD makes this dependency explicit by showing how political intent sets the boundaries of operational design, while operational assessments of access, risk, and intelligence shape what is tactically feasible. The implication is that a state that treats OCO as a primarily technical activity increases the probability of misalignment between intended outcomes and realised effects.

A second component of the argument concerns intelligence integration. Offensive operations depend on intelligence as a preparatory input and as a continuous structuring function that shapes target selection, access maintenance, timing, and assessment. This follows from three conditions that recur across the book: knowledge of the target environment is partial, the technical landscape changes rapidly, and adversaries adapt in response to exposure and countermeasures. Under these conditions, operational success depends on whether intelligence architectures can reduce uncertainty in time to shape operational choice. When intelligence is delayed, compartmentalised, or organisationally siloed, offensive actions are more likely to be launched with incomplete situational awareness, which increases operational failure risk and can widen escalation pathways. When intelligence is fused across sources and integrated into planning and execution, decision-makers can calibrate effects, manage risk, and maintain alignment with strategic intent.

Offensive cyber doctrine constitutes the third component because it specifies how a state conceptualises the projection of power in and through cyberspace, and under what conditions that power can be authorised and applied. Doctrine defines roles, thresholds, and coordination requirements between offensive and defensive measures, and it embeds legal and ethical constraints into operational expectations. Its strategic value lies in reducing ambiguity about authority, proportionality, and escalation considerations. When doctrine is unclear or contested, planners and decision-makers may lack shared definitions of authority, proportionality, and escalation exposure. This condition is likely to delay authorisation and weakens operational design, even when technical capability exists. In this sense, doctrine operationalises MLMD by translating political intent into planning constraints and decision procedures that can be executed under time pressure.

Taken together, the MLMD framework, intelligence integration, and doctrine form a system in which OCO can be planned, authorised, and executed in ways that support national strategy rather than undermine it. This convergence matters because offensive cyber capabilities are dual-use in practice: they can impose costs, deny advantage, or shape adversary behaviour, but they can also introduce instability when actions are poorly aligned with strategic objectives or inadequately governed. The book's argument is therefore conditional: offensive capability contributes to national security when it is embedded in structured planning, anticipatory ethical and legal review, and intelligence-driven control mechanisms that preserve strategic alignment over the lifecycle of an operation.

A further conclusion is that the integration problem is primarily institutional rather than technical. Many states can acquire tools and specialist skills, yet still lack organisational mechanisms that connect those capabilities to political decision-making and to intelligence-supported operational planning. The consequence is delay, authority ambiguity, and coordination failure, which weakens deterrence because adversaries infer that action will be slow, inconsistent, or politically constrained. By contrast, when authorities, command relationships, and intelligence architectures are aligned, offensive capability becomes a credible extension of state power because adversaries can reasonably expect coherent decision and follow-through.

Finally, the argument implies that credible offensive cyber capability depends on whole-of-society arrangements. Innovation capacity, privately owned infrastructure, and academic expertise shape both the resources available for offensive action and the vulnerabilities that adversaries can exploit in return. This duality means offensive capability development cannot be insulated from broader societal dependencies. Instead, states must organise for coordination across sectors to sustain talent pipelines, manage vulnerability governance, and preserve resilience against retaliation and counter-pressure. Within MLMD, these societal conditions occupy the political and organisational dimensions that determine whether offensive options are feasible and sustainable.

This reassembled argument establishes why technology expands what states can do, while strategy, intelligence, doctrine, and governance determine what states can authorise, control, and justify. On that basis, the next section derives cross-cutting insights that recur across the book's theoretical analysis and empirical material.

9.2 Cross-Cutting Insights

Across the book, a consistent finding is that OCO expose recurrent misalignment between strategic intent and operational capacity. Political objectives often require fast, precise, and reversible outcomes, while operational practice remains bounded by legal mandates, institutional divisions, and incomplete intelligence. When strategic guidance is underspecified or authorities are fragmented, planners cannot translate political aims into coherent operational design. This gap is not state-specific. It reflects a structural difficulty: integrating a high-velocity technical domain into decision architectures developed for slower, more observable forms of military activity.

A second insight concerns the relationship between offensive operations and intelligence. In cyberspace, vulnerabilities shift, adversaries adapt, and system architectures change without warning. Under these conditions, intelligence cannot function as a discrete preparatory stage that "precedes" action. It must accompany operations as a continuous interpretive function that supports target validation, access maintenance, timing, and assessment. The case material and the doctrinal discussion show that when intelligence structures are slow, compartmentalised, or misaligned with tactical requirements, operational decisions become unreliable. The result is a mismatch between perceived control at the political level and uncertainty at the operational and tactical levels.

A third insight is that vulnerability management is a strategic governance problem rather than a technical choice. Decisions to retain, disclose, or weaponise vulnerabilities distribute risk across time and across actors. Retention can increase short-term operational opportunity, yet it also increases systemic exposure because the same weakness can be discovered, repurposed, or leaked and then used against the retaining state and its society. EternalBlue illustrates how exploit loss can transform an intelligence advantage into broad societal harm. The underlying dynamic is temporal displacement: benefits accrue immediately to the state holding the exploit, while costs materialise later and diffuse across public and private systems. States therefore require decision processes that weigh offensive value against defensive and societal risk, and that incorporate legal and ethical review as part of operational governance.

A fourth insight concerns organisational coherence. The book's cases and doctrinal analysis indicate that technical capability is seldom the binding constraint. Operational performance is instead shaped by coordination: how agencies share intelligence, allocate authority, sequence decisions, and integrate legal and ethical review into planning. Where institutions remain siloed, outcomes tend towards delay or action without adequate consultation, both of which increase the probability of unintended effects and political loss of control. Where joint structures are institutionalised and authorities clarified, decision cycles shorten and planning aligns more consistently with the MLMD dependencies between strategic purpose, operational design, and tactical feasibility.

A fifth insight is that time pressure is not an episodic condition but a recurring feature of offensive cyber decision-making. High-velocity incidents reduce the opportunity for deliberation, and exercises reproduce the same constraint even when the operational environment is controlled. Under compressed timelines, organisations rely on pre-established playbooks, rehearsed procedures, and pre-authorised decision pathways. Preparedness therefore substitutes for missing intelligence during crisis response. When such preparedness is absent, states default to ad hoc sequencing that erodes strategic coherence and increases escalation risk.

A sixth insight is that cyber effects routinely generate cross-domain consequences. Although operations are executed through digital access, their consequences affect political signalling, military posture, and societal confidence. Tactical actions shape adversary perceptions, and those perceptions can tighten or expand political constraints on subsequent action. The operational implication is that planners must treat "cyber" as an interdependent component of wider state practice rather than as a self-contained technical activity. When this dependency chain is not anticipated—tactical exploit to operational effect to strategic interpretation—states increase the probability of miscalculation.

A final insight concerns the distribution of cyber power across society. Offensive capability depends on innovation environments, privately owned infrastructure, and academic expertise that sit outside traditional hierarchies. When these resources remain disconnected from national security institutions, states struggle to generate credible signals, sustain capability development, and recover from counter-pressure. When coordination is institutionalised, states gain access to specialised knowledge, training capacity, and technical infrastructure that support more disciplined operational design. The strategic conclusion is that national cyber capacity emerges from coordination across institutional boundaries, not from centralisation alone.

9.3 Institutional Implications for Cyberliterate States

Many cyber-literate states face an institutional design problem when developing credible offensive cyberspace capability. Offensive action can create strategic value only when political direction, legal authority, intelligence production, and operational planning are connected in ways that support timely authorisation and disciplined execution under uncertainty. When these functions remain fragmented, planners are pushed towards either delay or action under incomplete situational awareness, which increases the probability of misalignment between intended outcomes and realised effects. The implications below identify governance variables that condition whether offensive capability can be authorised, controlled, and sustained over time.

A first requirement is a national decision framework for authorising OCO. Offensive action demands explicit thresholds, legal mandates, and escalation pathways because cyber effects can trigger political consequences that extend beyond the immediate technical action. A decision framework may specify how requests are initiated and elevated, who holds decision authority, and how assessments of legality, proportionality, and national interest are integrated into the authorisation sequence. When political intent is converted into procedural guidance, operational planning becomes more consistent and signalling becomes more credible because external actors can infer a capacity for coherent decision and follow-through.

A second requirement is to institutionalise intelligence integration across the intelligence community. Offensive operations require multi-source intelligence that combines SIGINT, HUMINT, cyber reconnaissance, vulnerability analysis, and strategic assessment. Specialisation across civilian intelligence, military intelligence, and signals intelligence (SIGINT) functions can strengthen analytical depth, but it can also increase fragmentation between strategic assessment and operational targeting needs. Many cyberliterate states therefore face a design choice: whether to formalise joint analytical structures that produce a shared operational picture and support the lifecycle of offensive activity, from target development to assessment. When intelligence flows converge in institutional form, uncertainty is reduced in time to shape operational choice, and authorisation can be based on a clearer understanding of access, risk, and consequence.

A third requirement is a formalised operational planning structure for OCO. Offensive units require access to intelligence-driven target development, vulnerability research, and assessment of cross-domain implications. In many cyberliterate states, a joint planning function that links defence, intelligence, and signals-intelligence organisations provides a standing mechanism for translating political guidance into operational design under MLMD constraints. The purpose is to ensure that legal and ethical review, intelligence dependencies, and technical feasibility are assessed together rather than sequentially. This integration reduces the probability that tactical feasibility is assumed where access is uncertain or that political objectives outpace operational control.

A fourth requirement is a national vulnerability governance process. For highly digitalised societies, decisions to retain, disclose, or mitigate vulnerabilities shape both offensive opportunity and domestic exposure. Many cyberliterate states therefore institutionalise a formal vulnerability disclosure-and-retention governance mechanism that weighs offensive value against defensive risk and societal consequence. Such governance is more feasible when SIGINT, civilian intelligence, military intelligence, and national cyber security coordination functions can contribute distinct assessments of operational utility and systemic risk. A structured process can preserve offensive options while reducing the probability that retained vulnerabilities become long-term liabilities for national resilience.

A fifth requirement is to align offensive cyber capability with NATO cyber structures and coordination processes. For many cyberliterate NATO members, alliance participation expands opportunities for intelligence cooperation, operational planning, and integrated exercises. Offensive capability gains strategic value when it is interoperable with allied doctrine, information-sharing arrangements, and legal interfaces. Many cyberliterate NATO members therefore face an institutional design task: ensuring that national reforms produce clear points of contact and procedures that enable timely coordination with NATO structures. When offensive planning is embedded in collective defence planning, adversaries must account for coordinated response options rather than national action alone, which can alter their risk calculus.

A sixth requirement concerns specialised human capital. Offensive operations require operators, analysts, intelligence officers, and legal advisers who can work across technical, strategic, and legal constraints. States with access to joint intelligence academies and expanded training programmes can therefore integrate offensive doctrine, targeting principles, legal frameworks, and intelligence fusion methods into a shared curriculum. The purpose is to produce a professional community with common concepts and procedures. When the workforce shares doctrinal and legal frames, coordination costs decrease and operational control increases.

A seventh requirement is structured public–private coordination as a national security function. Infrastructure relevant to access development, vulnerability assessment, and operational preparation is often owned or operated by private entities, and resilience against counter-pressure depends on collaboration with telecommunications providers, cloud operators, energy companies, and other critical sectors. Many cyberliterate states therefore institutionalise coordination mechanisms that support selective information sharing, joint exercises, and cooperative risk assessment. When such coordination is routine rather than ad hoc, national situational awareness improves and offensive planning can account for domestic dependencies and retaliation pathways.

An eighth requirement is to integrate cyber planning into joint and multi-domain defence planning. Offensive cyber effects can enable or constrain military posture, crisis response, and information operations. Many cyber-literate states with alliance commitments and regional deterrence responsibilities therefore integrate cyber capability into joint planning cycles and rehearsals. This is often operationalised through cyber liaison functions within joint commands, shared doctrinal products, and integrated exercises that force explicit trade-offs between speed, control, and escalation risk. When cyber is planned as part of joint operations, seams between domains are reduced, and strategic coherence is easier to sustain under time pressure.

Finally, many cyberliterate states need to treat societal resilience as an enabling condition for offensive credibility. Offensive capability can impose costs and shape adversary behaviour, yet its strategic value is constrained if the state cannot absorb countermeasures directed at civilian systems. Preparedness measures—redundancy, incident response, and public communication—therefore function as enablers of offensive action rather than as separate defensive activities. When resilience is higher, adversaries face reduced prospects of coercion through civilian disruption, and decision-makers retain political space to authorise proportionate responses without domestic exposure dictating strategic restraint.

Taken together, these implications indicate that the main advantage for many cyberliterate states lies in institutional integration rather than tool acquisition. Institutional reforms can create an opportunity to connect authority, intelligence, and operational planning into a coherent architecture. The remaining task is to translate reform intent into decision frameworks, joint structures, and governance processes that preserve legality, control, and strategic alignment.

9.4 The Whole-of-Society Imperative

The preceding chapters show that the credibility of OCO (OCO) does not follow directly from technical capability. It follows from the societal structures within which offensive capability is developed, authorised, and sustained. States that rely on digitally integrated infrastructures, interdependent supply chains, and data-driven public services carry strategic exposure that adversaries can exploit during crisis and competition. For that reason, offensive capability cannot be separated from societal resilience. A state that cannot absorb and mitigate cyber disruption will face stronger political constraints on authorisation and will struggle to sustain offensive action under counter-pressure. The whole-of-society imperative therefore follows from interdependence between offensive operations and the resilience of the socio-technical systems that underpin national security.

A first dimension of this imperative is public–private cooperation. Critical infrastructures —telecommunications, energy, transport, cloud services, and financial systems—are largely owned or operated by private entities. At the same time, offensive cyber operations can generate cascading effects that propagate into civilian systems, and adversaries often exploit private networks as access paths to state targets. Without structured cooperation mechanisms between government and industry, neither side can form a complete picture of national cyber risk or the domestic dependencies that shape operational feasibility. Joint exercises, selective information-sharing arrangements, and coordinated vulnerability disclosure (CVD) procedures are therefore enabling conditions for both resilience and controlled offensive planning.

A second dimension concerns public trust and societal preparedness. Offensive operations are often covert, but their consequences—including retaliation and disruption—can affect the population. Governments therefore require communication practices and crisis-response protocols that preserve trust under uncertainty and reduce susceptibility to panic and influence activity. When the population understands basic cyber risk and trusts national institutions, societal responses to disruption become more coordinated, and decision-makers retain political space to authorise proportionate action without escalation driven by domestic instability.

A third dimension concerns the national innovation base. States with advanced research capacity and dense networks of technical expertise can develop offensive capability more quickly, but this advantage materialises only when research institutions, technology firms, and national security organisations are linked through structured pathways. Capability development accelerates when shared problem sets exist, when expertise can be exchanged under lawful controls, and when test environments allow techniques to be evaluated before operational use. Without such connections, research remains siloed and capability development lags behind adversary adaptation.

A fourth dimension concerns the relationship between resilience and offensive credibility. Offensive capability shapes adversary behaviour only when the state can endure countermeasures directed at civilian systems. This requires redundancy in critical services, diversified supply chains, and well-rehearsed incident-response arrangements across both public and private sectors. Higher resilience raises the threshold at which adversaries expect civilian disruption to translate into political concession. As a result, resilience functions as an enabler of offensive action, because it reduces the likelihood that domestic exposure dictates strategic restraint.

Taken together, these dimensions show that cyber conflict collapses conventional boundaries between state and society. Offensive operations do not occur solely within military or intelligence organisations. They unfold through privately owned infrastructure, research capacity, legal constraints, and public expectations. The strategic implication is that credible offensive cyber capability requires societal arrangements that can support capability development, absorb counter-pressure, and preserve political control during crisis. Whole-of-society integration is therefore a requirement for states that seek to employ OCO as a responsible and strategically usable instrument of national power.

9.5 Future Security Policy Directions

Future security policy will be shaped by the interaction between technological acceleration, sustained state competition, and the erosion of temporal advantages that previously underpinned national cyber strategies. Automation and AI-enabled tooling compress the interval between vulnerability discovery, proof-of-concept development, and operational use. When exploitation cycles accelerate, the value of intelligence integration, preparedness, and institutional agility increases because decision windows narrow while uncertainty remains. Security policy must therefore be designed for high-velocity adaptation rather than for linear planning assumptions.

A first direction is to treat national digital infrastructure as a strategic resource that requires continuous assurance. Objectives such as digital autonomy, trusted technology supply chains, and resilience acquire operational meaning when adversaries can probe for weaknesses at scale. The policy implication is that states must invest in preventive assurance mechanisms—secure-by-design procurement requirements, continuous auditing for critical systems, and national-level vulnerability observatories—rather than relying on patch cycles that assume long warning times.

A second direction concerns governance of dual-use technologies. AI, quantum computing, and autonomy can create strategic advantage, but they also generate dependency risk when states rely on external platforms, components, or service providers for core functions. The policy problem is therefore two-sided: maintaining access to innovation while reducing strategic exposure created by foreign control over critical technological layers. States that retain control over key technologies preserve freedom of action and can impose costs; states that accumulate dependencies risk coercive leverage and reduced operational autonomy.

A third direction is to institutionalise private-sector participation in national threat assessment and response structures. The technical terrain most relevant to cyber exploitation—software stacks, cloud services, managed infrastructure, and supply chains—is predominantly owned or operated by private actors. When adversaries move quickly, the intelligence gap is widened if public institutions cannot exchange information and coordinate analysis with industry in near real time. Policy must therefore establish legal and organisational mechanisms for time-sensitive information exchange, collaborative analysis, and coordinated response planning, while preserving clear safeguards for accountability and proportionality.

A fourth direction is to align future-oriented capability development with the MLMD framework. Questions concerning AI-assisted operational planning, post-quantum transition, attribution support, and cross-domain escalation dynamics cannot be addressed through technical measures alone because they combine strategic intent, legal authority, intelligence dependencies, and tactical feasibility. States that institutionalise interdisciplinary work on these problems will be better positioned to update doctrine, adjust governance arrangements, and design capabilities that can be authorised and controlled under compressed decision windows.

9.6 Future Research Directions

The analysis across this book identifies domains where academic and policy knowledge remains incomplete. OCO develop faster than the institutional frameworks designed to govern them, and this divergence generates uncertainty for policy-makers and practitioners. Future research is therefore needed to clarify the institutional and operational conditions under which offensive capability can be controlled, aligned with political intent, and sustained under counter-pressure.

A first research area concerns intelligence–operations integration. Although intelligence is a prerequisite for offensive action, empirical work seldom examines how intelligence flows translate into operational decisions, or how organisational design shapes this translation under time pressure. Comparative research is needed on how different intelligence configurations—civilian, military, SIGINT-centric, or joint—affect decision tempo, precision, legality, and assessment. Process-tracing studies of real or simulated operations can clarify how intelligence dependencies condition operational outcomes across MLMD levels.

A second research frontier concerns AI-enabled offensive operations. Technical literature describes what automation can do, but less is known about reliability, controllability, and escalation dynamics when systems conduct reconnaissance, exploitation, or payload delivery with reduced human intervention. Research can examine how machine learning models behave in adversarial environments, which forms of human oversight remain feasible at operational tempo, and how accelerated decision cycles alter signalling and deterrence. The central question is whether autonomy introduces structural instability because operational speed outpaces political control and legal review.

A third area concerns quantum risk and national security. Cryptanalytic risk is widely discussed, but broader strategic questions remain underexplored: how quantum-enabled intelligence might shift offence–defence relations, how harvest-now/decrypt-later practices shape state behaviour during the transition period, and how states can coordinate post-quantum migration without creating new vulnerabilities. Scenario analysis and modelling can help clarify how quantum asymmetries may alter strategic competition and alliance dynamics.

A fourth area concerns vulnerability governance. Policy interest in Vulnerabilities Equities Processes have increased, yet empirical evidence on how states weigh offensive value against systemic risk remains limited. Research can examine institutional incentives, interagency bargaining, and the long-term consequences of exploit retention for domestic resilience and allied exposure. The core question is whether structured governance can mitigate the collective-action problem created by shared software dependencies across states, firms, and societies.

A fifth area concerns multi-domain coordination. Cyber effects increasingly support operations across air, land, maritime, space, and information domains, yet doctrine often treats these interactions at a high level of abstraction. Research can analyse how cyber capabilities affect operational timing, escalation thresholds, and coalition cohesion in integrated campaigns. Because adversaries exploit seams between domains and institutions, understanding cross-domain coupling is central to contemporary defence planning.

Together, these research directions indicate a need for analytical approaches that keep pace with technological acceleration while remaining grounded in institutional realities. Advancing this agenda will strengthen both scholarship and the policy foundations for controlled and strategically coherent offensive cyber capability.

9.7 Final Reflections

This book has argued that OCO are a consequential instrument of state power because they reshape how states deter, signal, and defend under conditions of uncertainty and technical volatility. Offensive capability generates strategic value when it is embedded in institutions that translate political intent into operational direction and legally grounded action. When governance, intelligence integration, and societal resilience are limited, offensive tools increase coordination demands and narrow political control.

A recurring theme is that cyberspace tightens the coupling between offence, defence, and intelligence. Offensive operations depend on intelligence for access and timing; intelligence depends on offensive techniques for reach and granularity; and defensive resilience shapes whether a state can endure reciprocal pressure without strategic concession. This interdependence places OCO within a posture that links deterrence and defence to intelligence production, authority, and institutional decision-making.

The MLMD framework clarifies why this coupling persists. Strategic–political intent, operational–ethical and intelligence integration, and tactical–technical feasibility remain mutually constraining. Political objectives shape what can be authorised and what can be signalled; operational design translates those objectives into plans under intelligence and legal constraints; tactical execution remains bounded by access conditions and technical uncertainty. When these dependencies lack institutional management, misalignment becomes a recurrent outcome.

The normative significance of OCO follows from their potential to influence adversary behaviour below kinetic thresholds while still imposing costs and shaping decision-making. This potential creates governance obligations. Offensive action remains bounded by international law, and operational design remains bounded by requirements to limit harm to civilian systems and to manage escalation exposure. Legitimacy and control condition credibility and sustainability.

The future of offensive cyber capability will be shaped by how states organise authority, intelligence, doctrine, and societal resilience to govern its use. Integration and preparedness preserve political control under time pressure and widen the scope for operations that remain aligned with declared objectives. Technological acceleration, adversary adaptation, and institutional reforms will continue to compress decision windows and increase the premium on disciplined authorisation and planning.

This book began from a practical puzzle: cyberliterate states invest in offensive capability, yet struggle to translate that capability into credible deterrence and controlled state action under conditions of time compression, attribution frictions, and technical volatility. The analysis has shown that this difficulty persists because access dependencies and intelligence requirements propagate constraints across strategic, operational, and tactical levels. Tactical technical actions can generate political consequences, and political objectives can exceed operational feasibility. The implication is that offensive capability contributes to national security only when it is integrated across strategic, operational, and tactical decision-making and embedded in institutional, legal, and societal arrangements that enable coherent authorisation, planning, and execution under legal authority, political control, and oversight. Under these conditions, OCO can function as one instrument within deterrence and defence postures for contesting persistent adversary activity while preserving political control.

Decision Exercise: Credibility Test for OCO Under Integration Constraints

Scenario. Over the past eight weeks, a cyberliterate state observes a campaign that combines (i) persistent access activity against government IT and a defence-adjacent research environment, (ii) disruption attempts against an election-adjacent service provider, and (iii) preparatory indicators in a critical-infrastructure supply chain. Attribution remains contested, and intelligence reporting is uneven across agencies. A coalition partner requests coordinated signalling before a ministerial meeting in 72 hours. Domestic leadership requests an option set that can impose costs or deny advantage while preserving rule-of-law oversight and limiting escalation exposure.

Analytical question 1—Strategic purpose and credibility condition. State the purpose of authorising an OCO posture over the next 30 days (deny advantage; impose costs; shape expectations; reassure). Specify (i) one credibility condition under partial attribution and (ii) one observable indicator that would signal it.

Analytical question 2—Minimum integration threshold (go/no-go). Define the minimum integration threshold required to proceed beyond incident response:

1. **Strategic:** authority clarity, end state, escalation boundary.
2. **Operational:** intelligence integration, deconfliction, off-limits equities.
3. **Tactical:** feasibility, test-verified boundedness, reversibility.

State one reason for **no-go** even when a technically plausible option exists.

Analytical question 3—Option set under constraints (two packages). Propose:

- **Package A (denial/continuity):** one operational measure and one communication measure. State one private-operator dependency.
- **Package B (cost/signalling):** one diplomatic/legal/economic measure and one bounded cyber-related measure. State one partner consultation constraint.

For each package, specify one failure mode that amplifies uncertainty or erodes legitimacy.

Analytical question 4—IGL rule. Specify one gain/loss rule that governs escalation from access preservation to effect delivery: one trigger to act, one trigger to restrain, and one audit requirement.

Short task—MLMD mapping (3 lines). For **Strategic / Operational / Tactical**, list: *decision; key dependency; misalignment failure mode.*

Optional extension—Non-state coordination (3 actors). Name three actors and state for each: *information needed within 72 hours; assurance you can provide without implying undisclosed thresholds.*

Bibliography

Anderson, J., Ablon, L., Kuehn, A. and Libicki, M. (2017), *Zero Days, Thousands of Nights: The Life and Death of a Zero-Day Vulnerability*, RAND Corporation, Santa Monica, CA.
Retrieved from: https://www.rand.org/pubs/research_reports/RR1751.html

Army Technology (2024), 'Sweden's nato accession: A cyberattack-filled saga'.
Retrieved from: https://www.army-technology.com/features/swedens-nato-accession-a-cyberattack-filled-saga/

Arute, F., Arya, K., Babbush, R., Bacon, D., Bardin, J. C., Barends, R., Biswas, R., Boixo, S., Brandao, F. G. S. L., Buell, D. A., Burkett, B., Chen, Y., Chen, Z., Chiaro, B., Collins, R., Courtney, W., Dunsworth, A., Farhi, E., Foxen, B., Fowler, A. et al. (2019), 'Quantum supremacy using a programmable superconducting processor', *Nature* **574**(7779), 505–510.

Axelrod, R. and Iliev, R. (2014), 'Timing of cyber conflict', *Proceedings of the National Academy of Sciences of the United States of America* **111**(4), 1298–1303.

Bengtsson, J. and Huskaj, G. (2021), The manifestation of chinese strategies into offensive cyberspace operations targeting sweden, *in* 'Proceedings of the 20th European Conference on Cyber Warfare and Security', Academic Conferences International Ltd., Reading, UK, pp. 35–43.

Brey, P. A. E. (2012), 'Anticipatory ethics for emerging technologies', *NanoEthics* **6**(1), 1–13.
Retrieved from: https://doi.org/10.1007/s11569-012-0141-7

Bronk, C. (2016), Getting creative on what will do: Cyber espionage, conflict and covert action, *in* D. L. Borum and M. Fein, eds, 'Cyberwarfare and Cyberterrorism: Concepts, Methodologies, Tools, and Applications', IGI Global, pp. 501–515.

Buchanan, B. (2017), *The Cybersecurity Dilemma: Hacking, Trust, and Fear Between Nations*, 1st edn, Oxford University Press, New York.

Chas, C. and Barrinha, A. (2024), 'Exploring the uk's cyber statecraft'.
Retrieved from: https://riscs.org.uk/2024/07/03/exploring-the-uks-cyber-statecraft

Clark, R. M. (2019), *Intelligence Analysis: A Target-Centric Approach*, sixth edn, CQ Press, Thousand Oaks, CA.

Dahm, M. (2021), 'China's desert storm education', *Proceedings* **147**(3), 1–417.
Retrieved from: https://www.usni.org/magazines/proceedings/2021/march/chinas-desert-storm-education

Denning, D. E. R. (1999), *Information Warfare and Security*, Addison-Wesley.

Department of the Army (2006), 'Human intelligence collector operations'.
Retrieved from: https://www.marines.mil/Portals/1/Publications/FM%202-22.3%20Human%20Intelligence%20Collector%20Operations_1.pdf

DiMaggio, J. (2024), 'Humint and its role within cybersecurity'.
Retrieved from: https://www.sans.org/blog/humint-and-its-role-within-cybersecurity

Dubin, R. (1978), *Theory Building*, 2 edn, Free Press, New York, NY.

EBSCO Knowledge Advantage (2021), 'Estonia cyber attack, april–may 2007', EBSCO Research Starters.
Retrieved from: https://www.ebsco.com/research-starters/computer-science/estonia-cyber-attack-april-may-2007

Edquist, H. and Henrekson, M. (2017), Swedish lessons: How important are ict and r&d to economic growth?, Technical report, The Research Institute of Industrial Economics (IFN).
Retrieved from: https://www.ifn.se/media/o3qeusrs/2017-edquist-henrekson-swedish-lessons-how-important-are-ict-and-rnd-to-economic-growth.pdf

Eriksson, J. (2019), Sweden: Small State, Middle Power or Moral Superpower?, *in* B. Veerbek and G. Giacomello, eds, 'Middle Powers in the 21st Century', Rowman & Littlefield Publishers., chapter 10.

Euractiv (2024), 'Iran ran special cyber op in sweden last year, local authorities confirm'.
Retrieved from: https://www.euractiv.com/news/iran-ran-special-cyber-op-in-sweden-last-year-local-authorities-confirm/

European Commission (2023), Digital decade country report 2023: Sweden, Technical report, Publications Office of the European Union.
Retrieved from: https://digital-strategy.ec.europa.eu/en/library/country-reports-digital-decade-report-2023

European Parliament and Council of the European Union (2024), 'Regulation (eu) 2024/1689 laying down harmonised rules on artificial intelligence (artificial intelligence act)'.
Retrieved from: https://ai-act-service-desk.ec.europa.eu/en/ai-act/article-113

Fischerkeller, M. (2017), 'Incorporating Offensive Cyber Operations into Conventional Deterrence Strategies', *Survival* **59**(1), 103–134.
Retrieved from: https://www.tandfonline.com/doi/full/10.1080/00396338.2017.1282679

Fischerkeller, M. P. and Harknett, R. J. (2017), 'Deterrence is not a credible strategy for cyberspace', *Orbis* **61**(3), 381–393.

Fischerkeller, M. P. and Harknett, R. J. (2018), Persistent engagement, agreed competition, cyberspace interaction dynamics, and escalation, IDA Non-Standard Report NS D-9076, Institute for Defense Analyses, Alexandria, VA.

Fischerkeller, M. P. and Harknett, R. J. (2019), 'Persistent engagement, agreed competition, and cyberspace interaction dynamics and escalation', *The Cyber Defense Review* .
Retrieved from: https://cyberdefensereview.army.mil/Portals/6/CDR-SE_S5-P3-Fischerkeller.pdf

Frizell, S. (2015), 'NSA Director on Sony Hack: 'The Entire World is Watching''.
Retrieved from: https://time.com/3660757/nsa-michael-rogers-sony-hack/

G7 (2023), 'Hiroshima process: International guiding principles for organizations developing advanced ai system'.
Retrieved from: https://www.mofa.go.jp/files/100573471.pdf

Garrity, P. (2025), '2024 trends in vulnerability exploitation'.
Retrieved from: https://www.vulncheck.com/blog/2024-exploitation-trends

Gartzke, E. and Lindsay, J. R. (2017), 'Thermonuclear cyberwar', *Journal of Cybersecurity* **3**(1), 37–48.

GCHQ and National Cyber Security Centre (2021), The equities process, Public guidance, Government Communications Headquarters.
Retrieved from: https://www.gchq.gov.uk/information/equities-process

Gill, R. (2023), 'What is open-source intelligence?'.
Retrieved from: https://www.sans.org/blog/what-is-open-source-intelligence

Government (2020), Totalförsvaret 2021–2025 (prop. 2020/21:30), Technical report, Försvarsdepartementet.
Retrieved from: https://www.regeringen.se/globalassets/regeringen/dokument/forsvarsdepartementet/forsvarsproposition-2021-2025/totalforsvaret-2021-2025-prop.-20202130.pdf

Government (2024*a*), 'Totalförsvaret 2025–2030: Prop. 2024/25:34', Government Bill (Proposition).
Retrieved from: https://www.regeringen.se/rattsliga-dokument/proposition/2024/10/prop.-20242534

Government (2024*b*), Totalförsvaret 2025–2030 (prop. 2024/25:34), Technical report, Försvarsdepartementet.
Retrieved from: https://www.regeringen.se/contentassets/5c98b885c2cc40d58aa3693d34d915d3/totalforsvaret-20252030-prop.-20242534.pdf

Granåsen, M., Huskaj, G. and Varga, S. (2019), Data collection and research in cdxs – command and control, cyber situational awareness and intelligence perspectives on cyber defense, *in* '24th International Command and Control Research and Technology Symposium', Laurel, p. 20.

Greenberg, A. (2012), 'Meet the hackers who sell spies the tools to crack your pc', *Forbes* .
Retrieved from: https://www.forbes.com/sites/andygreenberg/2012/03/21/meet-the-hackers-who-sell-spies-the-tools-to-crack-your-pc-and-get-paid-six-figure-fees/

Group-IB (2025), 'Understanding osint in cybersecurity'.
Retrieved from: https://www.group-ib.com/resources/knowledge-hub/osint/

Group-IB Threat Intelligence Team (2025), 'Human intelligence (humint) in cybersecurity'.
Retrieved from: https://www.group-ib.com/resources/knowledge-hub/human-intelligence/

Harper, D. (2024), 'Doctrine (n.)'.
Retrieved from: https://www.etymonline.com/search?q=doctrine

Healey, J. (2019), 'The implications of persistent (and permanent) engagement in cyberspace', *Journal of Cybersecurity* **5**(1), 1–15.

Hellerstedt, L. (2023), 'Espionage against swedish higher education institutions continues to increase'.
Retrieved from: https://universitetslararen.se/2023/03/30/espionage-against-swedish-higher-education-institutions-continues-to-increase/

Henriksén, N., Lexert, I., Dahn, J. B. and Hacks, S. (2025), Assessing sweden's current cybersecurity landscape: Implications of nato membership, *in* 'Proceedings of the 11th International Conference on Information Systems Security and Privacy (ICISSP 2025)', Vol. 1, SciTePress, pp. 209–216.

Herman, A. (2018), Quantum computing: How to address the national security risk, Technical report, Hudson Institute.
Retrieved from: https://www.hudson.org/national-security-defense/quantum-computing-how-to-address-the-national-security-risk

Huskaj, G. (2017), Cyber deterrence: An illustration of implementation, Master's thesis, Department of Computer and Systems Sciences, Stockholm University, Stockholm, Sweden.

Huskaj, G. (2019), The current state of research in offensive cyberspace operations, *in* T. Cruz and P. Simoes, eds, '18th European Conference on Cyber Warfare and Security', Academic Conferences and Publishing International Ltd., pp. 660–667.

Huskaj, G. (2023*a*), Digital geopolitics: A review of the current state, *in* 'Proceedings of the 18th International Conference on Cyber Warfare and Security (ICCWS 2023)', Academic Conferences International Ltd., pp. 305–314.

Huskaj, G. (2023*b*), Offensive cyberspace operations for cyber security, *in* 'Proceedings of the 18th International Conference on Cyber Warfare and Security (ICCWS 2023)', Geneva Centre for Security Policy (GCSP), Academic Conferences International Limited, Geneva, Switzerland, pp. 476–479.

Huskaj, G. (2024*a*), Eight principles for intelligence sharing: A holistic and strategic approach, *in* 'Proceedings of the 23rd European Conference on Cyber Warfare and Security (ECCWS 2024)', Geneva Centre for Security Policy (GCSP) and Stockholm University, Academic Conferences International Limited, Stockholm, Sweden, pp. 704–711.
Retrieved from: https://www.academic-conferences.org/conferences/eccws/

Huskaj, G. (2024*b*), Future elections and ai-driven disinformation, *in* M. Wasinger, ed., 'Aspects of Cognitive Superiority: Shaping Beliefs and Behaviours', TMW Horizont Gesellschaft mbH, Vienna, Austria, pp. 48–59.

Huskaj, G. (2024*c*), Offensive Cyberspace Operations: Implications for Sweden, PhD thesis, Stockholm University, Department of Computer and Systems Sciences, Stockholm.
Retrieved from: https://urn.kb.se/resolve?urn=urn:nbn:se:su:diva-231078

Huskaj, G. (2025*a*), A global policy perspective on offensive cyberspace operations, GCSP Policy Brief 22, Geneva Centre for Security Policy, Geneva, Switzerland.

Huskaj, G. (2025*b*), 'Revisiting the Letter of Marque: Leveraging the Private Sector in Offensive Cyberspace Operations – An Analytical Reflection on Historical Analogies and Contemporary Policy Debates', *Cyber Operationer* .
Retrieved from: https://cyberoperationer.github.io/2025/revisiting-the-letter-of-marque/

Huskaj, G. (2025*c*), The role of intelligence services in cyber security, *in* B. Lins and J. Schröfl, eds, 'The Cyber and Information Space Matrix: A Conceptual Framework', Peter Lang International Academic Publishers.

Huskaj, G. (2025*d*), 'Sverige måste svara offensivt på cyberhot', *Forskning & Framsteg* .
Retrieved from: https://fof.se/artikel/sverige-maste-svara-offensivt-pa-cyberhot/

Huskaj, G. (2026), 'Ai-enabled cyberspace operations', *The Defence Horizon Journal* .

Huskaj, G. and Axelsson, S. (2023), A whole-of-society approach to organise for offensive cyberspace operations: The case of the smart state sweden, *in* 'Proceedings of the 22nd European Conference on Cyber Warfare and Security', Academic Conferences International Ltd., pp. 1188–1196.

Huskaj, G. and Blix, F. (2022), 'Validating a framework for offensive cyberspace operations', *Journal of Information Warfare* **21**(3), 26–42.

Huskaj, G., Blix, F. and Axelsson, S. (2024), A theory of offensive cyberspace operations and its policy and strategy implications, *in* 'Proceedings of the 23rd European Conference on Cyber Warfare and Security (ECCWS 2024)', Department of Computer and Systems Sciences, Stockholm University, Academic Conferences International Limited, Stockholm, Sweden, pp. 214–223.

Huskaj, G. and Iftimie, I. A. (2020), Toward an ambidextrous framework for offensive cyberspace operations: A theory, policy and practice perspective, *in* B. K. Payne and H. Wu, eds, 'Proceedings of the 15th International Conference on Cyber Warfare and Security (ICCWS 2020)', Academic Conferences and Publishing International Ltd., Reading, UK, pp. 243–253.

Huskaj, G., Iftimie, I. A. and Wilson, R. L. (2020), Designing attack infrastructure for offensive cyberspace operations, *in* 'Proceedings of the 19th European Conference on Cyber Warfare and Security'.

Huskaj, G. and Moradian, E. (2018), Cyber deterrence: An illustration of implementation, *in* J. Hurley and J. Chen, eds, '13th International Conference on Cyber Warfare and Security', Academic Conferences and Publishing International Ltd., Washington, D.C., pp. 304–311.

Huskaj, G., Sallinen, M. and Nicander, L. (2021), Staters outtalade normer i cyberrymden, Report, Försvarshögskolan (FHS), Stockholm.

Huskaj, G. and Wilson, R. L. (2020*a*), An anticipatory ethical analysis of offensive cyberspace operations, *in* B. K. Payne and H. Wu, eds, 'ICCWS 2020 15th International Conference on Cyber Warfare and Security', Academic Conferences and Publishing International Ltd., Norfolk, USA, pp. 512–520.

Huskaj, G. and Wilson, R. L. (2020*b*), Anticipatory ethics for vulnerability disclosure, *in* B. K. Payne and H. Wu, eds, 'Proceedings of the 15th International Conference on Cyber Warfare and Security (ICCWS 2020)', Academic Conferences and Publishing International Limited, Reading, UK, pp. 254–261.

Huskaj, G. and Wilson, R. L. (2021), 'Offensive Cyberspace Operations and Zero-days: Anticipatory Ethics and Policy Implications for Vulnerability Disclosure', *Journal of Information Warfare* **20**(1), 96–109.

Javers, E. (2016), 'U.s. charges iranians with cyber attacks on banks and a dam'. Retrieved from: https://www.cnbc.com/2016/03/24/us-charges-iranians-with-cyber-attacks-on-banks-and-dam.html

Jefferies, S. (2025), 'What is osint? how cyber criminals use open source intelligence to target you online'. Retrieved from: https://www.sharp.co.uk/news-and-events/blog/what-is-osint-how-cyber-criminals-use-open-source-intelligence-to-target-you-online

Johnson, L. K. (2003), 'Bricks and Mortar for a Theory of Intelligence', *Comparative Strategy* **22**(1), 1–28.

Joint Chiefs of Staff (2018), Joint publication 3-12 (cyberspace operations), Technical report, U.S. Department of Defense. Retrieved from: https://www.jcs.mil/Portals/36/Documents/Doctrine/pubs/jp3_12.pdf

Joint Chiefs of Staff (2022), Joint campaigns and operations, Joint Publication 3-0, U.S. Department of Defense. Approved by the CJCS. Supersedes the 2017 edition.

Kaplan, F. (2016), *Dark Territory: The Secret History of Cyber War*, Simon & Schuster, New York.

Kehler, C. R., Lin, H. and Sulmeyer, M. (2017), 'Rules of engagement for cyberspace operations: A view from the USA', *Journal of Cybersecurity* **3**(1), 15–28. Retrieved from: https://doi.org/10.1093/cybsec/tyw015

Kerner, S. M. (2022), 'Colonial pipeline hack explained: Everything you need to know'. Retrieved from: https://www.techtarget.com/whatis/feature/Colonial-Pipeline-hack-explained-Everything-you-need-to-know

Klepper, D. and Tucker, E. (2024), 'Now armed with ai, america's adversaries will try to influence election, security officials warn'. Retrieved from: https://apnews.com/article/election-interference-facebook-tiktok-russia-putin-china-1b5e5ce56d64dc356c2ad332068e2f8c

Krelina, M. (2021), 'Quantum technology for military applications', *EPJ Quantum Technology* **8**(24). Retrieved from: https://doi.org/10.1140/epjqt/s40507-021-00113-y

Leidos (2025), 'Leidos ramps up cyber-physical protection of critical infrastructure'. Retrieved from: https://www.leidos.com/insights/leidos-ramps-cyber-physical-protection-critical-infrastructure

Lemos, R. (2025*a*), 'Generative ai shows promise for faster triage of vulnerabilities'. Retrieved from: https://www.darkreading.com/application-security/gen-ai-accelerates-triage-of-software-vulnerabilities

Lemos, R. (2025*b*), 'Proof-of-concept in 15 minutes? ai turbocharges exploitation'. Retrieved from: https://www.darkreading.com/vulnerabilities-threats/proof-concept-15-minutes-ai-turbocharges-exploitation

Lenaerts-Bergmans, B. (2023), 'Human intelligence (humint) in cybersecurity'. Retrieved from: https://www.crowdstrike.com/en-us/cybersecurity-101/threat-intelligence/human-intelligence-humint/

Libicki, M. C. (2016), *Cyberspace in Peace and War*, U.S. Naval Institute Press, Annapolis, MD.

Libicki, M. C. (2021), *Cyberspace in Peace and War*, second edition, revised edn, Naval Institute Press, Annapolis, MD.

Lindemulder, G. and Forrest, A. (2023), 'What is open source intelligence (osint)?'. Retrieved from: https://www.ibm.com/think/topics/osint

Lindsay, J. R. (2020*a*), 'Demystifying the quantum threat: Infrastructure, institutions, and intelligence advantage', *Security Studies* **29**(2), 335–361. Retrieved from: https://doi.org/10.1080/09636412.2020.1722853

Lindsay, J. R. (2020*b*), *Information Technology and Military Power*, Cornell Studies in Security Affairs, Cornell University Press, Ithaca, NY.

Lynham, S. A. (2002), 'The General Method of Theory-Building Research in Applied Disciplines', *Advances in Developing Human Resources* **4**(3), 221–241.

Lynn, W. J. (2010), 'Defending a new domain: The pentagon's cyberstrategy', *Foreign Affairs* **89**(5), 97–108.

Mandiant (2013), 'Apt1: Exposing one of china's cyber espionage units'. Retrieved from: https://cloud.google.com/blog/topics/threat-intelligence/mandiant-exposes-apt1-chinas-cyber-espionage-units

Mandsager, D., Cole, A., Drew, P. J. and McLaughlin, R. (2022), *Newport Rules of Engagement (ROE) Handbook*, Vol. 98, U.S. Naval War College, Stockton Center for International Law, Newport, RI. Retrieved from: https://usnwc.edu

Maschmeyer, L. (2021), 'The subversive trilemma: Why cyber operations fall short of expectations', *International Security* **46**(2), 51–90.

Military Intelligence and Security Service (2024), MUST Årsöversikt 2024, Technical report, The Armed Forces, Stockholm, Sweden. Retrieved from: https://www.forsvarsmakten.se/contentassets/546bbe13064a4c739e1cbc4b5e4571f7/2024-must-arsoversikt.pdf

Miller, C. (2007), The legitimate vulnerability market: the secretive world of 0-day exploit sales, *in* 'Workshop on the Economics of Information Security'. Retrieved from: https://api.semanticscholar.org/CorpusID:12423218

Ministry of Defence (2024), 'Myndigheten för civilt försvar – ett nytt namn för myndigheten för samhällsskydd och beredskap och vissa organisatoriska förändringar'. Retrieved from: https://www.regeringen.se/pressmeddelanden/2025/11/msb-blir-myndigheten-for-civilt-forsvar/

Montgomery, M. and Borghard, E. (2021), 'Cyber threats and vulnerabilities to conventional and strategic deterrence', *Joint Force Quarterly* (102). Retrieved from: https://www.ndu.edu/News/Article-View/Article/2684986/cyber-threats-and-vulnerabilities-to-conventional-and-strategic-deterrence/

Moore, D. (2022), *Offensive Cyber Operations*, Routledge.

Mosca, M. (2018), Cybersecurity in an era with quantum computers: Will we be ready?, *in* 'IACR Cryptology ePrint Archive'.

Nakasone, P. M. (2019), 'A cyber force for persistent operations', *Joint Force Quarterly (JFQ)* **92**(1). 1st Quarter.

National Cyber Security Centre (NCSC), Netherlands (2018), Coordinated vulnerability disclosure: The guideline, Technical Report Version 2.0, The Hague.
Retrieved from: https://english.ncsc.nl/publications/publications/2019/juni/01/coordinated-vulnerability-disclosure-the-guideline

National Cyber Security Centre (NCSC), Switzerland (2025), 'Coordinated vulnerability disclosure (cvd)'.
Retrieved from: https://www.ncsc.admin.ch/ncsc/en/home/infos-fuer/infos-it-spezialisten/themen/schwachstelle-melden.html

National Cybersecurity Centre (2025*a*), 'Myndigheter inom cybersäkerhetsområdet', Official government web page.
Retrieved from: https://www.ncsc.se/sv/om-centret/cybersakerhet-ur-olika-infallsvinklar/

National Cybersecurity Centre (2025*b*), 'Om centret', Official government web page.
Retrieved from: https://www.ncsc.se/sv/om-centret/

National Defence Radio Establishment (2022), Årsrapport 2022, Technical report.
Retrieved from: https://fra.se/download/18.54ed4de8186313dc3566d/1678969166868/FRA-arsrapport-2022_TGA_Enkel.pdf

National Defence Radio Establishment (2024), FRA Årsrapport 2024, Technical report, National Defence Radio Establishment, Stockholm, Sweden.
Retrieved from: https://www.fra.se/download/18.766e440918f572e7335195/1740753605133/FRA_arsrapport_2024_uppslag.pdf

National Institute of Standards and Technology (2024), 'Post-quantum cryptography: Fips approved'.
Retrieved from: https://csrc.nist.gov/News/2024/post-quantum-cryptography-fips-approved

National Security Agency (2024), 'Signals intelligence (sigint) overview'.
Retrieved from: https://www.nsa.gov/Signals-Intelligence/Overview/

Newman, L. H. (2018), 'The leaked nsa spy tool that hacked the world', *WIRED* .
Retrieved from: https://www.wired.com/story/eternalblue-leaked-nsa-spy-tool-hacked-world/

North Atlantic Treaty Organization (2019), Allied joint doctrine for the planning of operations, Allied Joint Publication AJP-5, NATO Standardization Office. Authoritative UK and NATO doctrine for the planning of joint operations.

North Atlantic Treaty Organization (2025*a*), 'Joint intelligence, surveillance and reconnaissance (jisr)'.
Retrieved from: https://www.nato.int/cps/en/natohq/topics_111830.htm

North Atlantic Treaty Organization (2025*b*), 'Nato's approach to counter information threats'.
Retrieved from: https://www.nato.int/en/what-we-do/wider-activities/natos-approach-to-counter-information-threats

Nye, Joseph S., J. (2017), 'Deterrence and dissuasion in cyberspace', *International Security* **41**(3), 44–71.

Oleson, P. C., ed. (2016), *AFIO's Guide to the Study of Intelligence*, Association of Former Intelligence Officers, Falls Church, VA.

Omand, D. (2021), 'The ethical limits we should place on intelligence gathering as part of an integrated CT strategy', *Studies in Conflict & Terrorism* **44**(4), 290–301.
Retrieved from: https://doi.org/10.1080/09546553.2021.1880225

Park, J. and Kim, D. (2025), 'Forging forward: South korea's proactive cyber defense and strategic cooperation with the united states'.
Retrieved from: https://www.csis.org/analysis/forging-forward-south-koreas-proactive-cyber-defense-and-strategic-cooperation-united

Pfleeger, C. P. and Pfleeger, S. L. (2012), *Analyzing Computer Security*, 1 edn, Prentice Hall, Upper Saddle River, NJ.

Psychological Defence Agency (2024), 'Vårt uppdrag'.
Retrieved from: https://mpf.se/om-oss/vart-uppdrag

Pupillo, L., Ferreira, A., Varisco, G. and Zarra, A. (2018), 'Protecting europe against software vulnerabilities: It's time to act!'.
Retrieved from: https://www.ceps.eu/ceps-task-forces/software-vulnerability-disclosure-in-europe/

Reitz, A. S., ed. (2024), *Operational Law Handbook*, The Judge Advocate General's Legal Center and School, U.S. Army, Charlottesville, VA.

Rhysider, J. (2019), 'Ep 50: Operation glowing symphony', Podcast episode, *Darknet Diaries*.
Retrieved from: https://darknetdiaries.com/transcript/50/

Rid, T. and Buchanan, B. (2015), 'Attributing cyber attacks', *Journal of Strategic Studies* **38**(1-2), 4–37.

Roussi, A. and Roberts, H. (2025), 'How a hacking gang held italy's political elites to ransom', *POLITICO Europe* .
Retrieved from: https://www.politico.eu/article/italy-milan-hackers-carmine-gallo-enrico-pazzali-samuele-calamucci-equalize-mercury-advisors/

Saltzer, J. H. and Schroeder, M. D. (1975), 'The protection of information in computer systems', *Communications of the ACM* **17**(7), 388–402.
Retrieved from: https://www.cs.virginia.edu/~evans/cs551/saltzer/

Schelling, T. (1966), *Arms and Influence*, Yale University Press.

Schmitt, M. N., ed. (2017), *Tallinn Manual 2.0 on the International Law Applicable to Cyber Operations*, second edn, Cambridge University Press, Cambridge, United Kingdom. Prepared by the International Group of Experts at the Invitation of the NATO Cooperative Cyber Defence Centre of Excellence.

Security Service (2025), The security service 2024/25: Threats and vulnerabilities (summary), Technical report.
Retrieved from: https://sapo.se/ovriga-sidor/other-languages/english-engelska/press-room/the-swedish-security-services-annual-assesments/the-security-service-2024-25/threats-and-vulnerabilities.html

Shor, P. W. (1994), Algorithms for quantum computation: Discrete logarithms and factoring, *in* 'Proceedings of the 35th Annual Symposium on Foundations of Computer Science (FOCS)', IEEE, Los Alamitos, CA, pp. 124–134.

Snyder, G. H. (1960), 'Deterrence and power', *Journal of Conflict Resolution* **4**(2), 163–178.

Snyder, G. H. (1961), *Deterrence and Defense*, Princeton University Press.

SOCRadar Cyber Intelligence Inc. (2025), 'The adversarial misuse of ai: How threat actors are leveraging ai for cyber operations'.
Retrieved from: https://socradar.io/blog/adversarial-misuse-of-ai-how-threat-actors-leverage-ai/

Spriet, J. (2024), 'What are the strategic applications of electronic support measures?'.
Retrieved from: https://www.crfs.com/blog/what-are-the-strategic-applications-of-electronic-support-measures

Sundelius, B. (1995), Sverige bortom småstatsbindningen: men smart i ett internationaliserat europa, *in* B. von Sydow, ed., 'Utvidgning och samspel: EU:s östintegration ur historiskt och ekonomiskt perspektiv', Statens offentliga utredningar (SOU) 1995:132, Stockholm, pp. 61–90. Expert report to EU 96-kommittén.
Retrieved from: https://lagen.nu/sou/1995:132

Säberg, K. and Huskaj, G. (2024), Intelligence agencies' move to the cloud: Challenges and opportunities, *in* 'Proceedings of the 19th International Conference on Cyber Warfare and Security (ICCWS 2024)', Department of Computer and Systems Sciences, Stockholm University and Geneva Centre for Security Policy (GCSP), Academic Conferences International Limited, Stellenbosch, South Africa, pp. 565–573.
Retrieved from: https://www.academic-conferences.org/conferences/iccws/

The Agency for Growth Policy Analysis (2015), How digitalisation drives productivity and competitiveness in sweden (report 2015:02), Technical report, Tillväxtanalys.
Retrieved from: https://www.tillvaxtanalys.se/en-GB/publikationer/rapport/rapportserien/digitaliseringensbidragtilltillvaxtochkonkurrenskraftisverige.820.html

The Armed Forces (2024), 'Cyberförsvar', Official agency web page.
Retrieved from: https://www.forsvarsmakten.se/sv/var-verksamhet/det-har-gor-forsvarsmakten/cyberforsvar/

The Armed Forces (2025), 'Nytt cyberförsvarsförband försvarar civil infrastruktur'.
Retrieved from: https://www.forsvarsmakten.se/sv/aktuellt/2025/04/nytt-cyberforsvarsforband-forsvarar-civil-infrastruktur/

The Riksdag (2018), 'Säkerhetsskyddslag (2018:585)', Svensk författningssamling.
Retrieved from: https://www.riksdagen.se/sv/dokument-lagar/dokument/svensk-forfattningssamling/sakerhetsskyddslag-2018585_sfs-2018-585

The Riksdag (2025), 'Förordning (2025:237) om det nationella cybersäkerhetscentret vid försvarets radioanstalt', Svensk Författningssamling.
Retrieved from: https://www.riksdagen.se/sv/dokument-lagar/dokument/svensk-forfattningssamling/forordning-2025237-om-det-nationella_sfs-2025-237

The Swedish Civil Contingencies Agency (2024), 'Msb:s arbete med informationssäkerhet och cybersäkerhet', Official agency web page.
Retrieved from: https://www.msb.se/sv/amnesomraden/informationssakerhet-cybersakerhet-och-sakra-kommunikationer/samhallets--arbete-for-okad-cybersakerhet/msbs-arbete-med-informationssakerhet-och-cybersakerhet/

TONEX (2024), 'Signals intelligence (sigint) faqs'.
Retrieved from: https://www.tonex.com/signals-intelligence-sigint-faqs/

United States Government (2017), Vulnerabilities equities policy and process for the united states government, Policy directive, National Security Council, Washington, DC. Unclassified.
Retrieved from: https://trumpwhitehouse.archives.gov/sites/whitehouse.gov/files/images/External%20-%20Unclassified%20VEP%20Charter%20FINAL.PDF

U.S. Cyber Command Public Affairs Office (2022), 'CYBER 101 – Defend Forward and Persistent Engagement', *U.S. Cyber Command News* .
Retrieved from: https://www.cybercom.mil/Media/News/Article/3200413/cyber-101-defend-forward-and-persistent-engagement/

US Joint Chiefs of Staff (2013), 'JP 2-0 Joint Intelligence', *US Department of Defense* (October), 150.

USAF LeMay Center (2023), *Air Force Doctrine Publication (AFDP) 3-12: Cyberspace Operations*, Department of the Air Force.
Retrieved from: https://www.doctrine.af.mil/Portals/61/documents/AFDP_3-12/3-12-AFDP-CYBERSPACE-OPS.pdf

Valeriano, B., Jensen, B. M. and Maness, R. C. (2018), *Cyber Strategy: The Evolving Character of Power and Coercion*, Oxford University Press.

Van de Velde, J. (2023), 'Cyber deterrence is dead! long live "integrated deterrence"!', *Joint Force Quarterly* **109**(2nd Quarter), 41–50.
Retrieved from: https://ndupress.ndu.edu/JFQ/Joint-Force-Quarterly-109/Article/ArticleID/

Ware, W. H. (1967), Security and privacy in computer systems, Technical report, RAND Corporation. Unclassified.
Retrieved from: https://nsarchive.gwu.edu/document/21676-document-01-willis-h-ware-rand-corporation-p

Warner, M. (2014), *The Rise and Fall of Intelligence: An American Secret History*, second edn, Georgetown University Press, Washington, D.C.

Wasinger, M. (2023), 'Aspects of cognitive superiority: Shaping beliefs and behaviours'.

White, S. P. (2018), 'Understanding cyberwarfare: Lessons from the russia–georgia war', Modern War Institute at West Point.
Retrieved from: https://mwi.westpoint.edu/understanding-cyberwarfare-lessons-russia-georgia-war/

Wikipedia contributors (2015), 'Office of personnel management data breach'.
Retrieved from: https://en.wikipedia.org/wiki/Office_of_Personnel_Management_data_breach

Wunder, A. P. (2016), 'What is cyber isr?', *Air National Guard News* .
Retrieved from: https://www.ang.af.mil/News/Commentaries/Article/863777/what-is-cyber-isr/

Zetter, K. (2016), 'Hacking team's leak helped researchers hunt down a zero-day'.
Retrieved from: https://www.wired.com/2016/01/hacking-team-leak-helps-kaspersky-researchers-find-zero-day-exploit/

For Product Safety Concerns and Information please contact our EU
representative GPSR@taylorandfrancis.com
Taylor & Francis Verlag GmbH, Kaufingerstraße 24, 80331 München, Germany

www.ingramcontent.com/pod-product-compliance
Ingram Content Group UK Ltd.
Pitfield, Milton Keynes, MK11 3LW, UK
UKHW052052230926
475702UK00025B/1139
* 9 7 8 1 0 4 1 1 0 4 6 5 0 *